STALKING THE HEADHUNTER:
The Smart Job-Hunter's Guide to Executive Recruiters

STALKING THE HEADHUNTER:
The Smart Job-Hunter's Guide to Executive Recruiters

John Tarrant

A Stonesong Press Book

BANTAM BOOKS
TORONTO · NEW YORK · LONDON · SYDNEY · AUCKLAND

STALKING THE HEADHUNTER
A Bantam Book / September 1986

A Stonesong Press Book

Library of Congress Cataloging-in-Publication Data

Tarrant, John J.
  Stalking the headhunter.

  1. Executives—United States—Recruiting.   2. Job
hunting—United States.   I. Title.
HD38.25.U6T37   1986   650.1'4'024658   86-47579
ISBN 0-553-05181-4

Published simultaneously in the United States and Canada

Bantam Books are published by Bantam Books, Inc. Its trade-
mark, consisting of the words "Bantam Books" and the por-
trayal of a rooster, is Registered in U.S. Patent and Trademark
Office and in other countries. Marca Registrada. Bantam
Books, Inc., 666 Fifth Avenue, New York, New York 10103.

PRINTED IN THE UNITED STATES OF AMERICA
DH   0 9 8 7 6 5 4 3 2 1

To Pat and John

Acknowledgments

MANY PEOPLE HAVE HELPED me to write this book—more than I can possibly acknowledge. Some of those to whom I am deeply grateful are Ken Cole, Kent Straat, Bob Taylor, John Lucht, Gerry Roche, Russell Reynolds, Linda Weiss, Linda Meagher, Allan Stern, Bob Cox, Tom Buffum, Heath Boyer, Bob Dingman, Bob Murphy, Lynn Gilbert, Carl Menk, Jerry Fields, Pam Hayes, John Hellman, Lucie Adam, Ann Board, Adele Ribolow, Gardner Heidrick, Robert Baird, Janet Jones-Parker. And then there are Joan Fee, Elaine Shepherd, Janis Roche, Jay Mettler, Claudia Gertner, Arch Whitehead, Peg Phalen. Also Carl Pierson, Ed Miller, Warren Wasp, Duncan Muir, Jack Erdlin, Dick Conarroe. I cannot omit John Lytle, Pat Tarrant, Don Foley, Ken Murton, Jack Kiermaier, Ted Diamond, Charles Lamb, Richard Kuusela, and Peggy Tarrant.

Paul Fargis's creativity and perceptivity gave rise to this book. Linda Cunningham's editorial strength has helped to shape it. Sheree Bykofsky's resourcefulness at Stonesong Press was a constant support.

And my wife Dorothy Tarrant is a wonderful resource, helping with information, direction, and understanding.

Contents

Introduction

THE EXECUTIVE-SEARCH CONSULTANT, or headhunter, is a key figure in the lives of executives and professionals. Career success can depend on attracting the attention of the recruiter and then making the most of that attention. This book focuses on several specific areas of importance in maximizing the interaction with the headhunter.

First it is important to have a grasp of the search industry and to know how recruiters work.

Then the manager or professional should be aware of some significant trends in the search industry. These trends mean that the person who contacts you may not be the kind of recruiter you're used to hearing about. Some new entrants in the recruiting field are coming to it with sharply different approaches. There are dangers for the individual who doesn't know about them, and advantages for those who do know about them.

Next, the book provides a comprehensive plan for achieving the kind of *visibility* that brings you to the attention of the recruiter.

Good visibility leads to *contact* with the recruiter and eventually the employer. The skill with which you handle the initial steps in the contact phase can make or break your chances of landing the job.

Today, recruiters are also deeply involved in the *negotiation* between candidate and potential employer. The executive who is not familiar with the advantages and pitfalls in this kind of three-way bargaining may get far less than the best possible deal. The book provides a thorough guide to the bargaining process and how to use the involvement of the headhunter to your advantage.

In addition, the book contains more than 150 capsulized profiles of recruiting firms, big and small, generalists and specialists, along with information on independent researchers, a new and important factor in the search scene.

Since the executive-search field is undergoing considerable changes, this book brings the reader up to date on the industry, tells what he or she must know, and lays a complete plan for career enhancement with the help of the headhunter.

CHAPTER 1

The Evolution of Executive Search

THE VOICE OF THE headhunter is heard in the land. "Good morning. I'm Barrett Wimpole, representing Manning, Mack & Morgan, executive recruiters. We're working on a very interesting job search on which you might be able to help. Your name came up as a good source for names of people who might fit this position. It's a *Fortune* 500 company. . . ."

Business careers are made by the attention of the executive recruiter—or harmed by the indifference of the recruiter. Successful career management requires that you be able to attract the attention of the search consultant and have the knowledge and skill to use the consultant as a resource and ally in negotiating the conditions of the job.

There's a certain parallel between these executive recruiters and the mythological Greek and Roman gods who reached down from Mount Olympus to touch the lives of mortals. Suddenly Zeus or Athena singled out an individual and whisked that individual into a more exalted station in life. (The gods were just as likely to intervene in negative ways as well, turning people into bears or trees, but this was the downside risk of life in those days.)

Today, elevation to higher rank for the career manager is apt to be accompanied by the intervention of not a god but a mortal called an executive search consultant, who sometimes seems to perform a godlike function. Search consultants, recruiters, or "headhunters," as they do not like to be called, are a basic part of business life in the United States. They are a necessary factor in the age of the mobile manager, when executives change jobs as a career strategy and when companies change managers for all sorts of reasons.

Although recruitment agencies are commonplace today, executive search is a relatively new field; it began after World War II. By 1950 there were a few firms in the business of seeking executives and professionals to fill jobs. They were different from the employment agencies. Employment agencies are basically clearinghouses. They screen those job applicants who fill out applications, and refer applicants to employers who have listed jobs with the agency. In many cases the employment agency charges the employee a fee.

Executive-search firms *never* charge the employee. They are paid by companies to go out and *find* qualified candidates, irrespective of whether those candidates are looking for jobs. This distinction between search firm and employment agency is still not clear to many people today.

The mission of the executive search professional is reflected in the term "recruiter." The searcher not only locates the candidate but also helps to recruit that candidate. In the early days this function was loudly denounced as piracy. The word "headhunter" came into use as a pejorative, designating someone who ruthlessly stole employees from their employers. Today "headhunter" is a generic term for executive recruiter, although recruiters themselves are not altogether happy with the word.

Though there are great variations in size and approach, the function of the executive recruiter, and the basic nature of the search, are fairly standard. First comes the *assignment*. The client—usually a company, though nowadays it may be a nonprofit organization or a government agency—has a job to be filled. The executive recruiter is called in. If the recruiter is being paid a retainer—as are most of the big and active recruiting firms—that recruiter is apt to be handling the search exclusively, meaning they are the only ones looking for candidates.

The search consultant finds out what the client is looking for. Good recruiters don't just sit there passively writing it down; they participate with the client in coming up with a workable description of the ideal candidate. Sometimes clients want too much qualification for too little money. Or sometimes the client will place conflicting qualifications on the job (for example, requiring exceptional youth and entrepreneurial vigor in combination with extensive experience). Another difficulty arises when the client places too many qualifications on the job, eliminating people who would be, in the recruiter's opinion, good candidates. The recruiter will try to straighten all these problems out, emerging from the process with a coherent position description and with assurance that the compensation package will be hefty enough to attract the right people.

Now the headhunter has a specification. The "spec," with the identification of the company removed, is frequently made available to candidates, or potential candidates, by the recruiter early in the proceeding, perhaps before the first face-to-face meeting. (If the recruiter doesn't volunteer to provide a spec, the candidate should request one.) Following are two actual specs.

SENIOR VICE PRESIDENT AND GENERAL MANAGER

COMPANY: This division, a developer and marketer of microprocessor-based process control systems headquartered in the Midwest, has revenues approaching $4 million. The parent company, involved with a broader range of industrial products, has revenues of $70 million from its worldwide operations. The management of the company has been resourceful and innovative in increasing the productivity of this long-established company.

RESPONSIBILITIES: The General Manager will lead this small but established division in a broad penetration of the market, which provides computerized systems to transport, process, and store materials sensitive to moisture, pressure, and temperature. The products are programmable controllers that accept a number of analog inputs and return control information. Geographic focus will be dominantly (but not exclusively) North American.

Responsibilities will include: product line development, market definition, building a direct sales force, the development of training programs, and advertising, all to the objective of maximizing profitable market penetration. The objective is to build on the installed base of more than 60 systems and to create a significant systems business within five years.

QUALIFICATIONS: The successful candidate, a "hands on," "get it done" type, will have marketing experience with microcomputers and applications in process industries. Familiarity with the integration and installation of these systems is required, as is sensitivity to a customer's requirements, and the ability to devise a system and explain to the customer (often through others) how it provides him greater profitability.

Experience in management and the development of people within a profitable framework are essential. Demonstrated high energy and entrepreneurial drive are attributes of all members of the company's management team.

COMPENSATION AND
FUTURE PROSPECTS: An attractive package of base plus incentive approximating $100,000 is provided. The ideal candidate will have the skills to become the General Manager of a $50 million business and to play a major role in the management of the parent company.

NATIONAL SALES MANAGER

COMPANY: A rapidly growing, consumer products subsidiary of an Australian parent, this company is building its first organization in the United States. The product line contains 60 items of various designs and price points. The headquarters location is suburban New Jersey.

DUTIES: Reporting to the President, the National Sales Manager will be responsible for all sales, both direct and through representative firms. The objective is maximum distribution in retailers such as Sears, Wall-Mart stores, J. C. Penney, major department stores, discount chains, premium houses, hardware stores, and lawn and garden outlets.

The individual will build, manage, and motivate a select group of representative firms, handling accounts where he has a special familiarity himself. Travel could range from 30 to 40 percent. These products enjoy a 60 percent penetration of households in Australia, and the company believes that a significant share can be achieved in the United States with effective management.

QUALIFICATIONS: Sales experience with consumer products in national accounts is required, as is the imagination, creativity, and drive to sell a concept rather than price. Experience with products enjoying rapid growth is important, as various new product entries may cause a doubling of volume in each of next few years.

A comfort level with discounting is desired, as is experience with promotion and advertising at the local level. A knowledge of lead times and schedules of various catalogues and advertising is important, as is experience with television advertising. This is a building situation where a person who can get the job done with less than everything at hand is required—a resourceful doer.

COMPENSATION AND
FUTURE PROSPECTS: A package of base plus bonus is the high five-figure range plus an attractive benefits program are provided. Future prospects are exceptional due to the high growth targets and the planned acquisition of products complementary to the company.

Once the recruiter has the assignment in hand, the next step is to amass a list of names of possibilities. The recruiter may do all of this himself, or may farm out parts of the task to an in-house research facility or to an independent researcher who subcontracts to do this work. At this time also the recruiter is getting in touch with people who may be able to tell him or her of likely candidates.

The first contact may come by mail. Some recruiters send letters to potential candidates. This approach is most likely to be taken when the search is for a position below the highest level. Few recruiters send out a batch of letters at the inception of a search for a CEO of a major company because there is such a narrow range of qualified candidates to begin with.

But when it comes to positions outside the top echelon, conditions change. The factor conducive to the use of a letter is a "definable universe." This means quite a few potential candidates can be identified quickly. For example, if the search is for a management information specialist, or a C.P.A., or a chief appraiser, it is possible to get names off lists of members of professional societies or other organizations. However, if the search is for a general-line executive who must possess certain qualities that are discernible only through conversation, the letter is less likely to be used.

When a letter is sent, it may be a personalized word-processor note that says, in effect, "We have been retained to conduct a search for a West Coast construction firm. . . ." The recipient probably is not asked directly if he or she is interested in the job. The approach is more general: "I would like to hear any suggestions you might have. . . ." The letter will enclose the spec (without naming the client company). Or the letter will be longer than just a note and will incorporate information about the job.

Typically the recruiter may send out about 50 letters. Then the letters are followed up by phone. Not every letter may be followed up, however.

Or the recruiter will skip the letter stage and begin telephoning people who have been identified as possibilities. When possibilities have been identified, they are contacted. Recruiters often begin the conversation with something like this: "We've been retained to conduct a search for a large midwestern package goods firm. We're looking for a brand group manager. Compensation is in the $100,000 to $130,000 range. I understand that you might be able to recommend some-one. . . ." Those familiar with the stylized, almost ritualistic traditions of the discipline know that the other party is expected to say, "Well, I might even be interested myself. . . ."

Headhunter and candidate meet. If this goes well, the candidate meets the employer. And the search process proceeds to a conclusion when someone is hired for the job.

Today thousands of firms, big and small, are involved in executive search. At one end of the spectrum are the giants, of which Korn/Ferry International is the most gigantic. These are multifaceted companies, handling searches all over the world and boasting vast resources. Then there are many smaller firms, including one-person operations, which carry out the same basic job being done by the larger outfits: They are retained by the client company to fill a management job, and they pursue searches through various channels to identify and provide the best candidate for the job.

Overall, Kenneth J. Cole, publisher of *The Recruiting & Search Report,* says there are more than 20,000 active search firms in the United States, ranging in size from one to more than 100 recruiters, filling more than 1 million jobs a year, and generating $5 billion in fees. Other observers feel these numbers are too high: They estimate total billings at $2 billion to $4 billion. (Precise measurement is hampered by two factors: the varying reporting practices of recruiting companies, most of them private; and varying definitions of what constitutes an executive search firm—a point we will consider later.)

Whatever its exact dimensions, the search industry has become woven into the fabric of business—and, increasingly, the nonprofit area, including government. The concept is international; recruiters work around the world.

One of the indications of the acceptance and importance of the recruiting function is the extent to which the recruiter's role is acknowledged by those he or she serves. Today we take for granted that you just don't get most management and professional jobs by filling out an application. You must be sought out by the third parties who are hired to find the right people for those jobs.

That makes executive search decisively important to the career manager. And it makes it imperative that those who pursue the management career stay in touch with the evolution of the search profession. Otherwise they are unable to play their cards to maximum advantage when the headhunter calls.

THE HEADHUNTER CAPTURES HEADLINES

Once the executive recruiter worked totally behind the scenes. That's changing. With acceptance and clout have come higher visibility. In a way the heightened visibility of the recruiter is similar to a change that has come about in show business. Not long ago it was extraordinary, almost unheard of, for a producer or director to delegate the casting of a show. After all, what could be more important? But nowadays you will notice, as the credits roll after a movie or TV show, "Casting by So-and-So Associates."

Something similar is happening in executive search.

In the spring of 1985 the Bridgeport (Conn.) *Sunday Post* carried a story about a change in command at United Illuminating, the local power utility. George W. Edwards, Jr., would be taking over as president and CEO. Mr. Edwards, who was moving from the job of executive vice president of external affairs at Georgia Power Co., would be the first nonattorney and outsider in 21 years to head the utility.

The story features a tribute to Mr. Edwards: "He has a tremendous sense of the number of audiences he has to face as UI's leadership. He has good interpersonal relations skills, a terrific political sense and understands regulation very well." This quote came not from the chairman of the board but rather from Robert Welsh, the consultant from Heidrick & Struggles, Inc., who conducted the search.

Time was that search consultants took pains to remain behind the scenes. While the use of headhunters to fill executive jobs was nothing to be ashamed of, it was not boasted of, either. The consultant discreetly guarded his anonymity.

Many still feel that the search consultant should not be out front. But the growing importance of the function is exemplified by the public relations activities of some firms. Heidrick & Struggles, among the top three, is frequently in print, as in the story about the new UI president. Gerry Roche, chairman of Heidrick & Struggles, is a highly personable leader, as good at PR as he is at persuading management luminaries to take other jobs. One of Roche's most recent coups is the selection of John Sculley, once PepsiCo's top man, as chief executive of Apple Computer. Roche talks with relish of this spectacular episode, of his elation when he thought of Sculley, of the incredulity with which some people greeted the notion of a consumer goods titan taking over the reins of a computer company, of the amount of persuasion it took to get Sculley to consider the job.

As we consider the tendency of some headhunters to take center stage, one or two inferences come to mind. First, it would appear that the search consultant who publicizes his latest completed assignments would then have to bear some responsibility if the person does not work out. However, this doesn't happen as much as one might think. The business world does not blame the executive searcher when a high-level manager bombs out. Indeed, client companies themselves are amazingly tolerant. A leading consultant, telling the author of this book about his successes, mentioned a prominent company and said, "I'm finding my fourth CEO for them in seven years." It happens that two of the previous "finds" were fired and a third quit.

Second, it would seem that businesses would now be able to reach out much farther than before to fill top jobs, not just geographically but also in terms of background. This appears to be the case. For example, when United Illuminating, a company in some difficulty, needed an outsider and a nonattorney, it would have been significantly hampered in its efforts if the services of such a high-powered organization as Heidrick & Struggles had not been available.

Because recruiting services are so necessary these days, rather than staying out of the public eye, searchers are competing for attention doing what they can to differentiate themselves from one another. For example, John Lucht, who opened his John Lucht Consultancy after years with Heidrick & Struggles, is known as "the Mike Wallace of headhunters." Lucht qualifies for this sobriquet by supposedly spending unusually long periods—three to four hours—interviewing candidates, and asking questions like, "Were you the implementer or just the gofer?"

It has actually gotten to the point where it is considered prestigious to be associated with certain consulting firms. Just as Joe DiMaggio's endorsement confers stardom on a coffee-making machine (although, logically, hitting in 56 straight games does not make one an expert on kitchen appliances), so the nod of an illustrious headhunter will, to a greater and greater extent, bestow stardom on executives. It may not be long before executives are including on their resumes the fact that they were referred as candidates by leading headhunters—even though they did not get the jobs.

THE EVOLVING HEADHUNTER

One of the pioneers of executive search is Gardner W. Heidrick, once at the helm of Heidrick & Struggles, now chairman of The Heidrick Partners in Chicago. One major trend Heidrick sees is in the relationship between recruiter and client.

Once, says Heidrick, there was a close, warm relationship between the CEO and the consultant. Fees tended to be unquestioned, recommendations accepted. Now the choice of a recruiter is likely to be delegated to a human resource department, which is more hard-nosed and which may require "shoot-outs"—competitive presentations, as in advertising.

So the traditional executive search field has seen the rise of a new breed of more competitive entrepreneurs.

To understand how the change took place, one must first look at the type of individuals who were originally involved in recruitment.

Russell Reynolds Associates is the second-ranking search company (in terms of revenue) behind the leviathan Korn/Ferry. The former's story, and the background and personality of its leader, say something about the changing nature of executive search.

By and large, the pioneering executive searchers after World War II were general management consultants who got into it as a natural extension of their reorganization recommendations. The business quickly became more specialized. Full-line consultants set up separate search departments. Others began to concentrate on search full time.

In those days, headhunters came in all experiential sizes and shapes. Some were as primitive and voracious as their namesake, the real headhunters of New Guinea—but possibly less ethical than the tribesmen. (This is one of the main reasons that organizations such as the AESC—the Association of Executive Search Consultants—have tried to impose a modicum of standards and ethical practice on the industry.) Most of the early headhunters who did not come out of general-line consulting were personnel executives who got into it because their jobs called for interviewing and hiring people, or line managers who were "good with people."

This did not make the early days of executive search a model of professionalism or an electric circus of talent. Personnel managers of that era (before the function was renamed "human resources" and boosted up in the corporate hierarchy) tended to be executives who could not cut the mustard in the "important" areas of the business but who were well connected or well liked and thus were shunted onto a safe sidetrack, where they presided over moldy benefit files and never got involved in anything important. Those who drifted over to executive search brought along, in many cases, very little in understanding about the way an organization works, let alone the ability to find and evaluate people for key jobs in the organization.

Line executives who got into search during the first wave sometimes boasted as their chief talent the ability to order lunch in a good restaurant. Some of them were representative of the type of manager who makes a dynamite first impression but who just can't do the work. In their searches they tended to be drawn to similar types. Scholars might well investigate the effect of this phenomenon on

American management in the 1960s, when its level of high-level competence receded from its position as the envy of the world.

Of course, there were some very good people in the business from the earliest days—people such as Gardner Heidrick, Spencer Stuart, and Ward Howell. But there were a lot of mediocrities as well, and they were not all driven out of business by any means.

As executive search evolved, it began to attract more hard-nosed businesspeople. One such person is Russell Reynolds of Russell Reynolds Associates—today the second-ranking search company in terms of revenue.

Reynolds did not get into the search business because he was involved in human resource work or because he was a consultant or because it seemed like the natural thing to do. "I'm an entrepreneur," says Reynolds. "I could have gone into any business. I got into this business because I knew it had enormous potential and I knew I could be successful at it."

In 1969 Reynolds, who had been an investment banker at Morgan Guaranty, looked over the field of executive search with a cool, objective eye, concluded that there were a lot of washouts and turkeys in it, and decided that he could score with a company based on objective efficiency rather than subjective "feel." This does not mean, however, that Reynolds thought he could dispense with the human element and do it all with computers. Emphatically not; he had reached the conclusion that the industry was full of incompetent gladhanders and that better search work could be done by better people.

To Reynolds, "better people" comes pretty close to being synonymous with "Yale"—or at least the "Ivy League." He is a graduate of Exeter and Yale, where he was, among other distinctions, president of the Glee Club and a Whiffenpoof. He hires young people from distinguished universities, on the assumption that while a superior educational background by no means assures success in executive search, it means a lot. Since Reynolds is an active and enthusiastic alumnus of Yale, it is not surprising that the company's headquarters at 245 Park Avenue in New York have a noticeable Old Blue tinge, not in decor but in personnel. Associates tend to be Ivy M.B.A.'s.

It has worked. Russell Reynolds Associates has grown to a point at which it employs more than 400 people, including 100 associates, in 11 U.S. locations and in offices in London, Paris, Hong Kong, and Sydney. The median level of assignment is around $110,000, with more than 15 percent of searches exceeding $200,000 in annual compensation.

A class act. Reynolds says the hallmarks of the firm's approach include totally objective reporting ("We never introduce candidates for political reasons or out of 'reciprocity'"), superlative research, and thorough professionalism. Associates are expected to cooperate on searches and are motivated to do so by generous bonuses for "assists."

Reynolds doesn't want resumes. He expects his associates to go out and find the best possible candidate to fulfill a search, and he has great confidence in their ability to do so. How does a manager come to the attention of Russell Reynolds Associates? "Do your job well," he says. "We'll find you."

As one might expect, not everyone in the search business is a Russell Reynolds fan. Some mutter about the Ivy League emphasis in the firm, asserting that elitism is not consonant with finding the best management talent. Others deride Reynolds's professed fastidiousness about whom he will work for—for example, he talks of turning down the chance at a lot of lucrative search business because he would have nothing to do with a firm in the gaming industry. Still others claim that the buttoned-up Reynolds approach—which stresses such things as the ability to produce excellently written documents—ignores the basic gut values of intuition, warmth, and friendliness.

All of this bothers Russell Reynolds not at all. He has staked out as his paramount objective the attainment of undisputed leadership in executive search. He is convinced that the excellence of his people and the aseptic objectivity of his approach are among his principal assets. He is neither admiring nor sentimental about the old breed of headhunter. And why should he be? His firm is second among the top three—Korn/Ferry, Reynolds, and Heidrick & Struggles, all firms with reputations for getting the job done right.

Although Reynolds and Korn/Ferry and Heidrick & Struggles are the big ones, there are hundreds of small recruiting operations that carry on the same kind of general management recruiting as the large firms.

Kent Straat is typical. Straat conducts the Straat Group, in Stamford, Connecticut, as a one-man operation. He operates nationwide, and he also represents foreign clients in filling jobs in the United States. Straat, like practically all of his counterparts in small or single-proprietor search companies, worked for bigger firms before going on his own 13 years ago. He achieves an annual gross of about $250,000—minuscule in comparison with the business done by the giants, but enough for him.

THE CHANGING CONFLICTS

While recruiters throughout the industry have shaken off their old, weak image, they now face new difficulties. As corporations and executive search firms have gotten bigger, delicate problems of conflict of interest have become more common. The problem is reflected in these questions:

• Should a recruiter be able to use what he learns about a client company to, at a later point, recruit an executive from that client company?

• Should a recruiter who has been instrumental in placing an executive in a position at a client company later try to recruit that same executive for a subsequent client?

The code of ethics of the Association of Executive Search Consultants states that a member "will not recruit or cause to be recruited any person from the defined client organization for a period of two years after the completion of such assignment unless the member firm and client agree in writing to an exception." One practical problem with this formulation is the definition of the client organization. If the definition is broad, the recruiter who works for one division of a huge conglomerate could be deprived of a lot of business with other divisions. So it is in the interests of the search firm to try to define the "client organization" as narrowly as possible. As a practical matter, the recruiter usually will not commit him or herself to protecting divisions of the client organization that are essentially separate from the one he or she is serving. In the same way, a recruiting firm that operates internationally may not commit to protecting the client in countries other than the one in which the search is undertaken.

Many executive recruiters take issue with the section of the AESC code just quoted. They maintain that to give good service to all of their clients, they should be free to judge the degree of protection and negotiate it with the client. Nevertheless, the search industry accepts, in general, the concept that a client is off-limits for two years after the search is completed. There is further concurrence that, in general, a recruiter should never again try to recruit a candidate he has placed. In practice, however, there is continuing debate and sporadic conflict over the question of just how well the "off-limits" ethic is followed.

Another rift the modern recruiter has to contend with is the distinction between contingency and retainer firms.

All the search firms mentioned so far in this book are *retainer* firms, meaning they are paid a fee by the client for undertaking the search, whatever the outcome. The customary fee is 30 to 33⅓ percent of the annual compensation allotted to the job to be filled. Expenses— phone, meals, travel, etc.—are added.

However, some firms charge *contingency* fees instead, meaning the recruiter gets nothing up front and is not paid unless the job is filled. As we shall discuss, the retainer/contingency division is of tremendous importance within the search industry. The great bulk of the larger and longer-established firms are retainer firms. They maintain that they are the true professionals, that the retainer arrangement permits the research and painstaking professional work needed to conduct a true search.

There are well-established and highly professional contingency firms. Many of them are smaller organizations specializing in a particular industry or functional area.

Some firms, like Jerry Fields in advertising, have been specialists for many years. Now more companies specialize vertically—for example, searching for a wide variety of positions in the health care field, or horizontally by function, searching just for accountants, say, or engineers. This is a reflection of just how far the industry has come.

Today bona fide recruiters have to distinguish themselves from their look-alike cousins. Since executive search has become so important, all kinds of enterprises may try to wrap themselves in its mantle. Companies that are little more than employment agencies claim to perform a search function—search in this sense meaning they run ads and interview those who respond.

True executive search is a lot more than that. It is an exacting discipline. Its traditional dimensions involve these steps: The recruiter works with the client to develop valid criteria and a useful job specification; the recruiter defines the "universe," describing the general area in which likely candidates may be found; the recruiter collects names and information, meets and talks with possible candidates, applies critical judgment, and narrows the possibilities down to a short list from which the client will finally choose.

In recent years the field on which the executive recruiter deploys his or her skills has expanded in two directions. The opening stages of the search used to consist of the recruiter making some phone calls to reliable sources and obtaining some promising names. Today the sourcing phase frequently calls for more extensive, sophisticated, and aggressive ways of identifying possible candidates and getting information on them. (As we'll discuss, some of these new intelligence-gathering methods are causing furious controversy.)

The extension of the recruiter's function at the latter end of the search is equally important, particularly to candidates or those who might become candidates. The recruiter no longer just serves up candidates and leaves the client to do the interviewing and conduct the negotiations. Today recruiters are intimately involved in the bargaining over conditions of employment. They counsel the client on the size of the money offer. They are likely to present the package to the candidate, carry the candidate's response back to the client, decide how much should be given to get a particular executive, and decide when the demand is too high; in short, they orchestrate the negotiating procedure while playing a principal role in it.

There is still yet another way in which the field has changed greatly. That change reflects the changing role of women in business.

CHERCHEZ LA FEMME

At its inception, executive search was a stag affair. The executive world was all-male, with a few notable exceptions. Recruiters, like those they recruited, were men.

As the women's movement gathered momentum and as Title VII and its ban on sex discrimination began to take hold, a great many firms began looking assiduously—sometimes feverishly—for women executives. Recruiters started to look wherever they could for qualified women to fill jobs. Many firms initiated special programs; many set up departments, headed by women, devoted to female search. An assignment would be received, and a dual process would begin, with the conventional recruiters operating their old-boy networks, and the woman-oriented operation seeking female candidates for the same job.

A few search firms were begun by women. In 1972 Lynn Gilbert and Jan Tweed, who had been working for a New York employment agency, formed Gilbert Tweed Associates. Ms. Gilbert and Ms. Tweed acknowledge that some of their early success came about because they were a matter of curiosity, and potential clients wanted to see them. More of their success was keyed to ingenuity, persistence, and guts—

for example, in calling on Xerox, they left an umbrella behind to assure a second visit.

Today Gilbert Tweed is a leading firm, with offices around the world. Whereas in 1979 a total of 11 of the firm's 12 associates were women, now there is a more even male/female division. The company works as a general line search firm, with annual gross of about $2 million. About 15 percent of their searches are aimed particularly at women.

The need to run special searches for women has declined. Today it is becoming more of a matter of course for recruiters to search for—and clients to consider—candidates without particular regard to sex. While much of the steam has gone out of EEOC enforcement, the need for that club is not nearly as great as before. Haskell & Stern Associates was one of the first of the established general recruiting companies to assign someone specifically to searches for women. That search professional, Gretchen Long, now managing director of Haskell & Stern, no longer focuses so exclusively on women but rather recruits for general management and financial services across the board.

That's the way it has gone with quite a few firms. Some companies still undertake special efforts to recruit women. Others don't feel it's necessary, because women are included in the search as a matter of course.

Is gender totally eliminated as a factor in recruiting executives? Some maintain this is the case. Gerry Roche of Heidrick & Struggles says that women are making their way upward in the organization charts, that there is no more discrimination, and that the only criteria involves merit. These observers see a time not far off when men and women will be far more equally represented in the most senior positions, including those of CEOs of the biggest corporations.

But there are thoughtful experts who say the picture, in reality, is not quite that sunny. Many say that women still have to be at least 10 percent better than men. Women managers who found themselves eagerly courted for entry-level management jobs and who breezed up through the ranks into middle management are finding in some instances that the going is extremely tough as they move toward the upper-middle and senior ranks. Now, of course, the slope gets steeper and more slippery for both men and women. But there are indications that there is still a powerful male bond against which women must fight when they attain these levels.

Women, no matter how good they are, may tire of what they consider the unequal fight, or withdraw from the competition for other reasons. Women, after all, do confront the biological imperative. As they reach their middle thirties, in the decade that typically sees the consolidation of power, they must decide about motherhood, in addition to other decisions confronting the person pursuing a career in high-powered management.

Allan D. R. Stern, chairman of Haskell & Stern, feels he is seeing a trend in which there are fewer (or at least no more) qualified women for certain line management jobs—for example, CFO. Stern says that gifted women executives begin to leave the ranks as they move into the higher echelons because they weary of fighting resistance and see other options that look more attractive. For one thing, they meet men who are at comparable intellectual and career levels. There are a lot of marriages between executives in the midthirties. And the women, conscious that their time for starting a family is running out, may choose to move off the fast track, at least temporarily.

Of course, a woman can always elbow her way back onto the fast track in the big corporate world. But that isn't always practical or desirable. Other options seem better. Women executives go into smaller companies, or gravitate toward industries that already have a high percentage of women in senior posts—industries such as advertising, publishing, and public relations.

Some executive search people see another phenomenon: the tacit designation of certain corporate jobs as "women's" jobs. Director of corporate communications is one such job. In certain large corporations most of the senior human resource jobs go to women. These are gifted executives, as good or better than their male counterparts who are working in the line jobs, such as marketing. So the situation looks like a reversion to what existed 20 or more years ago, when it was natural to assume that men worked "where the action is" and women were kept in the corporate equivalent of the kitchen.

But today there's a difference. Some highly talented, self-confident women executives are voluntarily seeking alternate career paths that will permit them to choose among a full range of personal and professional options. Women M.B.A.'s are thinking these questions through. They no longer feel they have anything to prove. That women are as good as men in any kind of corporate job is beyond dispute. So women executives don't feel that they have to pick careers for any reason other than personal preference.

Today a recruiter will as a matter of course provide qualified candidates without reference to gender. Sometimes clients may indicate a preference for men (or, occasionally, women). The preference usually is hinted at rather than stated overtly. The consultant is likely to point out that, apart from the fact that such a policy would cut off a rich source of talent, it is against the law.

Talented women are not as hard to find as they were 20 years ago. Nowadays they are represented within the ranks of all areas of industry and therefore are as accessible to the headhunter's regular sourcing methods as their male counterparts. But some search professionals still like to make an extra effort, so they augment the regular sourcing by making contact with women's organizations and networks.

The search industry itself is offering more opportunities to women. Not long ago a woman member of a search firm was designated as a specialist in female recruiting. Then there were a few all-female firms, like Gilbert Tweed. Today, while there are not yet vast numbers of women working as general line recruiters, their numbers are increasing.

Linda Weiss is a vice president of PA Executive Search Group. She has never been designated a specialist in the recruitment of women; in fact, though she works in all functional areas, her particular area of specialization with this large international search firm is engineering and aviation, emphatically not a women's preserve.

Weiss is neither an engineer nor an aviator by training. After graduation from college she worked in the creative design department at *Seventeen* magazine and as an art secretary for an advertising agency. Then she formed her own company, selling sales incentives to business. She did not feel she was going anywhere; her husband remarked, "You're a career woman without a career."

Some friends in the executive search business suggested it was something that might interest her. It was. She has forged a successful career in recruiting. It's still hard for women, she remarks—"although it's not the way it was when I was starting, when the first question was, 'Can you type?' "

Men at the top levels of client organizations are, in many cases, still not used to women as recruiters. "So I prove in five minutes that I'm a professional," says Weiss. The candidates she interviews may be even less accustomed to a female in such a role. For most of them it is the first time they have been interviewed by a woman about a job. Weiss takes this into account, simply handling the interview with relaxed professionalism until the candidate is no longer conscious of gender. There are, of course, commonsense moves: "When I'm interviewing in a hotel, I take a suite. I never interview in a bedroom." But in fact, male or female, recruiters are apt to work out of suites. The bedroom interview seems a little below the top drawer, no matter what the sex of the participants.

Linda Weiss succeeds because she has what a good recruiter must have: quick intelligence; lively curiosity; and the ability to be a rapid study, learning overnight not only the facts and figures of an industry or a particular business, but also the intangibles that will influence the performance of the executive in the job. When experience is built on these attributes, the search consultant can recruit for all kinds of jobs, including such posts as one Weiss had just completed filling, the job of president of a security firm that protects executives against kidnapping from terrorists.

Women have come a long way in search, and search has come a long way in achieving scope and power in the world of business. Careers are profoundly affected by recruiters. So it's important for managers and professionals to know about executive search—how it works, where it is now, and where it's going.

CHAPTER 2
The Increasing Importance of Independent Researchers

THE MOST CRITICAL PART of a search is likely to be the opening phase, in which the "universe" is defined and the recruiter gets information on a broad range of possible candidates. Large recruiting firms have their own research facilities to conduct this part of the search. As a selling point for their services they describe their computerized memory banks containing thousands of names. In some big firms, associates are expected to assist each other by offering mutual support; each recruiter reviews assignments being handled by others in the firm and passes along sources, thus building up the reservoir of possibilities from which the list of candidates will be refined.

Smaller recruiting firms have no comparable research facilities. The job of conducting the initial research is time-consuming. Furthermore, it requires qualities that are different from those usually associated with a successful headhunter. Some of the most successful recruiters tend to be impatient with the painstaking requirements of good research. They are more comfortable when they are dealing with people face-to-face, whether clients or candidates.

So a new discipline has emerged—that of the *independent researcher*. This development and the list of researchers at the end of this book are of significant interest to potential candidates in a number of respects. When we consider visibility, we must consider the question of becoming visible to the independent researcher. Furthermore, an increasing number of independent researchers are performing an expanded function by actually making the first phone contact with the candidates.

The independent researcher (IR) is a subcontractor retained by the recruiter to conduct the first part of the search—locating target companies, getting the names of potential candidates, working up brief profiles and resumes, and talking with potential candidates to gauge the degree of interest. This might be called the legwork of the search—or, more properly, "wirework," since the independents make extensive use of the telephone. Their fees for all this work run from $40 to $100 an hour in most cases. An intensive search can take 100 hours.

SEARCHING SOURCES

Where is an IR likely to start the search? Typically with directories: *Standard & Poor's,* the *Standard Directory of Advertisers, D&B,* the *Directory of Corporate Officers.* Having defined the universe, the IR is likely to look, to a considerable extent, for people who are in the industry of the client company (unless the spec says otherwise). In seeking possibilities, one approach used by the contract researcher (as well as the full-fledged headhunter) is the "one step down" principle: If the job is vice president for marketing, look for directors of marketing in companies of roughly similar size. Or apply the "more room to swing" principle: Look for people with similar titles in smaller firms.

Another place the IR looks is in industry association directories, particularly those that are comprehensive and frequently updated.

Then the IR calls up key people in the industry whom she or he has gotten to know as sources. In this case the exploration is truly sourcing; the researcher is not calling the individual to determine interest but to get names of other people who might be candidates. Of course, if one of them turns out to be a candidate, that fact is reported to the headhunter.

The IR also uses printed material prepared specifically for search assignments. For example, Arch S. Whitehead Associates of New York generates highly detailed lists, including such categories as all the human resource professionals in the headquarters of *Fortune* 500 companies. There are more than 12,000 names on this particular list. Whitehead comments, "Con Edison alone has more than 300 people in human resources administration."

The Whitehead Associates people work this way. Say, for example, an edition of *American Men of Science* appears. The Whitehead approach is to go through every one of the 135,000 entries, classifying and coding each name according to such criteria as industry, company, geographic location, and academic degrees.

The products generated by Whitehead Associates are sold to search firms and corporate clients. They include, besides those mentioned, books in consumer package goods, finance/accounting, and other areas. The firm will also undertake customized research.

WHAT RESEARCHERS DO

Some independent researchers stick to the more traditional forms of research. Peg Phalen of Oberlin Park, Kansas, works with industry lists, periodicals, directories, and other printed sources to compile the lists she provides to her clients. She does not like to telephone, and she does not use ploys. She does, however, use live sources—for example, contacts with columnists for trade magazines.

Sometimes her clients—predominantly recruiters—give her instructions about the industry segments and companies in which they are particularly interested. In other cases she is asked to figure out the industry and companies to be researched.

Like many independent researchers, Ms. Phalen formerly worked for a large recruiting firm. She spent 17 years with Heidrick & Struggles and started that firm's research department. Later she worked with Pendleton James, who was a member of President Reagan's transition team, finding talent for the administration. (Mr. James now has his own recruiting firm.)

Peg Phalen now works mostly for smaller recruiters who do not have a research capability and who know, when they retain her, that they are getting a reliable, quality product. She undertakes every assignment afresh; she does not keep resumes.

But other independents work differently from Ms. Phalen. They expand their operations to take in more of the traditional search function. They meet candidates face-to-face, obtain organizational charts and other inside information, make judgments, and conduct what amounts to the first-stage screening. Other researchers prefer to limit their operations to more basic research. Still others go beyond basic research. They locate and identify candidates but stop short of some of the more elaborate intelligence-gathering aspects of the discipline.

Janis Roche of Redondo Beach, California, has been an independent researcher for five years. Before becoming an independent she worked for a couple of recruiting firms. She starts with a job specification and perhaps an indication of the industry segment within which the search is to be conducted. Her tool is the telephone. She calls companies and asks questions: "Who's in charge of consumer product testing? Who are the internal auditors who report to the vice president for finance?" She works patiently to dig out names and titles. Resistance and suspicion vary. Advertising and marketing-oriented firms, for example, are relatively free in giving out information. They're used to such inquiries, for all sorts of reasons. Hi-tech and Big Eight accounting firms, for example, are apt to be tougher. They have been "raided" many times, and their employees are instructed to be leery about giving out information on the phone.

After thoroughly working through the target companies, Ms. Roche has a lot of names. She begins calling these potential candidates. She is looking for interest, and if there is no interest, referrals. The product she feeds back to her client is resumes. She may talk on the phone with 300 people and get 25 resumes, which she turns over to a search professional, who undertakes the face-to-face contact.

In about three quarters of her assignments, says Ms. Roche, she is free to tell people the name of the company that has initiated the search. Obviously that makes her job easier.

IRs are proud of their ability to get information. An independent researcher who works in Chicago maintains that she and her counterparts can do the job better than even the biggest of the traditional firms.

She uses printed sources—*Standard & Poor's,* the *Standard Directory of Advertisers* (the *Red Book*), the *Directory of Corporate Officers,* and so forth. And she will use industry-oriented sources, retail chain guidebooks, and the like. But she emphasizes that these data "can be old in a month." So she relies heavily on the telephone, calling into target companies to get the information she needs. She disdains the more elaborate and controversial ploys, like pretending to be a big customer or bill collector. Often the researcher—who has a pleasant but authoritative telephone manner—gets results simply by getting through to a key person in the company and asking, in matter-of-fact fashion, for the names and titles required for the assignment. "When they ask me why I need it, I'm evasive. If they suggest that I forward the correspondence, I say, 'Sorry, I know it's dumb, but I have to send it direct.'" She points out that some people have a talent for it; she, for example, doesn't have much trouble getting what she wants on the phone.

What she wants is information: names, titles, places in the chart, reporting responsibility, etc. When this part of the universe-building task is completed, she will frequently call the potential candidate to get more information—perhaps compensation, receptivity to relocation, etc.—and to gauge the degree of interest in the target executive. If the potential candidate asks, she is likely to be able to send a specification, but she may not be able to identify the client.

This researcher's end product is apt to be brief biographical sketches on persons who are likely candidates. She may provide the client—corporation or recruiter—with six to 12 such possibilities. The client then pursues the face-to-face contacts.

"To me, where it is is not in the computer but in the discipline," says the researcher. A computerized setup is only as good as the discipline with which it is established and used. And information gets old so quickly. Nor does she feel that the old-boy network works as well as it used to. It's too limited in this day of extensive and complex organizations and sophisticated needs.

"The way I do it is better. It's pinpointed, it's fresh, and it fills today's needs," she says.

Some IRs, who started as information gatherers, are moving more boldly into "sourcing," which involves more the traditional executive search function—screening, preliminary interviews, etc. As this trend continues, it will be harder to tell where independent research stops and headhunting begins.

CHAPTER 3
Ploys and Scams and Flimflams

NOW WE TURN TO one of the more controversial aspects of recruiting research: the use of ploys and scams.

Turning up the names of excellent candidates who can't be found by traditional means has become a major concern. Some independent researchers offer a singular benefit. They say they will provide names, miniresumes, and organizational charts that are not easily available and that in some instances are closely guarded secrets. How do they do that? The corporations and search consultants who retain these specialists don't ask too many questions. They want results without necessarily wanting to know how they're attained.

Names and numbers are needed, and often they are just not available in *Standard & Poor's,* or *D&B,* or industry directories, or 10K's and 10Q's, which cover only corporate officers. This is the rule rather than the exception today. Organizational structures are extremely complex, unlike those of 30 or 40 years ago, when even a large company could be charted in a relatively simple pyramidal structure.

"The old-boy network just does not cover anywhere near all the possibilities anymore," says the researcher. "The old-line recruiters still depend on their networks, of course, but it doesn't really extend into all the nooks and crannies where the good candidates are stashed away. So you've got to get at those names. Fresh. Not through the lists and the networks and all the rest of the old-time apparatus."

Good, hard-boiled IRs don't settle for easily acquired referrals. Their stock in trade is up-to-date, important information that is not easy to get. To get the difficult facts, researchers may resort to some interesting devices.

TRICKS OF THE TRADE

A telephone operator at a large corporation answers a ring. An authoritative voice asks, "Who is the director of marketing in your Consumer Division, please?" The operator gives the information; the caller ascertains the correct spelling of the name and hangs up. This is a basic ploy. The IR has not identified himself, but he was not asked to.

But let's listen in on another call. The caller asked the switchboard for the secretary of the vice president for sales, Industrial Division. "Would you bring me up to date on the regional manager list, please? Names and regions." The secretary may not wonder at all why she is being asked for the information; she reads off the list. This is particularly likely to happen if the call is not identifiable as coming from outside. If the secretary asks why, the caller may say, "I have to send them some correspondence [or some new forms, or whatever], and I need the right spellings." If the secretary says, "Why not get them to me and I'll send them out?," the reply is, "I know it's a pain, but the instructions are to send this stuff direct. You know how it is."

A little misdirection is starting to creep into the conversation. A lot more misdirection may come into play if the caller runs into resistance. One enterprising researcher says the key to his success rests in three words: "Lie like hell." The caller may claim to be from another division of the company, or from a trade association, or from a well-known management consulting firm.

Certain researchers have developed considerable ingenuity, to say the least, in getting information. The approaches that say, "We're compiling a mailing list," or, "I am writing an article," are relatively straightforward compared to some ploys.

Some researchers are actresses and actors of a high order. (In fact, independent researchers will hire out-of-work actresses and actors to make the calls.) One of the most familiar roles is that of an important, impatient, and high-handed secretary of a senior executive in another division who wants the information and wants it now. But there are other interesting approaches. The caller says, "I was sitting next to one of your executives on a plane and we started to talk about some business I could do with your firm, but I've lost his card. . . ." Or, "I was talking with————[a well-known name in the industry] and he told me to call you. . . ." The ploys don't stop here.

Here's one scenario sometimes used. A caller reaches the manager of a key computer department in a large bank. The caller introduces himself as the bank's "official photographer" and says that he has been instructed to take a group picture of all the computer experts. He wants their names. The caller is really a researcher seeking information. (In this case the actual name of a photographer used by the bank was given to the manager.) In other variations on this ploy, the caller may represent himself or herself as the secretary of a senior executive in a remote division, or a member of a consulting firm retained by the company, or a member of the company's law firm. The "cover" always is that of someone who is in authority or who is entitled to the information. The information requested consists of names and titles. In some cases the caller will ask for more information, on compensation, for example. This is the case, for instance, when the researcher calls the Personnel Department pretending to be the executive assistant of the CEO and demanding capsule dossiers on a number of managers.

Here's another scenario. The CEO of a large corporation in the construction industry is told by his secretary, "There's a Mr. Gallman on the phone; he's from *Business Week* [or *Forbes,* or *Fortune,* or perhaps *Time* or *Newsweek;* an impressive and influential magazine, or, in the case of *The Wall Street Journal,* newspaper]." CEOs of major corporations do not brush off people who write for major publications. An article, or even a mention in an article, can have a profound effect on stock prices. So the CEO picks up the call.

Mr. Gallman says, "I'm working on a story about the people who are most likely to be the next generation of leaders in the construction industry—young managers who have been hired and are being developed by farsighted companies to guide them into the future." Mr. Gallman wants to ask the CEO some questions about his prudence and vision in building the next generation of managers. He also wants to know about the six or eight young tigers in the organization below the senior echelons. He will be talking with them next.

The CEO may say something about going through the firm's PR Department. But Mr. Gallman easily handles that. His approach gently implies that he and the publication are much too important to be fobbed off to the Public-Relations Department (which the CEO may think of as a bunch of wordsmithing flunkies, anyway). Mr. Gallman's manner further suggests that he might be offended. At the very least he would wonder why the CEO is not willing to talk, etc. Since these devices are the same as those used by legitimate reporters, the CEO, who is likely to have some considerable experience with the media, sees nothing odd.

Some senior executives, of course, have become quite cautious about responding to this sort of inquiry. They want to play for time, check it out. But Mr. Gallman has an answer for that. He is not on the masthead of the magazine. He is a stringer, retained to write this piece. He is on the road a lot, so it would be very difficult to call him back. He knows the people who work at the magazine, but the particular editor who is working with him is not available. And on and on. The CEO has the choice of blowing the possibility of a favorable mention that will make him and his company look good, or passing along some information that, after all, may hardly seem top secret. And Mr. Gallman seems intelligent, responsible, plausible, and in a hurry.

So the executive discloses the information.

Mr. Gallman—who is really, of course, a contract researcher—has gotten what he wants. The assignment is for a tough-minded young manager, a prestige M.B.A., who is moving up rapidly in a big company but who has not yet become well known in the industry. Once he has gotten the names, "Mr. Gallman" has little trouble finding out what he needs to know about compensation and reporting relationships.

How? One way is to ask the CEO—"I don't want to take up any more of your time"—to instruct his secretary to provide details. The secretary can come up with vital information in a short time, perhaps instantly if she is summoning it up on a computer terminal. Or the "reporter" is referred to other people in the company.

Through a combination of ploys involving misdirection, misrepresentation, and just plain lying, the researcher has what he wants. Now he, or the recruiter who retains him, can start calling the people who are his real targets. His approach may vary from the standard one of "We are conducting a search and I wonder if you could help me. . . ."

There are many other exotic variations of information-getting techniques. In one of the rougher ploys the caller pretends to be a bill collector, snarling threats until he is given the information he wants about compensation, job title, etc. There are further flights of imagination. In one case a researcher needed a hard-to-get name and some other information from a company that had been stung a number of times and had trained its people to be very closemouthed and suspicious about giving out *any* information, no matter how innocuous it might seem. The researcher taped the sound of dogs barking, turned on the tape in the background, then phoned into the company. With the dogs yipping he reported that this was the dog catcher, that a dog had been picked up, that only part of the tag was legible but it seemed to be someone in the company, and that the dog would be put to death immediately if the owner could not be located. Flustered and concerned, the secretary ran through names and other information while the caller said, "No, that's not it. Try again."

Some executive search consultants say that practically all the abuses are committed by researchers. The fact is that both recruiters and researchers can be guilty. The following vicious ploy has been worked by at least one bona fide search professional. The recruiter puts through a call to a manager—call him George Anderson. The recruiter has no interest in Anderson. He needs information on other areas of Anderson's company. He leads Anderson to think that he is being considered for a good job, at the same time milking the unfortunate "candidate" of the desired information. Anderson, at best, is in for a disappointment. It could be worse, though; buoyed by the spurious interest, Anderson may be led to make some disastrous moves—for example, trying to use the call to gain leverage inside his own company.

THE RUSING CONFLICT

Getting information through ploys and misrepresentations—"rusing" is the term often used in the profession—has become the subject of heated debate. It's standard practice for search consultants to denounce the practice and proclaim that no ethical firm will ever have any part of it.

Some headhunters and researchers say that's baloney. When rusing is advantageous, they all do it, according to this cynical view. Of course, the headhunter may not do it himself. He uses a "hired gun"—a contract researcher who is known to use this kind of approach. Some independents are quite forthcoming in describing their activities, even boasting of them. Others soft-pedal it, because they know the client does not want the details.

One thing is clear: Those who are willing to use such ploys, and are skillful at it, can obtain a lot of fresh, valuable information that is not easy to come by in any other way. Such information is getting tougher to dig out as companies, determined to protect themselves against the depredations of those whom they consider to be pirates, try to train their people to be cautious about telling anybody anything. But this is not always easy to do, and researchers can learn a lot this way.

There are those who become very upset about what they think IRs (and some headhunters) do. They call it spying. It is, of course, intelligence-gathering, but so far no one has determined that there are any laws against it. Nevertheless, the practice is not universal. There are IRs who deny using any subterfuges. But then, of course, those who do admit to a little skirting of the truth now and then are unwilling to be quoted. Since competition among recruiters and researchers impels them to find ways to come up with more and better information, it seems inevitable that the thrust will be toward discovering better ways to get information, even if that means cutting a few corners.

CHAPTER 4

Do-It-Yourself Search: A Trend Worth Noting

THE AVAILABILITY OF INDEPENDENT researchers is contributing to an interesting and potentially significant trend. A few companies have broken ranks. Instead of following the traditional route of retaining executive recruiters to fill management jobs, they are starting to conduct their own searches, working from bases in-house.

To some this seems like an astonishing departure from the established order. For four decades the executive search business has followed a distinct pattern. Headhunters, whether part of a big organization or independent operators, are retained by client companies to produce a small number of top-notch candidates who fit a set of specifications. The search consultants conduct research, or use research by members of their staffs. They activate their networks (some maintain that they are still "old-boy networks"), make the ritual phone calls, buy the customary lunches, and, when the search is complete, submit the customary invoices. Executive search has become a big industry. Many people cannot imagine how American business ever got along without it. The idea of business getting along without headhunters now seems bizarre.

But some handwriting is beginning to appear on the wall. The characters are as yet indistinct; but it is possible, if certain very embryonic trends grow, that the executive search field may be in for profound change. The effect of the change would be a considerable lessening of the role of executive search consultants in the recruiting of managers.

Some old-line search professionals, asked about such a possibility, dismiss the idea as unthinkable. Their reasons: Much recruiting for management jobs "always" has been done through the traditional search industry (always dating from the inception of executive search as we know it after World War II). And then, the search industry has done such a good job, the business community would have no reason to abandon the system. In-house searches could never be conducted with the same rigor as is applied by the professional. How would the company do the research and networking necessary for a successful search? Corporations don't want to be bothered with this chore. They will leave it to the professionals, as they always have.

This reasoning is shaky. At least a couple of trends may be contributing to a broad-scale revolution in the procedure for locating managers.

One such development is the growth in sophistication and clout of Human Resources Administration. When it was just the Personnel Department, stuck over in a dim corner, headed by a popular but no-longer-competent old-timer who was "good with people," run by a small gaggle of gorgons who presided over the benefit files, there is no doubt that the function was unable to handle anything so demanding as a search to fill an important position. But that's yesterday. Now it's the human resources function, reporting high in the chart, entrusted with the task of staff planning and development and wielding considerable influence in many companies to a degree that was unthinkable a few years ago.

Running this operation is a new generation of HRA professionals. They don't remember the old days. They hold no particular awe for the mystique of executive search. They focus on results and cost-effectiveness. Once a search company formed such bonds with a client company that it could do no wrong. A headhunter could boast that, for a certain client, he or she had found three CEOs in seven years, and nobody would even think there was anything odd about it. A lot of HRA people today feel that the traditional executive search approach has been getting something of a free ride, immune from the kinds of stringent criteria applied to other functions.

Looking at what the headhunter is supposed to do, human resources people in certain companies are beginning to say, "We could do that—or at least some of it—ourselves." From that the next logical step is trying to do it themselves.

A second contributing factor is the fledgling discipline of the independent researcher. This professional is called upon by a search consultant to make the preliminary identification of good candidates.

The headhunter then takes over and does his or her thing. Some independents stop after the research phase. Others make the preliminary contact by telephone, in a step that is a combination information-gathering and screening procedure.

MOVING TO THE CORPORATE SIDE

At first the independent researchers—a low-profile group—worked primarily for executive search people, being hired by the smaller firms without their own research facilities or the larger firms whose facilities were overloaded. But today a growing number of firms retain the independents directly. The independent researchers carry out the assignment up to a point, after which the corporate people take it over, doing the things that were formerly done by the headhunter. In some companies the search work is done by regular human resources staff. Other companies have set up special in-house recruiting units, more or less on the same principle as house advertising agencies. A few executive search firms have been bought by corporations. The recruiting companies continue to operate, according "most favored client" status to the parent firms.

When IR Janis Roche started her present business five years ago, she was retained exclusively by recruiters, most of them Los Angeles and Orange County firms not large enough to have in-house research facilities. Now she finds herself being hired by some companies conducting their own searches rather than using a traditional search consultant. The companies feel that they have the resources to complete the searches after the preliminary work has been done. One factor that impresses these companies is cost. Ms. Roche charges $35 an hour, plus expenses.

While Ms. Roche has no doubt about her competence to take the process to the next step and make face-to-face contacts and screening judgments, she prefers to continue doing what she is doing. "I get resumes. I don't usually build org charts or make judgments."

Joan Robbins, an independent researcher of Aurora, Illinois, near Chicago, says, "Yes, we are seeing more cases of corporations hiring us direct, and it's not just because it's less expensive. We cut the time necessary for the search. We know how to do it right."

Ms. Robbins was with the Executive Search Division of Kearney before starting her own operation. She works nationally; the search firms who retain her, like most of her counterparts, are likely to be the smaller ones who do not have their own research capability. She will work for contingency firms on a guaranteed-fee basis. She relies on cold calling—"We have ways of getting names." While she reports that most of her clients are recruiters, the trend is toward the corporation as direct client.

Primarily, says one independent researcher, it's a matter of money. "They got tired of paying those huge fees. There's a big difference between $5,000 and $45,000." The latter figure would be 30 percent of a first-year compensation of $150,000. The lower amount is what they would pay this researcher for a typical search. In 1985 she was charging $50 an hour plus expenses.

Of course, this does not figure in the time and expenses of in-house personnel engaged in the search. But many independent researchers, along with quite a few recruiters, feel that the early stages of the search are by far the hardest parts, and the things that take place once the candidates have been identified are largely a matter of handholding. Obviously there is still a vast body of opinion that the expert headhunter earns his or her fee through shrewdness in sizing up people, facility in understanding the real needs of the organization and matching people to them, and skill at persuasion.

But many human resources executives feel that they, too, possess these intangibles. And besides, the handholding, and the wining and dining, are the fun parts. Besides, say some of those who carry out in-house searches, they are more attuned to the plans and needs of the enterprise than an outsider could be, whatever his or her experience or reputation.

Large search firms maintain that their big data banks and research facilities give them a decisive advantage in identifying possible candidates. Smaller recruiting firms and independent researchers tend to scoff at these claims. They say that there may be more hot air than data in a lot of these memory banks. And they try to turn the proclaimed strength into a weakness by declaring that the best research is conducted fresh for each assignment, not based on old information. (However, many researchers, along with virtually all recruiters, acknowledge that they look at resumes and file promising ones.)

HOW COMPANIES DO IT THEMSELVES

Despite what many recruiting firms say about their services being irreplaceable, many executives disagree and even are starting their own searches. One such executive, Warren Wasp, left the Recruiting Division of Arthur Young nine years ago to join Warner Communications as director of executive compensation and recruiting. "I looked at the organization," he says, "and saw that Warner had more than 50 searches, all over the lot."

Wasp installed guidelines for the retention of search firms. But then, in a much more sweeping move, he began to undertake Warner's searches himself. Unlike in-house recruiters who hire independent researchers to handle the early parts of the search up through the first phone contact, Wasp and his staff do it all themselves. Typically Wasp will buy a list from a company specializing in lists for headhunters. "We might ask for all the names of financial executives in companies in a certain area."

Then Wasp does direct sourcing, calling people up and saying, "Hi. I'm Warren Wasp of Warner Communications. We have a unique opportunity. . . ." His in-house unit handles searches from $50,000 up.

"We were able to save half a million on fees the first year," he says. He feels that his approach gets good people at a fraction of the charges of headhunters by dispensing with a lot of the ritual that headhunters claim as part of their unique ability but that some other people dismiss as techniques more likely to impress the CEO of a corporation than to hire the right manager.

Wasp believes the trend toward in-house search is swelling, although slowly. There are still, he remarks, a great many corporate leaders and unsophisticated personnel people who rely on the old ways. But more companies will put in their own operations, he says. For one thing, there will be a greater supply of recruiters available for corporate work. "A lot of the guys working as independents are going to be shaken out," he remarks. "The field is too crowded. These guys are going to be able to go to the corporations and say, 'Let me run the thing for you. I can save you money.'"

Here's how another successful in-house operation works.

Ed Miller is manager of professional recruitment for Standard Oil

(Ohio). He is a professional recruiter, having spent four years with Peat, Marwick and six years on his own before being brought in to set up Sohio's department nine years ago.

Miller has four professionals on his staff. Each has about 10 years' experience in recruiting. The department handles practically all of the corporation's recruitment at the incentive level. The unit works as a profit center, serving the line divisions of the company. The fee schedule is based on a fee ($5,500 in 1985) and expenses plus 10 to 15 percent of the fee as a service charge. So searchers, even at the highest level, cost the line department client no more than about $6,000 to $7,000, considerably less than what outside consultants charge.

At rare times the client department will express a strong preference for using an outside recruiter because of special circumstances pertaining to the assignment—for example, one of a particularly technical nature. When this happens, three headhunters may be invited in for a "shoot-out" competitive presentation, demonstrating their methods of operation and selling their effectiveness. Miller remarks, "In the case of a shoot-out we never really have to make a decision. At least two of the presenters shoot themselves in the foot." When all three shoot themselves in the foot, the in-house department conducts the search.

At Standard of Ohio there are now very few searches farmed out to traditional recruiters—only two or three in each of 1984 and 1985.

The Sohio recruiting unit uses a highly structured approach in conducting its searches. The job description is the beginning. Working with the line division, the internal recruiters develop a detailed specification. They designate target industries and perhaps target companies toward which the search is to be directed. Then the recruiting unit turns to an independent researcher. (Standard of Ohio makes extensive use of the services of Elaine R. Shepherd Company, near Denver.) The researcher obtains names, makes phone calls to potential candidates, and provides resumes and written reports. Then Miller's department takes over, just as an outside recruiter would, interviewing candidates; bringing them in for interviews with the client divisions; and administering psychological tests, in which Sohio believes strongly.

Miller says the Sohio approach is far superior to the long-dominant custom of retaining conventional search firms. The most striking difference is cost. The internal department runs the search for far less than the recruiting firm would charge—30 percent of first-year compensation (sometimes going up to 33 percent) plus expenses.

Miller feels that recruiters charge too much. He is particularly critical of such practices as the 10 percent additional service charge that some firms request, and the additionally dubious practice of generating needless expenses.

A greater value of the Sohio approach, according to its architect, is the ability of the internal search unit to get a better sense of what the position really calls for and what kind of person is needed to fill it. Every company has its own culture, Miller maintains, and an outside recruiter, dealing with the spec and his conversations with senior managers, is far less apt to divine the true nature of the intangibles that will affect results. The Sohio unit, says Miller, is better able to give the line manager/client what he or she needs.

Miller feels it is inevitable that more corporations will move in the direction of setting up their own search units—though the move will be slow and, in many cases, reluctant. For one thing, senior management in a lot of companies has no idea of what the company is paying for the services of search consultants. The bills are neither analyzed nor questioned. Moreover, there is the feeling on the part of the senior executive that one should remain on good terms with prominent recruiters, because, after all, one fine day the phone could ring with the possibility of an even more magnificent job. The mystique of executive search has been bought totally by a lot of corporate people who are hardheaded, even cynical, about other things but who are surprisingly uncritical about the headhunter.

And then there is the safety or "cover your ass" factor. When the wrong person is hired, if the agency has been one of the top executive recruiters, the CEO can always say to the Board, "We got the best." Whom do you blame if the internal department blows it?

But the reasons to consider establishing an in-house facility are becoming more compelling. The escalating cost of the headhunters is one factor. Another problem is the extent to which a major search firm may be precluded from covering all the possible sources because, if it did, other of the firm's clients might be "raided." (The degree to which headhunters keep hands off their clients is a matter that is subject to some argument. Some firms maintain that they will keep hands off a client organization altogether for, say, two years after the search. Others limit their hands-off pledge geographically, divisionally, and functionally. And there are those critics who say that when push comes to shove, the headhunter will go anywhere self-interest takes him or her, regardless of pledges.)

Miller and others say that another reason companies will be

thinking more about doing it themselves is the performance of the recruiting firms. Miller remarks that one problem often is that the person from the recruiting firm who signs up the client does not do the work. (He feels that, in dealing with an outside recruiter, it is essential that the company be able to meet and evaluate the people from the search firm actually assigned to the task.)

Then critics say that the work of headhunters sometimes can be amazingly sloppy. Candidates show up without having seen the specs and knowing only the most rudimentary facts about the company. (Of course, this is the candidate's fault. One who is contacted by a headhunter should learn everything possible about the client—and should, as a matter of course, ask for the specification early in the process.)

But for most companies who consider going this route, the primary appeal is apt to be money. There is a rule of thumb in the establishment of charges in a good number of search firms: One third is compensation, one third is overhead, one third is profit. The in-house operation can save a lot on overhead and most or all of what goes to the headhunter as profit.

But Miller warns that the in-house operation should be made up of people who are primarily search professionals. He says, "You can't do it with a hotshot HR executive and a couple of ambitious M.B.A.'s. The HR guy will be afraid to recruit from companies where his buddies work. The M.B.A.'s will want to hire themselves."

The staffing of the in-house facility is a critical point. Elaine R. Shepherd runs one of the larger independent research companies, in Aurora, Colorado, near Denver. She has seen her business shift from a point at which she worked almost exclusively for recruiters to a situation today in which a great deal of her work is for corporations. Ms. Shepherd prefers to work only for corporations that have established a search unit staffed by people with recruiting experience. She feels that human resource people without recruiting experience, whatever their level of ability, often are not equipped to carry out a search as it should be done.

Others take a different view. They hold that a strong Human Resources Department can handle the latter stages of a search after a researcher has carried out the sourcing and, perhaps, initial contact. One HR professional says, "I'm not just a booking agent for headhunters." In any event, as the concept of in-house search spreads, it will be set up in a variety of ways—sometimes with experienced recruiters, sometimes completely by human resources staff.

Another factor in the success of in-house recruiting is company structure. A corporation with a centralized orientation and strong staff resources would seem to be a better bet for the approach than a decentralized company.

Some years ago a very large multinational company was structured as a highly centralized firm. There were senior HR people available, and there was a multiplicity of searches to be conducted. The HR director had become somewhat disenchanted with many recruiting firms: "A lot of what search firms get is gravy. They overcharge. And they don't necessarily do a full job of sourcing. They go to the usual sources and hope they get lucky. I mean, the pulp and paper industry publishes a blue book with resumes and pictures, which you can get for about $60. Why pay a lot of money for research based on that book when we could buy it ourselves? We found we could do for $15,000 what we would have to pay $60,000 to a recruiter for. And besides, senior staffing is fun."

Now, under new leadership, this corporation is being drastically decentralized. The strategic business units do their own staffing and, since they do not have large human resources departments, tend to use headhunters. But, says the corporate human resources director, in-house recruiting with the proper setup is a first-rate idea: "When the circumstances are right, I might do it again."

Various factors combine to make it likely that more companies will try in-house search. Independent researchers are available. The fees of the recruiters are coming under increasing scrutiny. Corporate human resources departments are growing in strength, sophistication, self-confidence, and influence within the organization. And as competition increases within the executive search field, experienced recruiters will be attracted to the idea of going to work for corporations rather than battling for business on their own.

CHAPTER 5

Visibility I: Being There When They Start Looking Up Names

WHEN A SEARCH BEGINS, there are basically two ways in which you can be included. You can be listed in a source, print, or computer memory bank that the recruiter or researcher consults. Or you can be mentioned by a source who is contacted by the computer. A less likely possibility is that the recruiter knows you already or, having talked with you in the course of a previous search, met you at a business gathering or socially.

Let's begin with the matter of getting your name into the recruiter's internal files. We'll look first at how the big firms handle their files.

GET YOUR RESUME OUT

Gerry Roche is a virtuoso who works on the basis of instinct and persuasive power that have brought him to the top of his profession. But his virtuosity has solid underpinning. He enjoys the support of Heidrick & Struggles's considerable research capacity, orchestrated for his use by Assistant to the Chairman Pamela Conway Hayes.

Hayes is the executive in charge of putting blips on Roche's screen. While the searches that Roche conducts personally are in the most rarefied heights of the corporate power structure, the procedure used in generating his initial list of possibilities does not differ in principle from that used by Heidrick & Struggles in running any of its searches.

Each of the firm's offices—in New York, Los Angeles, Houston, and other cities—has a Research Department and a computer terminal on line to the main computer in Chicago. When one of the consultants takes on a search, he is likely to sit down with a researcher and talk about the client, the job, the industry—the salient facts about the project. The researcher then checks the computerized files to look for possible candidates. The file is, of course, cross-referenced in all relevant respects—responsibilities, background, industry, compensation, etc.

The vital question: *How do names get into that file?*

The file contains names and information on people with whom Heidrick & Struggles recruiters have talked in the course of previous searches. Some have been actual candidates. Some were recommended and approached but were not interested. Some were sources of information.

Well, how else did those entries get into the files? Pam Hayes says, "A good researcher is a squirrel. We are constantly looking for useful bits of information and storing them away." Hayes, who worked in the Heidrick & Struggles Research Department before becoming Roche's assistant, reads newspapers, magazines, books, and newsletters, looking for mention of people who might someday fit a search. The obvious sources are the business pages and magazines, but interesting nuggets may be gotten from other places—gossip columns, for example. The alert researcher develops antennae that pick up indications of talent and accomplishment.

And here we confront another important question for the manager: *If I send them my resume, will it get into their files?*

A few executive searchers dismiss the "over the transom" resume almost totally. For example, Robert W. Dingman of Westlake Village, California, says, "Before sending your resume to a search firm, ask yourself, 'Am I so special that somebody would pay a fee to get me?' Our company is not a career-change medium. We're not particularly interested in taking the time to go through a lot of resumes."

But that's not true of Heidrick & Struggles. There, every resume is looked at. And unless the resume falls totally outside the bounds of any conceivable search, it is made part of the memory bank. Hayes says the firm's setup has the capacity to store so much information that few submissions are discarded.

So there is a great deal of sense in sending one's resume to Heidrick & Struggles. You get into the computer brain. And once you are in there, no matter how you got there, your number should come up as a possibility when a search seems to fit.

The pertinent information from the resume is punched into the computer. The resume itself, in its more primitive paper (or hard copy) form, is stored in a file. But before being filed, the resume is checked to see if it fits any current searches. It is checked manually in the office to which it has been submitted, and it is checked again at the central data source in Chicago.

What about the smaller firms, those without spacious research facilities or memory banks? They look at resumes, too. In fact, a glance at the profiles of search firms in the back of this book shows that the great majority look at resumes. And, in general, that is also true of the independent researchers on whom many smaller recruiters rely to identify possibilities.

Even in firms that maintain as a policy the proposition that unsolicited submissions are thrown away, individual recruiters will admit to keeping their own files of promising resumes. So part of any comprehensive visibility campaign is sending out resumes. If they are sent to responsible recruiting firms, the worst that can happen to you is that the resume is discarded.

Prepare an up-to-date resume in conventional reverse chronological order. Don't get fancy. The purpose of the resume is simply to place you in a category. Categories usually are those of functional area, industry, rank, compensation. Head the resume with your area— marketing, finance, etc.—and indicate at each career step your title, whom you worked for, what you were paid, and anything unusual about what you did. Don't lie or inflate; it can be fatal.

Write a short covering letter, which might say something like this:

> While I am happy with my present company and doing well, I feel it makes sense for me to bring myself to the attention of leading recruiters. For this reason I submit the enclosed resume. The kind of opportunity that might particularly interest me would be that of CFO of a larger energy-related company in the West or Southwest. . . .

Don't send it all over the place. Send it to established recruiters, usually those who work on a *retainer* basis. The exception would be those contingency firms you know, and particularly those that specialize in your particular area. Otherwise you may be sending the resume to firms that are, basically, employment agencies.

Send your resume to a number of branches of a large firm, particularly branches in parts of the country (or world) where you might like to work. Address a resume to the director of research where feasible, to the CEO of the firm, and perhaps to a principal who specializes in your line of work. (The profiles of some search firms in this book occasionally indicate the areas of specialization of principals, and also the names of research directors.)

Update your resume periodically, especially when there has been a significant step in your career. Allan Stern, chairman of Haskell & Stern, suggests you update the resume once a year. "If it's hard to list your accomplishments," he says, "your employer knows it, too. It's time to move on." Be sure to send updated resumes to recruiters with whom you've had contact, as a possible candidate, a source, or in some other way.

OTHER WAYS TO GET INTO THE GAME

For practically all recruiters the files are a first step. A snack-food client wants a merchandising executive. The recruiter checks the files, first by industry, to turn up possibilities. A few phone calls to sources within the files turn up some leads. And the recruiter is off and running. These leads may not turn out to be active candidates. But their names will go into the files.

Most file entries carry standard identifying data. Some may append comments: "slow-spoken but mentally quick . . . locked into Chicago area . . . very active in industry association . . ." In these files you're not apt to find really negative comments. Persons considered incompetent, alcoholic, or undependable are weeded out or never included in the first place. Sometimes these names may be relegated to an inactive file or flagged in some way. An individual may be a dead loss as a candidate but a potential source of leads.

Moving on from the files, the recruiter turns to the resource materials that often set the direction of the search. Basically these sources are lists of names of executives. They may be such basic references as *Standard & Poor's* or *D&B* listings. Then there are the extremely valuable possibilities inherent in lists of names compiled by industry associations.

Membership in an industry association may seem like a joke to a lot of people. The meetings are boring, the bureaucrats who run the industry office are drones, the newsletter is vapid. So the executive says, "Who needs this?" and forgoes enlistment in the association. All of the negatives about the association may be true, but just being listed as a member may be worth far more than the cost of membership in money, time, and boredom.

That's because lots of headhunters turn to these directories early in the game. Sure, the directories are just lists of names. Sure, membership in the industry association is no guarantee of ability. But the recruiter has to start someplace. He or she is searching for an executive who has experience with widgets. A list of people who belong to the widget association is a prime source. You may be the Lee Iacocca of widgets, but if the headhunter doesn't find your name on a list, your chances of being approached for a good job are somewhat diminished.

Diminished; not destroyed. The conscientious headhunter networks through sources until coming upon a live possibility—at least one. If you're good, someone may mention your name. But the big idea is to offer as many possibilities as possible to be contacted.

One of the best ways to do this is to get your name on as many lists as possible. After all, associations are not the only places where lists are compiled.

There are other lists. For example, every industry and functional area have trade publications. Many disciplines and executive categories have publications that cater to them. Sometimes the publications are not very exhilarating reading. Sometimes they contain little that is new. Sometimes there is just too much essential reading; that which is not essential goes in the wastebasket. So a good many executives do not subscribe to the trade publications in their categories, or they take some but not all.

But in career terms, that might be an oversight. These publications sell their subscription lists. Usually the lists are used for direct mail (another reason some people prefer to stay off the lists). But the lists also are used by executive-search professionals. It's a cheap way of getting a lot of names, addresses, and telephone numbers of people in a particular category.

So don't pass up the opportunity to get the magazines in your field, particularly those that come to you because you "qualify" by filling out a card with your title and other information, such as number of people supervised. Get on the list even if you don't read the magazine. And keep yourself updated.

These lists of names are only a starting point. The headhunter may try to narrow down the field by looking for things that provide some qualitative rating of people, even if that rating is subjective or whimsical. Stories in industry publications listing speeches, membership on committees, promotions, etc., help in the narrowing-down process.

The recruiter's file may also contain roundup stories that mention promising young executives, job movements, etc., without particular reference to industry. By cross-checking, the headhunter narrows down a list of people within the industry by focusing on those who have achieved mention of one kind or another.

Sending the resume is the beginning. Now proceed to build on that foundation so that you are able to implement a practical, effective visibility program.

Still another route to the attention of the recruiter may be the university alumni journal. This is particularly true for professionals, scientists, engineers, and younger executives who are graduates of the "prestige" M.B.A. schools—Harvard, Wharton, Tuck, Stanford, and the like.

Organizations that carry out networking on a systematic basis— Women in Media is just one that has found great value in this approach—also are helpful in assisting you to come to the attention of recruiters. In the case of women and members of minority groups, some recruiters—as a matter of course or when requested by the client—get in touch with such network organizations when looking for candidates.

But networking need not be confined to formal organizations, nor is it just for women and minority-group members. By keeping in communication with people who can offer advice and help, you also use another means of getting your name around, thus increasing the chance of appearing on the search organization's radar screen.

OUTPLACEMENT

If you're being fired and your company provides the services of an outplacement specialist, find out if the outplacement specialist is giving your resume to search firms. If not, why not? If so, which ones? You may want to follow up periodically.

Outplacement professionals understand that executive-search people look at resumes. Outplacement is, in some ways, the other side of the coin of executive search. In trying to place their clients, outplacement consultants define a "universe" of companies that might be prospects, conduct research to focus on likely candidates, then guide executives through the process of trying to get a job with these companies.

But outplacers recognize the value of broad-scale prospecting with search firms. Some search companies maintain regular contact with outplacers to supplement their reservoirs of candidates. Now, while the headhunter is not likely to proclaim to the client that a candidate has turned up because he has been terminated and is trying to find another job, it is nevertheless true that good people may be made available through the outplacement process. So part of the outplacement routine will involve mailing out resumes to quite a few headhunters.

Claudia Gertner, vice president of Seagate Associates, a Paramus, New Jersey, outplacement company, sometimes will recommend mailing resumes to 300 or more search firms. She may include the large across-the-board recruiters in the lists for practically all her clients. Among smaller recruiting firms she will help the executive to focus on those that tend to work most in the industry area in which the executive is looking for a job.

CHAPTER 6
Visibility II: Building a Favorable Image

EXECUTIVE SEARCH PROFESSIONAL DOES not mean ESP. Headhunters are searchers, not clairvoyants. They look for the best candidates, and they find those who can be found. If this were a perfect world every possible candidate would be unearthed, no matter how deeply buried that candidate might be. But it doesn't happen that way. The ideal job may be out there waiting for you. But if your name does not come up—out of the files, off a list, in conversations with sources—then you're not going to be found.

Image is important in getting jobs as well as in most other areas of life. Lester B. Korn says, "There's no doubt that it helps to be prominent in your profession." How do you become prominent in your profession? Achievement is essential. But you capitalize on achievement by using public-relations principles to enhance your prominence. When the search consultant starts calling people to ask if they know of somebody who might fill a given job, these contacts are far more likely to mention you if they have seen your name in print, watched you speak or appear on TV, read your articles. This is why the creation of personal PR programs for executives has become a major source of income for some PR practitioners. But you can do a lot of it yourself.

Personal public relations is not just a matter of becoming known. It consists in becoming known in the right context—creating a favorable image. When the recruiter telephones a source, you want that source to mention your name. It's even better, though, if the source says, "I've heard he has a lot on the ball." It's better yet if the source can say, "I've heard him speak [or read his articles], and he has a lot on the ball." Best yet is when they say, "I've seen him in action, and he is good."

There are a number of elements in planning and carrying out a strategy that will enhance your reputation and attract the right kind of attention at the right time. With thought and care you can handle most of them yourself. And if your company has a public-relations or corporate-communications director you may be able to take advantage of free professional advice and help.

Corporate PR directors need cooperation from line or staff managers. They are often frustrated because they learn about significant developments too late. Get to know your in-house PR person. Keep her or him informed about what's going on. In turn you may reasonably expect that when you're involved in something newsworthy the public-relations department will prepare and distribute a release about it.

In working with your PR professional, share every fact and idea. Don't screen out the things you deem not newsworthy. Let the PR person decide that.

Of course, the Public Relations Department's principal mission is fostering corporate image. Sometimes this involves keeping things out of print as much as it does getting them in. Here is where the PR person really needs help. Top management often has a tendency to keep the lid on bad news until very late in the game. That includes the person who will be responsible for managing the news. If, without breaking specific confidences, you can warn public relations about an incipient problem, you may help that function to operate creditably when the crunch comes.

The PR people always are interested in getting the name of the firm around in a favorable light. Skillful practitioners of the craft don't need much of a hook to prepare a good story. So even though you may not be in the top echelons of the company, some activity involving you—a speech, a product change, a personnel shift, a promotion, a new process—can serve as the medium for a good story.

Don't think you are keeping in adequate touch with PR simply by directing information copies of memoranda "FYI." Provide some help. Point out the significance of the information. For example, a memo describing a newly installed machine might bear the notation, "As far as I know, this is the first in this area. Imported from Germany." The plan for rearrangement of a warehouse might be explained: "Faster access. Easier inventory. Possible because of new forklifts."

The point is that any event within the company should have meaning in terms of the company's goals. (If not, why is it being done?) When you help the PR person to see the significance, you are performing a service.

So when you tell public relations about your own activities, point up the angle that enhances the corporate image. You give a talk to your local Rotary Club. Whatever it's about, use the company as a good example: "Here's how we solved that problem at Global." Give the PR Department advance information about the talk, including a copy, if you've got it. Underline the parts that feature the company. Even though the group you're addressing may not be earthshaking, it can be a hook. A release goes out headed, *Global Problem-Solving Process Revealed*. The PR person is happy, and you've gotten some free publicity.

WRITING ARTICLES

Another good way to bring yourself to the attention of your colleagues, your industry, and executive-search professionals is to write an interesting magazine article. Authorship of an article says you have something interesting to say and that you can say it in a way that gets across to others.

There are a number of areas in which you can be published. The most obvious are the major business magazines: *Forbes, Fortune, Dun's Review, Nation's Business, Business Week,* etc. These are also the hardest in which to be printed. Some, like *Business Week,* are essentially staff-written. Others will carry articles signed by outside contributors, including executives. "The Manager's Journal" in *The Wall Street Journal* is a prized space open to submissions. Many of the pieces by-lined by senior managers are actually written and placed by public-relations professionals, either on staff in the executive's firm or in a PR agency retained for the purpose. (Personal PR programs for executives can be highly successful. When you see a manager appearing all over the place—in print and on the screen—you can be practically certain that the phenomenon is not accidental; it has been orchestrated by an astute PR mind.)

This also goes for other high-visibility outlets, such as the in-flight magazines you pull out of the pocket in front of you on the plane. Usually the stories are very well done. The in-flights are able to get high-quality work for extremely low fees because the stories usually are PR efforts to achieve notice for a company, a product, or a person. This is not to say you should not try the major business magazines or the inflights if you have a good idea. But they are a tough market.

Fortunately, there are other possibilities. Usually the trade magazines relating specifically to your industry are looking for fresh material. Their editors are especially open to contributions from people who can provide something different and interesting.

Local business publications sometimes print articles. And then there are the business sections of the newspapers—but for that market you are better advised to prepare releases, which are quite different from magazine articles.

Don't overlook such possibilities as alumni magazines. An article in the alumni journal has been of significant help to a number of executives, because it has been seen and filed away by a fellow alumnus who also happens to be a search professional.

Note the kinds of stories these publications run. Think of several ideas that might fit. Then enlist the PR person's help: "I have an idea that might make an article for————. A lot of the people I know read it, and it would be a good way to tell people about our new process. . . ." The PR specialist may like the idea, prepare (with your help) a "query," or proposal, to submit to the publication, and perhaps may follow up with the editor. He may then ghostwrite the article. After all, that's his job.

HOW TO SELL AN ARTICLE

Editors work on the basis of "queries"—proposals submitted by writers. The query is a one-page selling piece that describes the article briefly; indicates what's different, interesting, and attention-getting; and tells how it will be done—with case histories, anecdotes, etc. Professional writers send queries to editors. The editor, if he or she likes the idea, sends the writer a contract that includes provision for a "kill fee"—what the writer is paid if the magazine decides not to use it.

Here is a typical query:

TAKING A BYTE OUT OF CORPORATE EXPENSES

by Joe Clyde, President
Polaris Payment Systems

A new application of computer technology is helping companies solve an age-old problem: controlling corporate expenses.

Travel and entertainment now is the third biggest expense item for most companies, after payroll and computers. Other expense items—including remote-location payments, performance allowances, cooperative payments, display allowances, and credits—generate thousands of transactions every day. When individual transactions cost more than they should, the cost leak per transaction is small—but the cumulative effect is like the "death of a thousand cuts," with the company bleeding money in a multitude of places.

Throughout the years various ways of controlling expenses have been tried. Cash advances and corporate credit cards facilitate spending but leave out the element of meaningful control. Actually, the most effective way ever found for controlling travel expenses is a business adaptation of the international banking concept of the letter of credit. However, some managers have resisted the idea because it seems to require too much effort.

Polaris, specialists in expense control for nearly a hundred years, has now developed a method of computerizing an effective means of expense control that works and runs by itself, with the need of little management attention day-to-day.

Financial executives are hailing this development as an important example of computer application. The author tells how to do it and describes how it's being done through case histories.

GETTING INTO THE PAPERS

When the market for your article is not a magazine but a newspaper, one of the essentials of your personal public-relations program is knowing how to write a press release. The release is the staple of communication between people who want to get into the papers, and editors who want to fill their news columns with factual and interesting reading.

Nowadays it seems that practically everyone involved with any kind of activity thinks about obtaining free publicity. Editors are swamped with releases, most of which are thrown away after the most cursory glance. Editors say they can tell at a glance whether the release is newsworthy. That's not quite what happens. The editor's first glance is devoted to finding out if the release is *usable,* if it can be put into print with a minimum of editing. When a release is an amateurish mess, a dedicated editor with time on his hands *may* read through it, trying to find the kernel of sense. But that's not likely. The bad release is lofted into the wastebasket. Some newsworthy ideas are lost to the world because people do not know how to do releases.

Most of us know that a newspaper story starts with a lead that distills the important facts into one paragraph, answering the questions Who?, What?, When?, Where?, and Why? Begin your story with a lead that contains the relevant facts, but don't go overboard in trying to be terse and snappy. Some releases that try too hard for compression just give the editor a laugh.

Like this lead, for example: "Polaris Products Vice President of Marketing Gene Finchley's speech to the monthly breakfast meeting of the South Side Sales Club on the topic of 'keeping your sales options open' was greeted by an audience of 93 marketing executives on October 17, 1985, at the Grand Ballroom of the Mayfair Hotel with enthusiasm. . . ." Too much in too brief a space. When you try to jam everything into one sentence, you confuse the reader. Give yourself two or three sentences:

> "Keeping sales options open is one of the most important things marketing executives can do today," said Polaris Products' Gene Finchley to nearly a hundred top managers at the October breakfast meeting of the South Side Sales Club. Finchley, vice president of marketing for Polaris, told the enthusiastic gathering at the Mayfair Hotel . . .

Study the publications in which you would like releases to be printed, and come as close to the style as possible. But don't worry too much about copying the style identically.

The form in which you send out the release is important. Make it as easy as possible for the editor to read and use. Leave space at the top—a quarter of a page or so—for the editor to "slug" the copy. When all the editor has to do is slug (scribble a few words of instruction) on the release, it's easy for him to approve it. Write the date you want it to be published. Usually you want it ASAP, so you write "For Immediate Release." Unless the release is typed on your letterhead, type your name and address. Then "Contact—[your phone number or numbers]."

Next, write a brief headline. The publication will almost invariably write its own headline, so you don't have to go into agonies of creativity about this. Our release could be headed:

"Keep Your Options Open,"
Marketing Executives Are Told

Type the release double-space. Keep it short—one page if possible, no more than two. Then photocopy it and send it to the editors of all of the relevant publications. It's a gamble, but you haven't risked much, and you may be pleasantly surprised at having your release picked up.

COMPOSING LETTERS

An additional way to get your name in print is via the "Letters to the Editor" column in business publications. It's free, it's good visibility, and it enables you to position yourself in a way that corresponds to your job-getting strategy.

Many publications run reader-response features. These features are found in the major business magazines such as *Fortune* and *The Wall Street Journal,* in the local business press and in the more sharply focused industry magazines. These are widely read features. By getting a letter printed you help yourself by:

• letting people inside and outside your company know you have some interesting ideas

• getting your name before executive-search people and those to whom they turn for recommendations

• becoming a potential resource for editors.

Print has great authority. People who work with you, or have lunch with you, or socialize with you, tend to take you for granted. While the old saying "Familiarity breeds contempt" may not be altogether true, familiarity rarely engenders awe. When you have a letter published in a column read by your colleagues, you may experience some kidding, but they will wish they had written the letter—and they may form a new, albeit grudging, respect for you.

Headhunters start with names. When they see the name of an executive signed to a letter that makes an interesting point, they may add it to their files.

Editors like to have a file of experts to whom they can turn for comment. If you've become identified as having special knowledge, or being articulate, or possessing a special point of view, journalists may call you for quotes.

And it's not as hard to get into the letter columns as many people think. Editors are always looking for good letters.

What's a good letter? One that's short and clear and makes a contribution.

Scan the letters columns of the business publications you read. Get a sense of the length and type of letter they favor. Look for articles that will serve as hooks on which you can hang letters. For example, if an author makes a statement with which you disagree, you may have a chance of getting a letter printed. Most publications like enlightened controversy in the correspondence sections.

Don't write in anger. Don't protest too much, or denounce the author. Your letter will be discarded, and you may be tabbed as a crank. Disagree with a fact or an interpretation: "A closer look at industry performance statistics . . . Another way of looking at these facts . . . This result may be seen in a new light when we consider . . ."

Keep it short. Choose one point that can be made distinctly and briefly. Make your point and close.

Another excellent basis for a letter is the provision of additional information or insight. Don't just write with a comment that translates into "I think this is a good idea." Add to the knowledge or understanding of the reader: "Another way of achieving this result . . . Here is additional proof . . . This may help those who want to put this theory into practice . . ."

Good letters do one or more of several things: They give the reader something new and interesting to think about; they make a civilized argument in opposition to a previously made point; they provide the reader with new information; and they offer helpful suggestions.

As with press releases, write your letter in a form that makes it easy for the editor to print it. Leave room at the top of the page for slugging (in which the editor writes a headline or caption and instructions to the printer). Print the letter double-space. Keep it to one sheet unless there is an extraordinary reason to go over to a second sheet. Long letters are losers.

Start by citing the material to which you are responding: "In his article 'Human Resources Merge with EDP' (January 1986), E. T. Case concludes that . . ." Say just enough about the subject to recall it for those who read it, and provide the gist of it to those who didn't read it. Ideally a letter should stand by itself and not be meaningless to those who missed the original piece.

Set up your point: Tell the reader the nature of what you're going to say: "Another relevant fact . . . I can help to clarify . . ." Then say what you have to say.

Some publications will print your title and company. Most won't. So, if possible, weave your identification into the body of the letter: "Here at Polaris Industries we have developed a system that alerts us to problems . . . Last year Polaris Industries confronted a similar problem. We found . . ."

Make sure your home phone number is on your letterhead. Write quickly, as soon as you've seen the article to which you're responding. The first acceptable letter often is the one that gets in.

Write as often as you can, to as many publications, big and small, as you wish. Don't write general letters, with copies to more than one publication. Tailor-make each letter to a specific publication by referring to something that has appeared there recently. If you do a good job you're very likely to see your name appearing in a variety of places.

MEETING THE PRESS

Don't forget to touch base with members of the press when you're looking for publicity. Where can you find a reporter?

When you attend a convention or a reasonably important luncheon meeting of an association—particularly one at which a prominent speaker appears—you're likely to see a number of journalists, if you look hard enough. They may be sitting at a press table, or they may be scattered around, indentifiable only by their badges. Most executives tend to steer clear of the members of the press—because they feel uncomfortable with them, or are afraid of them, or think it a waste of time to talk with them, or because they sense that the reporters may be sneering or laughing at them.

This last feeling is likely to be true in some measure. Journalists do not view business executives with awe. But then they do not view anybody with awe. They are inclined to cultivate an extremely cynical attitude toward most if not all of the human race. To the reporter, people who hold big jobs and make a lot of money are just as human as everyone else, only more so.

This cynicism, combined with a fear of the power of the press, makes a lot of executives wary of reporters.

Don't be wary. Get to know the press people. At a business occasion they may include staff members or stringers from business services and newsletter publishers such as Kiplinger and Research Institute of America. These people reach a lot of executives with their writings—and that includes executive recruiters and their sources. This is a very good reason to meet the press.

Mix with reporters. Introduce yourself. Don't worry about whether they may think you want publicity. Of course you do. And they want sources for fact and opinion. By becoming such a source, you can bring your name to the attention of a wider business world.

Ask press people what they think of the meeting. Tell them about your own particular area of expertise. Don't pretend to be expert in unfamiliar areas. But in your own field, make some definite, clear—perhaps controversial—statements. Say that you have information and would be glad to share it anytime the journalist wants your help in checking something out. Give him or her your card. Maybe you'll have the chance to write down a key word or two on the card—"regional banks," or "just in time." Make sure you get the reporter's name and affiliation right.

And leave it at that. Don't try a snow job, don't offer to buy drinks unless the reporter wants to continue the conversation. But at some point afterward, when you have what you think is a piece of news in that reporter's particular field of interest, call up and pass it along.

Then, when a journalist calls you as a source, be a cooperative source. If you don't know something, say so. If there's an answer you're not sure of, say what you think, add that you want to check it further, and then call back as quickly as possible. Be crisp and definite.

And you'll find yourself quoted. One quote may lead to another. Other media may get in touch with you. You're getting favorable visibility. Give good value for it. Understand what the journalist wants and provide it objectively, without hedging or propagandizing or exaggerating your own role. Being quoted as an authority is reward enough.

GETTING ON TV AND RADIO

The proliferation of talk shows and business shows on television also provides good opportunities for visibility. With the coming of cable, more and more local stations are putting on interview and panel shows. They need guests who combine expertise with effective presence on the tube.

Watch the shows aired in your region. Get into contact with the station. One way is to write the program director or producer of a particular program. Comment on a show that especially interests you. Then make a couple of suggestions about topics designed to appeal to an upscale business audience.

The producer will welcome a calm, positive letter, since most of the mail contains complaints. When you get a response, you may want to follow up with a phone call, offering additional comments and suggestions. The producer may not think of you as a fountainhead of TV wisdom, but you may be noted as someone who has authority, who has something to say and can say it.

When you're invited to appear on an interview or panel show, give some thought to how you want to handle yourself. Effectiveness on TV involves a lot more than knowing your subject.

Prepare for the show. Think of the likely questions you may be asked. You may find that there are really just a few basic questions, a dozen or less. Obviously they can be asked in any one of a great many ways, but the answers remain the same. Write highly distilled, punchy answers to each question—one answer to an index card. Combine attention-getting boldness with one dramatic fact. For example, the guest is vice president of a small suburban discount brokerage firm. The interviewer asks, "Why do investors come to you rather than the larger brokerage houses?" The answer could go on for many minutes, covering the pros and cons of investing. But the guest answers, "People around here are smart enough to call their own shots without paying for a lot of advice they don't need and can't use."

The answer is brief. It's in everyday language—no jargon. It's clear and strong; the speaker is taking a position without directly attacking anyone. And it's *short*. Keep your answers short: twenty seconds or less.

It's all right to pause and think about your next answer. Many inexperienced guests, dreading even a microsecond of dead air, tend to rush into their answers as soon as the interviewer ends the question. People who wait a moment, then answer, appear to be thinking, even when they are not. You've observed this yourself on talk shows when you've seen a thoroughly seasoned celebrity, who must have fielded similar questions a thousand times before, pause, concentrate, and then give an important-sounding answer that he or she has learned by heart.

By making yourself move your body, you help yourself relax. And by having headline-short answers to the basic questions, you can command the interview. (Don't be shy about reviewing your index cards before the show, although, of course, you must not bring notes of any kind on camera.)

But while you don't want to consult notes, it's a good idea to do something visual if it is relevant. A chart with big, bold, colorful graphics can enhance your answer and revive the watcher's jaded eye. You don't just spring your visuals on the show. Talk to the producer beforehand so they can prepare to train a camera on the material at the right time.

When you are able to perform as an interesting TV guest, you come before the eyes of a lot of people. Your skill and savoir-faire on the medium will help to build your visibility and credibility.

A VISIBILITY CHECKLIST

Have the headhunters been calling you? Not frequently enough? Then you need to increase your visibility.

Here's a checklist of visibility enhancers, some of which have been covered in depth. You should have as many of these angles going for you as possible.

Widen Your Network of Acquaintances. Meet, entertain, and play golf, tennis, racquetball, etc., with executives of other companies. Try to join a select luncheon group.

Befriend the Consultants. When outside consultants—not head-hunters—undertake projects within your firm, they need reliable resources. Some people steer clear of them. Don't make that mistake. Become a resource. Consultants talk to headhunters, and general consulting firms often undertake searches.

Use Your Community as a Showcase. Volunteer for local activities that show you at your best: speaker, meeting leader, analyst, coordinator.

Speak Up. Work up a good speech. Let community and business associations know you're available. Program arrangers are always looking for speakers.

Use Your Company's Outside Associations. Get to know your firm's bankers, auditors, and lawyers. Headhunters use them as primary sources.

Make the Convention Your Arena. At industry gatherings, make the scene in the suites. Don't get on a soapbox, but don't just engage in chitchat, either. Ask perceptive questions. And don't slight the formal sessions of the convention. Even if you're not on the program, you can attract favorable attention with a short, penetrating comment from the floor—illustrated with an anecdote that makes you look good.

Screen Headhunting Firms. Your company may work with one executive-search firm. When a job is to be filled, suggest that other headhunters be screened. Volunteer to handle this chore.

Keep in Touch with Old Colleagues. Executives who have left your firm may well mention you to headhunters—if they think of you. Make sure they don't forget you.

Be an Officer in the Trade Association. Some people think volunteer work with business associations is a pain in the neck, but such involvement builds good visibility, especially if you become an officer.

Get into Print. An article with your by-line can be valuable in arousing the interest of the search professionals. It's not that hard to get into print; Pages 50–53 shows you how. And you don't need to confine your writing to articles. Letters to the Editor are heavily read and can be extremely helpful.

Get on the Air. You can be on radio and TV. The proliferation of UHF and cable TV has created more opportunities for articulate guests.

Retie the Old School Ties. Attend alumni get-togethers. Make sure that old grads who are managers know what you're doing and where you work.

Be Kind to the Headhunter. If called by a search consultant, be very helpful even if you have no interest in the job. Let it be known that you are judicious in recommending other candidates.

Leak the Numbers. Is your salary/bonus arrangement higher than that of your peers? You may be encouraged to keep this under your hat, but it may not be a bad idea to let the word get out. Often you are rated on the basis of what you're paid.

Get More Than Money. Concentrate on promotions, not just more money. Even when a promotion does not bring all that much more power, a boost in title can be helpful.

Be a Board Member. Take any opportunity to serve as a director for another company or an institution (hospital, community association).

Spread the Good Word. Get news of your job changes and promotions in newspapers, trade magazines, alumni publications, etc.

When You're Abroad, Let Them Know You're Around. When traveling for business or pleasure, get to know other executives and officers of industry associations. Keep in touch with these persons.

With the help of any one or any combination of these attention-getters you're apt to be hearing from someone soon.

CHAPTER 7
First Contact I: The Recruiter Reaches Out

THE PURPOSE OF VISIBILITY is to attract the attention of the recruiter. When that attention comes, how should it be handled?

The first contact may be by letter or telephone. In a way it's easier when it's by mail. You have a chance to look over the spec and decide on your response. The letter probably will invite you to respond, by phone or mail. The ostensible purpose of the response may be leads for the headhunter to follow: "I'd be very grateful if you can suggest anyone who you think would be right for this position. . . ." But, in fact, the recruiter's higher priority is to determine if *you* have any interest.

More often than not, such letters are followed up by phone. But not in every case. So you have to decide whether to respond by letter or phone. The first consideration here is: What do you know about the recruiter who has sent the letter? Is it a legitimate firm? Will your reply be kept confidential? A good deal of the discussion in this chapter, along with the profiles of executive recruiters at the back of the book, will be of help in determining your response.

But there may not be a letter. The first contact may be by telephone: "Mr. Anderson? I'm Steve O'Brien, with Brown and Smith Associates, the executive-search organization. I'm working on an interesting assignment. It's a blue-chip company looking for a senior vice president of finance at a very attractive compensation level. Since this is your area of expertise, I'm wondering if you might be able to suggest a qualified candidate."

You're at least curious. But you're also cautious. How do you proceed?

Unless you are absolutely uninterested in exploring the possibilities, you will go along with the process. You'll be asked some questions; you'll give some answers; *and you should have questions of your own.* The nature of your questions and the extent to which you should insist on answers are subject to your informed judgment. There are certain risks. But these risks are implicit in the executive-search process.

The person who calls you may be an executive-search consultant who has been retained by a client to find someone to fill a job. This is still the norm—but there are other possibilities. The caller may be a contingency recruiter, not working on retainer. The caller may be an independent researcher hired by a recruiter or a corporation to handle this part of the search. Or the caller might be on the staff of the company doing the hiring.

The caller wants to get information about you and to gauge your interest in the job. At the same time, the caller is likely to be forming first impressions about you, impressions that may be quite important.

You have four considerations in handling this first contact:

- making the right impression

- learning as much as you can about the caller

- learning as much as you can about the caller's client

- protecting yourself.

WHO'S THE CALLER?

As we have seen, the person who calls may not be a traditional executive recruiter but rather an independent researcher retained to do this part of the search. You can't always tell. Some researchers describe their function. Others find it easier to let you assume that they are full-fledged recruiters. Here's the opening frequently used by one researcher:

The researcher says, "Good morning. I'm———. You don't know me. If you choose to call me a headhunter, I can't object. The reason for my call is a bit out of the ordinary. My client has gotten an excellent line on you and is really impressed. He would like to talk with you. The client is Polestar Industries. The job is vice president of administration. . . ." The researcher proceeds to give a lot of details of the job—compensation range, operating budget, reporting relationship, and so on.

Then: "Obviously I don't know your feeling on this. But unless I've turned you off, it seems to me that you ought to talk with my client."

The manager may say "Sure." Or he or she may say, "Well, I'd like to think it over," in which case the caller applies techniques that have proven to be quite effective in pushing hesitaters over the edge. Or the target may say, "I don't think so. I'm happy right here."

"Ever play poker? You're being invited to sit in on a table stakes game. Your only ante is your presence. You have everything to win and nothing to lose. If you don't like your hand, you fold. At worst you will have met some people who might be able to do you a lot of good in the future."

The approach of this particular researcher has obvious differences from the approach of the average headhunter. He is using a battery of appeals to obtain hard-to-get information. He likes to tell the candidate more on the phone than most headhunters do. He sells very hard. And he does not meet the candidate face-to-face.

The researcher is apt to be calling to get information and an indication of interest from you rather than to make judgments about you. The information—including the resume you may be asked to send—is then turned over to the search consultant or the in-house recruiter, who takes it from there. You may find that on some things the researcher does not have the latitude possessed by the recruiter. For example, the researcher may be precluded from disclosing the name of the client company, whereas the search consultant, if pushed hard enough, may have the option to disclose it.

If you are not sure whether the person calling is a recruiter or a researcher, ask: "Are you the executive recruiter handling this assignment, or are you doing research?" It's useful for you to know— but it should not be the main criterion on which you base your decision on how much you will tell the person on the phone.

Some people make a bad mistake when they learn that the person making the call is not an executive recruiter but rather a researcher working for an executive recruiter. They regard the caller as a flunky. This is dangerous. While it is true that the researcher's role is likely to be confined to gathering information and measuring interest rather than making judgments, judgments are, of course, made in the caller's mind and may well be reflected back to the client. One researcher says,

"Some guys will patronize me, or be abrupt with me, or call me 'honey.' You're most likely to run into that with sales types. I note it on my report."

Treat the researcher who calls you with every iota of the courtesy you would use with a full-fledged recruiter. This is not just courtesy, it is common sense.

How much should you say on the phone?

In *The Wall Street Journal* of February 28, 1985, Alix M. Freedman suggests, "Assuming the recruiter is legitimate, don't divulge much beyond name, rank, and serial number when returning the call."

The reason: to prevent a capsule resume of your background and financial situation from being spread throughout the industry by the consultant. The story in *The Wall Street Journal* relates that just such a thing happened to a systems analyst who did not even know the resume existed—until he was told about it in an embarrassing confrontation with his boss.

It's sensible to be cautious in talking about yourself on the phone with someone you've never met. However, to limit your answers to those of a prisoner of war may not be the right tactic. Executives who are candidates for big jobs are assumed to be sure of themselves and able to size up situations quickly. Uptight caginess can convey the impression of someone who is scared about hanging on to a job. This may be a thoroughly wrong impression. But impression is all the recruiter has to go on at this stage, and while the self-assurance to talk about yourself on the phone may be unrelated to the specific demands of the job, remember that we are dealing here with perceptions as much as we are with facts.

If the recruiter is "legitimate," as Alix Freedman says, the facts about you will *not* be shopped throughout the industry. Legitimate recruiters don't work this way. Shopping you around is the last thing they want to do. The recruiter is working on a specific assignment for a specific client. If you are a prize, he wants to deliver you to *his* client without risking losing you. Nevertheless, there is reason for caution. You can be victimized by the "phantom search."

The executive takes the call and hears the usual, "I am conducting a search for an important firm. . . ." They meet. The headhunter asks a lot of questions. The executive, in turn, wants to know more about the company, the job, and the kind of person being sought. The headhunter furnishes a lot of general information—"*Fortune* 500, diversified, looking for leadership"—but is short on specifics. And, of course, the headhunter will not identify the client: "You understand how these things work and that we have to keep confidentiality. . . ."

There is no client. The "search" is phony. The searcher is indeed a headhunter, but he has faked this mission.

Why? The searcher may be collecting information. The "candidate" could very well find that his willingness to consider another job becomes known to people around the business world and ultimately to the members of his own Board. But often those who conduct bogus searches have another reason. They are simply widening their networks, making contacts, enabling themselves to say, casually, "I was talking with Jerry McKee of Polaris last week and he said . . ." In a business where knowing people is so important, it is not surprising that some will go to considerable lengths to strike up acquaintanceships. The pretext of a search is a perfect cover. It has become so widely accepted that many managers talk to the guy who approaches them about all sorts of things without thinking.

But even though we can acknowledge that it can be risky to open up on the phone, the reality of the situation is that you may have to do so or forgo your chance at an interesting job. The more you can learn about the situation, the better you can assess the risk.

Obviously one vital piece of information would be the name of the client.

WHO'S THE CLIENT?

The possibility of beiing victimized by a phony search is just one reason that it would be useful to know the client's name at the very beginning. There are more compelling reasons. You may not want to work for them. You may be aware of some special circumstance, for example, that a key person in the client firm is very close to someone in your own company, making it more likely that your interest in the job would become known.

And the earlier you know about the client company, the more quickly you can begin finding out about them so that you are better equipped to decide how much you want the job, what you should ask for, and what problems you may encounter.

But don't make instant disclosure of the client's identity an absolute must. For one thing, the recruiter may have been specifically forbidden to give out the name on the phone. If the caller is an independent researcher, it is more likely that there is such a restriction.

If you demand the client's name before saying another word, you may only turn the recruiter off, missing out on what might have been a very interesting and profitable experience. Headhunters have emotions, too. They can get mad when people seem to get tough with them. One search consultant says, "After that *Wall Street Journal* article appeared, the next six guys I called clammed up. 'Who's the client?' was all they'd say. It drove me nuts."

This doesn't mean you should not ask the client's name on the telephone. You should. And in many cases you'll get the answer. Recruiters like to be open with potential candidates. The veteran Tom Buffum says, "If I don't want the candidate to play games with me, then I can't play games with him. I will tell him who the client is unless there is some overriding reason why it can't be done."

How much you should *insist,* however, is partly a function of the level you have achieved. Heidrick & Struggles chairman Gerry Roche says, "Make him identify his client. Be blunt. Ask, 'Who is it?' If he won't say, tell him to call back when he can disclose the name." But Roche conducts very high-level searches indeed. After all, you can't call people like John Sculley at PepsiCo and refuse to name the client. However, most people may not feel they are in a position that lets them be quite so unyielding.

Researchers are less likely than executive recruiters to be free to disclose the name of the client on the telephone. If the caller is a researcher, accept the limitation and use judgment. Ask questions. Get the caller to spell out the nature of his or her business. Learn the name of the researcher's company. (You may want to check it against a list of researchers, which can be gotten from a source described elsewhere in this book.) If it sounds okay, go ahead. Elaine Shepherd says that on most of her assignments her people are not privileged to disclose the name of the client. She adds, "But we have no trouble. Most people are used to having to make up their minds quickly about whether to trust another person or not. They certainly have to trust us. After all, we are asking them how much they make, along with other fairly sensitive information. They do trust us. For one thing, it happens that we are trustworthy, and it comes through." Ms. Shepherd remarks that scientific types are most likely to be cautious about opening up on the phone.

It may help to keep in mind that you are just as safe in talking with a legitimate researcher as you are with a bona fide executive recruiter.

WHO'S THE HEADHUNTER?

Maybe you can learn, on the first phone call, the name of the client. Maybe not. But you can learn about the person who is calling and about the search firm he or she represents.

The caller just might be an independent researcher. If so, ask him or her the name of the search consultant that person is working for. Ask other questions about the recruiting firm—how many principals, what kind of clients they serve, and how they get paid.

When, as is likely, you're talking directly with the recruiter, you have a chance to ask questions that will help you decide on your next move. If the firm is familiar to you—if it's one of the big, well-known ones, for example—you may not have to ask as many questions. In any event, the caller should be willing to talk with you about his or her company—type of practice, degree of specialization, size, number and type of clients, etc. Reticence about the identity of the client may be understandable. Evasiveness about the search firm should arouse your curiosity if not your suspicion.

The key question to ask the recruiter is the basis on which the client is paying her or him—*retainer* or *contingency*. Since this question is central to your decisions on how to continue the process, it is appropriate to discuss it at further length here.

The San Andreas Fault of the headhunter business is the distinction between companies that charge on a retainer basis and those that charge on a contingency basis.

The heavy hitters in the industry are retainer-basis firms. They are paid a retainer for undertaking the search, regardless of its outcome. The retainer is part of a basic service charge (the predominant method of payment), or a charge based on time and expenses. The fee is typically 30 percent of the first-year annual compensation of the occupant of the job. This may go up to 33⅓ percent. Some firms undertaking international assignments will charge 35 percent or more.

Some firms receive one third of the estimated service charge in receiving the assignment, with another third paid during the search, and the final payment when the search is completed. There are variations; for example, a company may charge 20 percent on signing and 20 percent per month up to a preset limit. Yet other companies receive payment on a fixed-charge basis. Overall, however the payment is made, the retainer-basis firm charges 30 to 33⅓ percent, and sometimes more.

Contingency-basis firms do not charge retainers. They get paid if and when the client hires a candidate (just like an employment agency, except that the payment is always made by the employer, never the job-seeker). The contingency-basis firm does not necessarily charge less. For example, Houser, Martin, Morris & Associates, of Bellevue, Washington, charges 30 percent of estimated first-year compensation on jobs paying $30,000 or up. That's the top percentage. They charge on a sliding scale: 18 percent for jobs between $18,000 and $18,999; 25 percent between $25,000 and $25,999; and so forth. But since the vast majority of retainer-basis firms do not recruit at those lower levels, the top fee is the only one that merits comparison.

The contingency-basis people maintain that their approach is the most cost-effective because they get paid only if they do the job. The fee-basis firms say, with considerable justice, that a truly professional job cannot be done on a contingency basis. The contingency firm, they maintain, just cannot afford to put in the high-quality time needed to conduct a first-class search for an important executive.

The argument of the retainer-basis consultants is represented in the following statement by Whittlesey & Associates of West Chester, Pennsylvania:

FEES, EXPENSES, AND GUARANTEES

Our minimum fee is thirty percent (30%) of the estimated first year compensation for the position to be filled, including estimated bonus, commission or other compensation, plus reimbursement of all expenses such as travel, accommodations, meals, postage, advertising and any other direct costs associated with the assignment. Expenses are billed monthly, and any major travel requirements are reviewed in advance.

We believe that the "full retainer, no contingency" fee system of many executive search firms does not provide the proper incentive to the search firm. We also believe that the "no retainer, full contingency" fee system of employment agencies (and so-called contingency fee search firms) seldom results in a truly quality search, because assignment turnover, not client service, becomes the firm's principal concern. We feel that our system of a non-refundable retainer of one-third of the total fee upon commencement of the search, with the remainder due upon our successful completion of the assignment, captures the best features of both systems.

We guarantee any individual recruited for three months; if that individual should terminate during the first three months of employment (either voluntarily or involuntarily), we will find a suitable replacement without additional cost to the client (except for expenses).

Executive-search people who work on a retainer basis are frustrated about what they see as general indifference to the distinction between them and the firms that work on contingency. Heath C. Boyer, who runs a recruiting firm in Atlanta, speaks for many of his colleagues when he says, "The business press just does not convey the importance of this point. The difference between fee and contingency is crucial. People who get a telephone call have got to ask the question 'What is your fee basis?' "

Boyer is right. It's an important question. The method of payment of the recruiter is emblematic of the way the search is being handled. A retainer arrangement is likely to mean that one recruiter has the exclusive assignment for filling the job. And, while there will be exceptions, corporations use retainer firms to fill jobs to which they attach importance. (Among the exceptions are jobs in specialized areas—advertising, accounting, data processing—in which smaller, specialized search firms work on a contingency basis.) When the recruiter is on contingency, there may be other recruiters—some of them more employment agencies than search firms—on the assignment.

Ask, "What is your fee basis? Retainer or contingency? Have you done other work for this client? How often have you met with this client? How recently?" If there seems to be vagueness about how often the caller meets the client, or even if they meet at all, this may signal that the "executive recruiter" is handling this by phone or mail—not an auspicious circumstance for the person called.

The business world has long since bought the argument of the retainer-basis search consultants. Higher-level searches are, to an overwhelming extent, entrusted to the fee firms. Contingency-basis firms are used by many companies to fill middle- or lower-level jobs. They can have several contingency-basis firms working on the same opening, whereas retainer-basis search consultants are likely—except in extraordinary circumstances—to handle the search exclusively.

So the retainer-basis firms are ordinarily accepted—certainly by themselves—as the elite, the professionals of the business. Contingency-basis people sometimes mutter that the other guys are selling a lot of mystique without much substance.

The retainer-basis headhunters are bigger, work on a higher executive level, do more research, and generally dominate the upper levels of the business. This has been true for some time. But, as we will discuss, *there may be clouds on the horizon.* Some new developments in the area may threaten the domination of the traditional elite—not because the business world will turn back toward the contingency option, but because a growing number of companies may think of contracting out the initial research part of the assignment (at considerably lower charges), then handling the rest of the search in-house.

In one sense, it does not matter at all to the candidate how the headhunter gets paid. If, through the medium of a search firm, you get a better job, you could not care less about the fee arrangements.

But it is vital to know whether the search person who gets in touch with you is from a retainer or a contingency firm. If it's contingency, there may be other headhunters working to fill the job. Also, the retainer-basis partisans say, you run a greater risk of having the news of your interest in the job leak out. The contention is that some contingency operatives may shop your resume all over town.

If you have any experience of the world you will be skeptical of the proposition that charging a retainer fee automatically confers sainthood on a search firm. There can be sharp practices among the "elite." One cannot always be absolutely sure of confidentiality. However, it is reasonable to assume that a retainer-basis headhunter is likely to be more professional in many ways than the contingency counterpart.

The Association of Executive Search Consultants (AESC), at 151 Railroad Avenue, Greenwich, CT 06830 (tel. 203-661-6606), promotes ethics and professionalism in the business. Membership is confined to retainer-basis firms. There is a code of ethics setting forth standards for professional conduct, confidentiality, etc. Fewer than 80 search firms are members. This is not because they can't or won't measure up; a good many search professionals—including some of the biggest companies in the business—abstain from membership because of politics and rivalries within the industry. (Search is an industry that has no shortage of gossip, resentment, backbiting, and intrigue.) Search companies may subscribe to the AESC code of ethics without belonging to the association. It can be interesting and sometimes instructive to ask the headhunter about AESC membership and the code of ethics.

Find out whether the headhunter works on a retainer or a contingency basis. You will have a better sense of how to handle yourself.

And avoid anyone who presents himself or herself as a search consultant but who proposes to charge *you* for getting you a job.

WHY NOT MEET THE RECRUITER?

Having learned what you can on the phone and having formed some gut feelings about the caller and the situation, you must decide whether to proceed with the process.

When the search consultant approaches you, he or she does not bring a job offer but instead is offering the opportunity to apply for a job. Successful executives who occupy top-level positions don't see themselves as job applicants. Gerry Roche is keenly aware of this. Roche is famed for his audacity in going after the executive he considers the best available, whatever that executive's present position, degree of satisfaction, or level of compensation.

It's easy to see that some headhunters, confronted by the unwillingness of a candidate to pursue an opportunity that may not pan out, can be led into exaggeration. They may tend, consciously or unconsciously, to give the candidate the idea that all he or she must do is agree to go along with the process and the position will be offered that person.

Of course, Roche and other ethical search professionals do *not* operate in this way. Roche is apt to say something like, "Look, they're interested in you. I know you're not looking. But why not talk? I know you make it a point never to stop learning. Here's a chance to learn something." The executive *is* interested in learning new things, and it is certainly a universal characteristic to be curious about the value others place on us. And there's one more thing to be said for Roche's approach: It provides a good rationale for the executive who might really be very eager to go after another job but does not want to admit it.

Understand what the headhunter is asking of you. He is asking that you be an applicant twice: first, that you apply to become a candidate; second, that you submit yourself for the job. In practically no case can the headhunter, however the approach is worded, offer you anything else than that. You haven't been picked out of a hat. You have somehow been identified as a possibility for the job. But possibility is a long way from certainty. You will do well to assume that you are going to be up against at least one other candidate.

This situation may be unwelcome. You may be so totally happy with your present job that under no circumstances would you take another. You may be absolutely unwilling to run the risk that your employer will learn of the contact. If the risk is too great, then no potential reward justifies it.

But if you do not have overriding reasons to avoid the headhunter, and if you are reasonably sure that the search is a legitimate one and the searcher is a bona fide professional, then *why not*? Why not talk? Gerry Roche's point is compelling. At the very least, you will learn something. If nothing else, you will gain experience in a process that may be of vital importance at a future point in your career.

Don't go into the first meeting with the search consultant with a chip on your shoulder. Some do. They are suspicious, or they resent being put in the position of having to apply for a job. Resolve your mental dissonance about these matters before talking to the headhunter. They are the realities of the situation. There is no guarantee. You may be screened out right at the start. You may go through a series of interviews with the client company and get to the point where you are eager to get to the job—even counting on it—only to be rejected at the end. If you can't deal with any of this, don't begin the process.

Having agreed to meet the consultant, be realistic about the situation and the possibilities. You may decide, after talking with the headhunter, not to pursue the thing. So determine to use the time to get enough information on which to base the judgment of whether to go ahead or not.

Understand at the same time that even though you may wish to keep on, the matter may not be pursued with you. This need have nothing to do with your qualifications, especially if the searcher has gone through a thorough screening process. But three good candidates may have been contacted, and the client may decide to look at only two. Or the client may have changed the specifications. Or a reorganization may have eliminated the need to hire someone. Or any one of a dozen other things may affect the situation.

The process can be long and frustrating. You will find yourself resenting the search professional, telling yourself you were promised things that have not been delivered. Bring yourself up short. Nobody promised you a rose garden. You are only a possibility until they actually offer you the job.

But what if your present employer finds out? Take a moment to think through *that* scenario.

Everyone knows that executive search is a commonplace of business life worldwide. Your boss probably has talked more than once with a headhunter, perhaps landed his present job through a headhunter. There is no basis at all for the reaction that you are somehow disloyal for having such a conversation—no logical basis, that is. The subjective reactions, on both sides, are something else. Within the most sophisticated, self-confident, and up-to-date executive is often a core of illogical fear, a feeling that the relationship resembles that which exists between Dagwood Bumstead and the terrible-tempered Mr. Dithers. If Mr. Dithers learned that Dagwood was talking with a search consultant, the next panel would find Dagwood being booted out of his swivel chair; but the following day's strip would show that Dagwood and his boss have resumed business as usual.

When you talk with a recruiter it's not a bad idea to assume that, before long, word is going to leak back to your company. At least think a little about the implications if that does happen. Would your boss be angry or hurt? Maybe. Would he be justified in feeling that way? No. Would he penalize you? *Would your job be endangered?*

If your answer to the last question is *yes,* or even *maybe,* think about the implications. If your employer holds you in such low esteem that you can be imperiled by merely talking with a headhunter, then you have not been doing a good job, or your boss doesn't know you've been doing a good job. If you are of real value to the firm, news that you may be "looking around" should motivate your employer to find ways to keep you on board.

In most cases when the company learns that a key person may be looking around, the reaction is neither extreme anger nor hurt (although there is usually some resentment), nor feverish efforts to retain the new employee. The employer is apt to become somewhat wary and start thinking, "What should we do in case he [or she] leaves?" But that's nothing to worry about. These days most savvy employers do that anyway.

It may be desirable to have a conversation with the boss (when it is certain the boss has learned of the contact). The exchange could be opened something like this: "I like it here and I have every intention of sticking around and giving it my best shot. But, of course, I wouldn't be human if I weren't curious when a headhunter calls. I hope you feel I'm doing a good job and have a real future in this company." Without making apologies or commitments you can lead the conversation into a discussion of your prospects for greater opportunity. In short, you shouldn't let unrealistic fears of losing your job keep you from meeting the recruiters.

WHAT DO YOU NEED?

When you do make an appointment to talk with the recruiter, before the meeting you should, if at all possible, be sent a specification. This is a brief rundown of the job, describing the company, the duties and responsibilities, the qualifications being sought, and the compensation range. First-class professionals prepare these specs, basing them on the more elaborate specifications prepared by the client, and send them out to potential candidates as a matter of course, omitting the name of the client.

If there is no written specification, ask why. If the search professional has been given specs by the client, he or she should be willing to share them with you. If the search professional isn't, you're entitled to consider whether he or she may be playing games, implying the existence of a search that the person is not, in fact, pursuing. Another possibility is that there is some ambiguity about the nature of the job, or even whether there is a job to be filled at all. This ambiguity is not uncommon among clients. Good search consultants try to get all the doubts resolved and questions answered before they undertake a search, but that is not always possible.

Such cloudiness need not be detrimental to your chances. You may be able to impress the headhunter, and then the client, so much that you persuade them that they need to create a job for you. And even if you don't, the establishment of contact with the headhunter can be worthwhile for the future. But you need to know the reason for lack of a specification so you can decide what you want to do.

The spec is the basis for your discussion with the search professional. Early in the proceedings you should obtain the missing piece: the name of the client. From then on you're finding out as much as possible about the company and the job.

Look for potential trouble spots. Does the authority seem limited in comparison with the responsibility? To whom would you report? Is the compensation arrangement reasonably precise as to bonuses? What you must do to earn them?

You may find that the specification asks for something you don't have: minimum years of experience in a certain discipline, let's say. Don't let it alarm you. Don't fake it. Lay out your background and qualifications for the headhunter. Then talk about the discrepancy. The consultant may not feel it is a weighty factor. Or even if it does loom large in the eyes of the client, the headhunter may feel that you could handle the job in spite of the divergence from the specification, and so he or she will bring you in anyway.

Search consultants try to get clients to be flexible. When a consultant is faced with an unwieldy spec he or she may take the "two from Column A, two from Column B" approach. As described by Kent Straat of the Straat Group, the consultant finds a couple of candidates who fit the letter of the specification. He also locates one or two candidates he feels could do the job well, even though they don't fit the paper profile in all details. The headhunter doesn't try to steer the client in a particular direction. Often the impressiveness of the nonspec candidate changes the client's mind.

So while you should certainly look the spec over before you meet with the recruiter, don't let any discrepancies intimidate you. You have been invited to apply for the job.

CHAPTER 8

First Contact II: Face-to-Face with the Recruiter

YOUR FIRST FACE-TO-FACE meeting with the recruiter is a pivotal occasion. You are meeting with someone who may be very important to you. If this session goes well, you will move on to interviews with the client. The recruiter is likely to be involved, in front of the scenes or behind them, every step of the way.

Most of us like to know as much as we can about the people with whom we deal in important matters. So at this point it is appropriate to make some observations on the nature of the recruiting industry and the concerns of those who make it up.

Recruiters have to be quick studies. They are called upon to size up new people and new companies rapidly. They're "good with people"—able to establish good relationships quickly. They are very persuasive. And, as part of that persuasiveness, the recruiter dons the mantle of authority and certainty. A search consultant doesn't say "I don't know" or "I'm not sure about that" often. While they don't give screen tests for headhunters, a reasonable degree of physical attractiveness is definitely not a drawback in the business. Nor is the elusive quality called charm. An hour with a search professional will usually pass quite pleasantly; most recruiters manifest engaging personalities in their contacts with clients and candidates. (Sometimes the recruiter can be so engaging and persuasive that the other party can be lulled into agreeing to something that should have been examined more closely.)

But one also finds a lot of defensiveness among recruiters. There is, for example, heavy emphasis on ethics. Many professions are, by and large, ethical as a matter of course, and there is not much discussion of it. But in executive search there is a lot of talk about it.

Because of difficulties in the area, the Association of Executive Search Consultants has drawn up a code of ethics covering client relationships, qualifications, practices, confidentiality, and so forth. While the AESC boasts, at last count, only about 80 members, more endorse the code. But there are cynics who say the code is followed only when convenient. For example, it is unethical to misrepresent when gathering information on candidates—for example, by claiming to be a reporter from *Business Week*. However, one may be told that they all do it, if necessary, code or no code; or if they don't do it themselves, they hire an independent researcher who does it and then accept the results produced by the independent researcher without asking how she or he got them.

Some of the sensitivity of search professionals stems from the public perception of the business. The word "headhunter" itself is a problem. Some recruiters carry on the fight to expunge the word; others have given up. They are hurt by public confusion between what they do and what employment agencies do. They are embarrassed at being lumped together with fly-by-night operators who proclaim themselves as executive recruiters without having the remotest resemblance in integrity and stature to the established organizations. And they seem to be ever suspicious of being misunderstood, falsely reported, and sold short.

It's useful for the candidates to be aware of this sensitivity in working with the search consultant, who may thoroughly resent— without showing it—any hint that he or she is not being accorded a full measure of respect.

To understand the insular world in which the executive-search consultant lives, it is useful to look at the industry's trade press. That's easy to do. The basic organ of communication in the recruiting industry is a monthly newsletter, *Executive Recruiter News,* founded, edited, and published by James H. Kennedy.

Jim Kennedy is a former trade magazine editor and publicist who runs a publishing business in Fitzwilliam, New Hampshire. The long-standing staple of his operation has been *Consultants News*. *ERN* was started in 1980 to cover just the search industry. The monthly is, for the most part, a routine industry letter set in typewriter type, full of gossipy little notices about personnel changes, news of industry associations, speeches, and the like. *ERN* is the sort of publication that might exist around the fringes of any number of industries, supplementing the more substantial print media with chitchat.

But *Executive Recruiter News* is not on the fringes. For many it is the alpha and omega of coverage of the industry. Practically everyone in executive search reads it. Moreover, these recruiters are, in many cases, very anxious about Jim Kennedy's opinion of them. Some are afraid of him.

Well they might be. The newsletter's content is usually breezy and innocuous. But every so often the letter seems to go into a Lilliputian rage, issuing thundering pronouncements and anathemas from the stronghold in Fitzwilliam. Some of its most celebrated tirades have been against recruiters who, in Kennedy's view, have acted unethically by doctoring their resumes. *ERN's* exposures of some such situations have been accompanied by the alleged culprits leaving their jobs. But Kennedy's attention did not stop with running the stories. At times when the targets have gotten other jobs—with firms that are aware of the credentials brouhaha—the newsletter hounds its quarries. For example, the April 15, 1985, issue reported, "FOLLOW-UP ON RECRUITERS WITH BLEMISHED RESUMES (ERN-Mar '84): LAST OF 'CHICAGO 3' FINDS WORK . . ." The story went on to tell how, after one miscreant had been "picked up" by another firm and a second had been noted as "quietly slipping" into a new job, the third of the trio had joined a search company. In an *"ERN COMMENT"* (the newsletter is lavish with editorial comments), Kennedy writes that "after all, credentials is what search is all about, right? One wonders, however, if concern for the environment (recycling soiled merchandise) has replaced good old-fashioned ethical standards!" The excerpt is a reasonable sample of the letter's style and approach.

The two largest search firms, Korn/Ferry and Russell Reynolds, have incurred Kennedy's disapproval. The newsletter carries stories with headlines like "Two Largest Search Firms Accused of Violating Off-Limits Canons . . . Korn/Ferry Officer's Claims Mar Boston Newspaper Story . . . Does Russell Reynolds Assoc. Really Violate Client Off-Limits Canons?" The two firms have canceled their subscriptions to the newsletter, a fact that Kennedy gleefully reports.

Some executive-search professionals are embarrassed by all this and wish the industry's communications were more of a class act. Others see Jim Kennedy and his letter as a necessity: "Sure he goes too far sometimes. But somebody has to police the industry. Faking resumes is a really lousy thing." Still others despise what they see as the bias, meanness, and vindictiveness of *Executive Recruiter News.* Some recruiters, particularly younger ones, tend to smile at the letter: "It's schlocky and I don't really read it, but it's good to get him to print your releases."

There is another curiosity about *Executive Recruiter News*. Most newsletter editors do not solicit anything except subscriptions from those on whom they are supposed to be reporting. But each issue of *ERN* carries this notice:

> SERVICES AVAILABLE TO ERN READERS: Confidential counsel to firm owners. Merger/acquisition. Referral service for partners & senior staff. Contact Publisher Jim Kennedy in complete confidence . . .

In 1984 *USAir Magazine* observed that Kennedy charges $1,000 a day for consulting and 15 percent of annual salary for job referrals: "He bristles at the suggestion that such activities represent exactly the kind of conflict of interest that he would normally pounce on himself in his newsletters. 'I grant you it has the appearance of a conflict,' he admits, 'but it doesn't impair my objectivity. I zap my clients in the newsletter as much as anyone else.'"

Of course, none of this is of the least importance to anyone outside the recruiting business—except for the light shed on the nature of a profession so deeply involved in selecting corporate leaders. A thoughtful observer says of Jim Kennedy, "He's our only source of information. Most of the companies are small and privately held. This is the way we find out about each other."

There are a few paradoxes here. An industry that depends on information maintains as its own information channel a mechanism that many acknowledge to be biased and inadequate. A discipline that is intensely concerned with ethics leaves the task of ethical policing to a newsletter editor. It seems ironic that professionals of great ability and achievement fear the whims and judgments of a newsletter.

While ERN is still the most widely read trade publication in executive search, other publications are coming into the field, including *The Recruiting and Search Report*, published by Kenneth J. Cole. Robert Baird, who publishes *The Executive Grapevine*, a directory of English recruiting firms, has been investigating the possibilities of a directory and information service for U.S. recruiters.

The fact remains that, right now, Jim Kennedy's letter is the primary source of information in the business. It has a large readership and is quite influential.

Acceptance and positive image are important to the recruiter. It's a good thing to remember when you deal with her or him.

SCREEN TEST

Your first meeting with the headhunter is part interview, part audition. The search professional probes for your qualifications. At the same time he or she is looking at you as a casting director looks at an actor auditioning for a part, wondering how you will "play in Peoria."

"Peoria"—the executive suite of the client company—has its own tastes and peculiarities. You can't know anything about this before you know the client's name. That's a big reason for you to push hard to identify the client early in the proceedings. But even after you learn the name of the potential employer, you may not know much more about the particular management style of the firm, at least not while you're still sitting across the lunch table with the headhunter. In this situation some people worry about saying something that will turn the headhunter off before the process gets to its next stage.

If the consultant has anything on the ball, that worry does not have much basis. Professionals don't nitpick during the first interview. They are looking at the fundamentals. If you fit most of the specifications of the search and if there isn't anything about you that will cause really big problems, search people assume you will make the small adaptations most of us make—often unconsciously—to be more acceptable in a job-application situation. After all, the manager who knows that some relatively inconsequential thing—insistence on voicing a strong political view, for example—will make it harder for the client to accept him or her is not apt to display that. If the manager does, he or she is saying something personal, perhaps that he or she doesn't really want the job.

But there are certain things you can do right from the start of the first contact, things that will help the searcher to see that you can not only do the job but also play the part.

Be active, not passive. One of the problems headhunters encounter is the candidate who just sits there, listening, weighing, and judging. This may be appropriate behavior when the executive is being presented with alternatives on which to base a major decision. But it's not helpful to the consultant who is trying to figure out not how the other person will handle the job but how he or she will handle the first meeting with the Board chairman of the client company. One headhunter sums up the feelings of many when he says, "It's embarrassing when your candidate clams up. The client is frustrated and insulted. A client said to me, 'I don't have to prove myself to this fellow. The hell with him.' What good is it to find a real high-quality person if the guy won't help himself in the interview? I don't want to look bad with my clients. I look for signs of that. If the person won't open up to me, I figure we've got trouble."

Some potential candidates who would really like a crack at the job look passive when they're just being polite. They assume it's a courtesy to let the other fellow talk; after all, he's buying the lunch. And that's okay—for a few minutes. But then you have to start to respond.

Your first initiative is to insist on the name of the client. You've tried to get it on the phone. Now you must get it. However, when you do find out, don't give your reaction away.

The consultant as casting director is looking for certain qualities. The role being cast has all kinds of individual ramifications, but one factor is practically universal: The candidate must not look too eager. After all, the mystique of the headhunter depends to some extent on the proposition that he or she not only searches the world for the best candidate but also has to do a hell of a job to persuade this paragon even to consent to an interview. A manager who acts as if he or she would have answered a want ad may make the client wonder if this is, after all, the right person and if the search consultant has done all that much searching. A candidate who is just trying to be cordial may convey so much agreeability as to look like a pushover.

So take over the interview. Find out who the client company is, and then ask some good questions about the company's position in the industry, plans, style, etc. Even if you think you know all about them, ask anyway. You're auditioning. The fact that the lines are familiar is secondary. In fact, when you know the answers, you can ask better questions.

Another mistake made by managers, particularly younger ones, when they first talk with a headhunter is overdeference. Some people seem to worry most about saying the right thing. This is an interview with another person trying to make a living, not an audience with the pope. The search consultant is not going to utter words of wisdom to which you must listen as if to the Delphic oracle. The search consultant is not an expert on the business you're in. *You're* the expert. Act like it. Talk to the headhunter about what you do with authority and confidence.

And don't worry too much about his or her opinion of you, at least not enough to try to pretend to be something you're not. To begin with, the search consultant can spot it. "It's painful," says one consultant. "I see people going through contortions, trying to change themselves into different people right in front of my own eyes. Last thing I need. What I need is a clearer picture of the people they really are."

It's even worse, in many cases, if you are able to fool the consultant into thinking you are radically different from the real you. (This happens more often than headhunters admit.) The consultant is going to sell you on the basis of your representation of yourself. Your chances of moving ahead with client interviews are enhanced, and you may even get the job. But then what? "I've been conned," says a leading search professional. "Some of these people could act Olivier off the stage. Their big talent is looking like what you want. Then they get the job. They're not going to keep up the pretense, they'd crack from the strain. So off comes the disguise. Sometimes this doesn't matter. The things the guy faked about his personality are not essential. But often they do matter. The candidate figured that pretending to think a certain way was simply superficial. It turns out to be basic to the culture. Result, bad stuff."

We're talking here about faking in terms of personality—acting deliberative instead of mercurial, gregarious instead of aloof. This kind of pretense is less likely to be spotted by certain headhunters and clients than is the exaggeration of qualifications or the fictionalization of accomplishments.

You're auditioning for a part when you talk with the headhunter. But the part is one that must suit you. If you have to distort yourself too much to fit it, it's just not there. Forget about it.

HOW LONG HAS THIS BEEN GOING ON?

One worthwhile question to ask during the meeting is, "When did the search start?" There's no particular reason for the headhunter not to tell you. The answer may be illuminating.

If the search consultant just got the assignment a few days ago, he or she has not gone through a painstaking process of examining every possible candidate. The headhunter has looked into some sources and gotten to you. (Where he got your name, from files or from a current recommendation, is another worthwhile question.)

Some search professionals profess to find a distinction between the "recruiter" and the "executive search consultant." In *How to Select and Use an Executive Search Firm* (New York: McGraw-Hill, 1984)— a book directed at the companies that use search people—search pioneer A. Robert Taylor writes that the process of careful sifting is one standard that identifies the higher-class professional: "A recruiter or headhunter is simply that. His mission is to find someone who is qualified—never mind whether the candidate is among the best that can be found for your particular position. It is the added dimension of finding and filling the position with the best-qualified executive that is part of the reason for paying retainers to a search consultant rather than a 'finder's fee' to a recruiter or headhunter.''

Some companies give the recruiting firm a greater role than others do. When the recruiter takes weeks or months to sift through all the possibilities and present the "best," obviously a large chunk of the decision-making process has been delegated to the recruiter. When the headhunter sets out to get a number of good candidates reasonably quickly, without exhaustive screening, the client is retaining more of the decision-making power.

So the length of time the search has been going on before it got to you is a matter of some interest. If it started a few days ago, chances are the recruiter is looking for good, qualified candidates rather than the best-qualified candidate. The field is larger. Ask how many candidates the search professional is likely to present to the client. You're unlikely to be told a number, but the nature of the answer may give you an idea of how many people you are competing against.

Another question that will help you to get a handle on the nature of the selection process is, "How long before the final decision is made?" Maybe the job has to be filled very fast, so the headhunter is moving at top speed to generate good possibilities without going through an extensive process of refining.

If the decision is being made quickly (and under some pressure), you will want to ask other questions:

• Why so quick?

• Why is the job open?

• What happens if they don't fill it quickly?

As we discuss elsewhere, if the process involves urgency, then the company probably is looking for someone who can get up to speed and start doing a decisive job almost immediately. Action will be more important than contemplation.

What if the search has been going on for months? That may mean the contact with you is the culmination of an intense process of elimination. It may also mean that others have been presented to the client and have not been hired, or have turned down the job.

It's important that you know whether other candidates have been presented, and if so, how many. If there has been a number of contenders, you are not merely being considered with respect to your qualifications and how well you match the requirements. You are also being looked at with the implicit question, "How is this person better than the people we've already seen?"

The ideal situation is one in which the client has great confidence in the search professional and has given carte blanche for a thorough search for the best-qualified candidate. If this is the case you are going in there with the full endorsement of the searcher. You will also be the beneficiary of the full cooperation of the consultant, who wants you to get the job because he or she is convinced you can handle it better than anyone else.

In most cases you are one of a number of competitors. If the search has been going on for a while, you're probably on the "short list," and a decision will be made fairly quickly. If the search just started, you may have to resign yourself to a lengthy process. Even if you look very well qualified, the client will not want to select until looking at all the goods in the showcase—unless you give the client a reason for moving quickly.

Find out, to the extent you can, how long the search has been going on and how many candidates have been involved. These considerations should be important in helping you shape your strategy.

HOW MUCH INFLUENCE DOES THE RECRUITER HAVE WITH THE CLIENT?

Ask, "How long have you been working with this client?" And, "How many searches have you handled for this firm?"

If the headhunter has been working with the client for a long time, he or she may be in a position of some authority in influencing their thinking. Get the headhunter to talk a little about the relationship. If he or she has clout, the headhunter may be able to get them to modify the specifications to fit you more closely—if you have impressed him or her.

SHOULD YOU REVEAL WEAK SPOTS?

Yes. Not weak spots in your basic skills or talents, but rather in your preferences. For example, it's not recommended that you say, "Never could make heads or tails of numbers. Can't tell one end of the P&L from the other."

But it's okay to say (if you mean it), "Heavy emphasis on production details bores me. I fall asleep at meetings where the R&D people walk you through the new model, step by step. I want to get to the bottom line."

HOW WILL YOU BE MEASURED?

Chances are the headhunter has no direct knowledge of how well you do your job. You're a name and a possibility, that's all. His first impression will be formed over the phone and then the lunch table. These impressions will be based on the likelihood of your impressing the client—how well you "come across."

So a key question is, "How much do you know about my business and the kind of work I do?"

Some experts recommend that you ask the headhunter this question point-blank. But there's a better way. Act toward the headhunter as you would toward a job candidate. Work into the topic this way:

Do you conduct many searches in the widget industry?

The headhunter is not likely altogether to deny knowledge of the business. So ask a couple of questions that test his or her familiarity with the ins and outs of widgets:

• What do you think of the trend toward disposable widgets?

• Does Widget Wizard's TV campaign impress you?

• Do you know of a company in the business that had a better return on investment than we did?

Okay, the headhunter is supposed to be asking the questions, not you, and it probably will be revealed that his knowledge of the minutiae of the industry is slim. He's interested in you. Then on what basis will he decide how hard to push you? On the basis of your likelihood of intriguing the client.

Help the search consultant. Tell him what you're good at, why that's important, how it can be measured.

WHAT NOT TO BRING UP

Veteran search consultant Tom Buffum, whose firm is now part of the Korn/Ferry empire, says it's important for the search professional to suspend judgment on some of the more obvious personal "signals," like a limp handshake or failure to make eye contact. However, there is one thing that bothers Buffum very much: a candidate being harshly critical of present or former employers.

It can be easy to slip into the critical mode. We do it even when we don't have any serious complaint about the employer. When two managerial colleagues get together over lunch, how often do they sing the praises of the boss and their organization? The tendency is to knock. Often it doesn't mean much. We're not unhappy; we go back and do our damndest after having had a gripe session.

But ripping the company to an outsider is different. Some candidates quickly feel right at home with the headhunter, a savvy and sympathetic friend. (The search professional is, of course, skillful at inducing this feeling.) So the candidate feels he can indulge in the same degree of bitching that he would with any other old friend. It's a mistake. The headhunter is likely to understand what's happening and discount it, but must anticipate the reactions of the client, who is highly unlikely to feel good about a manager who knocks the employer.

INTERVIEWING THE HEADHUNTER

Rather than wasting valuable time complaining about an employer, spend it interviewing the headhunter. Because that's what you should be doing—interviewing him or her as well as having the headhunter interview you. In fact, in a proper interview the candidate will ask far more questions than the search professional. The professional is there to listen to and size up the candidate against the needs of the client. The questions you ask and the skill and persistence with which you go after information are important factors in forming the headhunter's judgment.

The recruiter can tell you a lot that you need to know. Headhunters implore their clients to be as specific as possible. They are not always successful. The tendency, particularly among employers who have not worked with headhunters much, is to say, "Find me an executive vice president." Pressed, they say, "Well, the person has to have great leadership qualities, be fast on his or her feet, terrifically decisive, tough but understanding, an executive employees like and respect—and, of course, must have many years of experience in our industry but be able to come in with a lot of fresh ideas."

Faced with such utopian wishes, seasoned search people work with the client to develop something more useful.

The recruiter needs information about the company as well as the position; here are some of the questions asked (since you want to know the answers to the same questions, and since a good recruiter will already have asked them, you should get what you can out of the headhunter):

• What are the company's overall objectives?

• How well are those objectives being met?

• How does the company rank in the industry?

• What are the company's product lines?

• How does the company stand in volume, profitability, return on investment?

• How many people work for the company?

• What rate of growth does management project for the next five years?

Then the recruiter wants to know a number of things about the job to be filled. The basic specifications are not hard to come by:

• What's the compensation range?

• What experience is required?

• What's the age range?

• What educational background are you looking for?

These things the employer is able to state. But experienced recruiters earn their fees by probing beyond these basics. Sometimes they find that the specifications don't fit expectations, or that the specifications contradict each other. For example, a company asserts it is looking for a marketing vice president with extensive package goods experience combined with advertising agency account management—for a salary of $60,000. The recruiter must point out that the legitimate possessor of such qualifications cannot be gotten at that bargain price. The candidate would be a fraud or a loser.

Having obtained some consistent guidelines, the recruiter will try to put them in perspective:

• How does the job tie in to the company's plans?

• How important is the job?

• What functions will the executive perform?

• To whom will the executive report?

• Who will report to the executive?

• How will the executive relate to other executives in the organization?

• What are the responsibilities of the job?

The recruiter will want an organizational chart and position descriptions of those jobs that impinge on the job to be filled, whether they are higher, lower, or on the same level.

Now the conscientious recruiter will move onto ground that is a little more precarious. Tangibility and specificity are fine, but sometimes the intangibles are more important. It is necessary to get a sense of the situation into which the candidate will move. One way to get at this important but elusive reality is to probe into the reasons for the search:

• Why is the position open?

• What happened to the previous occupant?

• What are all the circumstances connected with the opening?

• Why isn't the opening being filled from within?

• What reasons disqualify the present second-in-command from moving into the job?

• Who in the company might reasonably have hoped or expected to be promoted into the job?

• Was there any sentiment among senior management to fill the job from within?

• What efforts have been made to fill the job so far—formal and informal?

• Has anyone, inside or outside the firm, asked about the job or been talked to about it?

At this point a good recruiter will move into an area that may be even more touchy. There are, in most cases, "hidden" specifications, imposed by the individual who is commissioning the search, the culture of the company, and the attitudes of those with whom the executive will work. Often management is unaware of these factors, or underestimates them, or is defensive about them.

• Do the executives with whom the candidate would work socialize with each other?

• What personality traits make an executive successful in this company?

• What are the strengths and weaknesses of the company as a whole and the division in which the candidate will be working?

• What informal networks exist in the organization? How do they work? Are they based on time with the company? Work background? Schools attended? A combination of these factors?

• How is an outsider likely to be viewed and treated?

• To what extent is a newcomer likely to be frozen out?

• Is there anyone who, consciously or unconsciously, would want to see the candidate fail?

• What is the company's "style"? What unwritten rules and traditions does it observe?

Then the search consultant will cover the ways in which the successful candidate will be judged within this context:

• What goals will be set for the new incumbent?

• How will progress toward these goals be measured?

• How long will the executive have to achieve the goals?

• What happens if the goals are not achieved?

• To what extent will success or failure be influenced by factors outside the executive's control?

• Assuming reasonable success, what are the further opportunities for the executive?

• What could happen to impede the executive's progress?

The search consultant can't get answers to all these questions but gets enough to gain a sense of the intangibles as well as the objective factors. The candidate must "debrief" the headhunter to the extent possible. What the recruiter knows bears on how much you want the job and how best to go about getting it.

Asking effective questions calls for a variety of techniques. Start with this basic question: "Why is the job open?"

"The present vice president for production, Peter Redford, resigned effective May 30."

Your next question is *why:* "Why did he resign?"

"Redford decided to explore some career possibilities on his own."

Aha! When the consultant gives you bland jargon like that, you can easily infer there's more to it—and the consultant probably would be disappointed in you if you didn't pursue the facts tenaciously. One way would be to ask, "What career possibilities? What job is Redford going to?" If the answer is that he has not altogether firmed up his plans, or is considering several possibilities, or has suddenly become an independent consultant—or if the headhunter simply says, "I don't know"—you can figure out what happened.

But why go through all that? When the reason for the previous incumbent's leaving is ambiguous, why not just ask, "Was he fired?" If that's the case, the search consultant should tell you.

Probing questions about the firing of the former holder of the job can tell you many things of great importance about the climate you would be entering and the problems you would be facing. But you may have to dig for the facts. Ask how long the manager had been in the job, the principal reason for the dismissal, who else got fired, whether it was a general purge or was confined to one person, etc.

The search consultant may be reticent about giving you all of the gory details lest you be scared off by the possibility of entering a bloodbath. Be reassuring: "I'm not afraid of getting fired. If I were, I wouldn't be where I am. But I want to know what makes your client tick, and one good way to do that is to talk about what they expect of the person in this position and how their expectations were frustrated. So let's talk about it—unless there's some reason you're not willing to talk about it."

The headhunter must agree to talk about it. Pursue it: "What was Redford's biggest failing?" The answer may be vague: "Oh, it was a combination of things. . . ."

And here is where you probe for the real truth. One such technique is exaggeration:

"You mean he suddenly started to louse up in every aspect of the job?"

"No, of course not. Primarily I guess it was the fact that he was pushing up the output levels to a point where they felt they were getting an unacceptable number of product failures."

"Product failures . . ." Reflection is another technique. You echo the last couple of words spoken by the other party and tail off, inviting elaboration.

"Yeah, breakdowns in the power units on the 1500 line. That's their consumer line, you know, the one they were counting on to penetrate a new market. . . ."

Now we're getting someplace. The implications of this go beyond the reasons for firing Redford. Is a major division in trouble? Might the whole operation be spun off or shut down? The perceptive candidate will keep asking sharp questions—and *listen* to the answers.

Listen—not only to the words of the answers, but also for what S. I. Hayakawa calls the "metamessage"—the meaning behind the words. The ways in which the consultant gives you answers, what he leaves out or wants to leave out, his body language—all go toward helping you form a useful working impression of the situation.

In questioning skillfully, you are using abilities you have very likely developed as a manager. You have ways of getting information out of people and of reading between the lines. Some executives don't use these skills in dealing with the search consultant. They don't view the encounter as an information-gathering session. But that's what it is, and the way in which you go about learning what you want to know is important in helping you move toward the next steps in the process.

Throughout the interview, keep in mind that you may not be the only candidate the headhunter is serving up to the client. Some clients feel most comfortable when they are able to choose among several people. Occasionally the search consultant provides an alternative candidate on his own, as part of a strategy to make his prime candidate look good. In this ploy the idea is not to wheel in someone who is arrantly unqualified—the headhunter would look like a fool—but rather to provide a look at someone who is in the ball park but who will be perceived as being inferior and whose shortcomings will contrast effectively with the strengths of the preferred choice.

What can you do about this? What should you do?

To begin with, unless the search consultant is clumsy, you will not know you're being used, so you'll never get a chance to resent it. You may suspect this is what's happening—but don't give way to that suspicion by acting on it or saying anything about it.

You could be wrong. Rejected job candidates look for scapegoats sometimes. It's easy to blame the consultant, to say you've been set up. If you say this, it looks like sour grapes. Even if you're right, you look bad. And you alienate the consultant—and perhaps other headhunters who might approach you in the future.

And anyway, so what if you have been included as just a member of the lineup? You may get the job. Search consultants sometimes are surprised by the client's passing over the seemingly obvious choice to pick one of the long shots.

More important, you are now in the headhunter's memory bank, in his head, and probably on his computer. By handling yourself well throughout the process, you have enhanced your chances of being tapped the next time around.

You have made contacts at the client company. They may not offer you a job this time around, but they will remember your name. You are, after all, someone who was recommended by the search expert in whom they have confidence. Perhaps one of the people who interviewed you will move to another company, perceive a spot to be filled, and recall your qualifications.

And in any event you have had the experiences of interacting with the headhunter and handling interviews with the client. You are a little more seasoned and better prepared for the next time.

Ask the search consultant if you are the only candidate currently being presented, or if there are others. You may be told the exact situation, or the person may hedge. Show that you understand the realities and have no problem about competing. Then go ahead and give it your best shot.

HOW FRANK SHOULD YOU BE?

Anything you tell the recruiter should be the truth. Lying is not only dishonest, it's also dumb. If you continue to move through the process, toward the point at which you will be a favored candidate, there will be pretty complete checks made on your background, including (but not limited to) thorough reference checks. One point on which people are tempted to lie is getting fired. The recruiter asks a candidate why he left a previous job, and the candidate answers, "It was a question of disagreement over basic company policy. I couldn't go along with the Board's policy thrust, and so I felt it incumbent to leave." Now, the recruiter suspects this is baloney, as indeed it is; the executive was fired. It's not necessarily a major black mark against the executive, but it's not good. It would be better to say, "They didn't like some of the things I was doing, and they let me go." Nowadays, getting fired is not a disgrace. Disclose this as well as other sore points in your business history; they're apt to come to light anyway.

The more delicate question is how much to volunteer about one's personal situation, or about things that fall into the gray area between business and personal. The key word here is *relevant*. For example, the breakup of a marriage is a personal matter. But if the breakup entails litigation that could involve the company, then the recruiter should know about it. In the same way, the occupation or status of one's spouse or partner may not be a matter for discussion—but that situation changes if the relationship might limit travel or transfer required in the job.

The headhunter has heard it all anyway. While he or she is not presiding in a confessional, it is fair, reasonable, and prudent to talk with the headhunter about anything that might reasonably seem related to the job.

CHAPTER 9

Negotiation I: The Dynamics of the Bargaining Process

YOU'VE REACHED THE POINT at which the employer would like to hire you. You'll be made an offer. Either you will accept the offer without question, or you will negotiate. The success of your negotiation will depend to some extent on your mastery of the dynamics of a bargaining situation in which a third party—the recruiter—is an influential factor throughout.

The first principle involved in this kind of job negotiation is that the negotiating process does *not* just begin when they make you an offer. Elements of the negotiation have been taking place since you first met with the recruiter. So it's important to do the things you can to strengthen your hand right from the start. In the early stages you are finding out what you need to know, and you are establishing a position. In the latter stages you are making moves and countermoves designed to get you the best possible arrangement.

A second vital principle is that the role of the recruiter shifts as the process goes along. You must understand the motivation of the recruiter at each specific point in the procedure so you can use the recruiter's involvement to your best advantage—or at least neutralize it so it doesn't work against you.

Another point is that the negotiating process should cover not just the compensation package but other matters of importance as well— your authority on the job, your upward career path in the firm, your protection against unwanted transfer or abrupt termination. And you may find it advantageous to turn the approach of the recruiter into leverage you can use to get yourself a better deal in your present job.

94

Let's begin with an overview of the bargaining process, with special emphasis on the recruiter's role.

The recruiter will be a factor throughout. At some points he or she may be negotiating with you directly. At other times the recruiter may be behind the scenes, assisting the client. The recruiter may play an ambiguous "floating" role, offering suggestions that do not have the force of hard offers. You may be sure the recruiter is conveying information to the client about you, not only what you say but also what he or she thinks you will settle for. At the same time a good consultant will lay it on the line to the client about what they must be willing to offer to get you.

THE STAGES OF RECRUITING

The pattern of the typical relationship between headhunter and candidate can be charted:

Stage 1: *Knockout.* At first the recruiter is trying to knock the candidate out of the box. The candidate, or potential candidate, is just one of a number of possibilities. The headhunter shifts into an elimination mode, driven by the necessity of narrowing the possibilities to a few.

Stage 2: *Embrace.* When you survive the knockout stage, you are likely to be embraced. Now you are a prime possibility. You may mean money in the consultant's pocket. The embrace is wide—there are others within its compass—but it is warm. You've become a kind of partner in the campaign for a successful search.

Stage 3: *Infatuation.* One candidate moves a little ahead of the others. The headhunter decides that Smith is a better choice than Jones or Brown, or at least that Smith has a better chance of getting the job. Now Smith becomes the pet. What drives the headhunter is the impulse to enhance Smith's strengths.

Stage 4: *Seduction.* The client likes you. Now the recruiter will go all out to get you. At this stage the legendary persuasive powers of some high-visibility consultants are said to be most valuable. The drive is the feeling that the affair should be consummated as soon as possible.

When you know which stage the relationship has reached, you have a sense of what strategies and tactics will avail you best.

Qualification stage. During your first meeting with the recruiter, you're being sized up. At this point you aren't negotiating. You're selling yourself, of course, and the best way to do that is to be relaxed, self-confident, candid, and forthcoming about your strengths and, on occasion, your weaknesses.

Now is the time to make maximum use of the recruiter as an information resource. You should be told the name of the client. There are other things you want to know about the client company—the basics about size, scope, nature of operation, location, etc. Also the vital intangibles:

• What's the corporate culture like?

• What stage of development is the company in? Entrepreneurial? Mature? Declining? How has it been doing recently?

• Where is the company going? What are its objectives?

The search consultant will be able to tell you a lot about the job. To begin with, you probably should get a printed specification. But there are questions that go beyond the spec:

• Why are they looking for someone?

• What happened to the last incumbent?

• Where does the position rank in the real hierarchy?

• What is the projected upward path for the holder of the job?

• Who will make the decision? Who else is involved in the decision?

These questions, and those like them, are not susceptible to precise answers. They provide the basis for discussion. Listen analytically to what the search professional tells you—and to what is not said as well. You will begin to form a good feel for the intangibles of the situation.

There's something else that's important at this early stage: *Avoid concessions,* even tacit concessions. It might happen this way: The recruiter says, "There is no participation in the stock-option plan for this position." Don't say, "I understand," or, "That's okay." Reserve it: "Well, I hear what you're saying. We can talk about that later." The recruiter may be just as willing as you are to finesse this point at this phase. Keep your negotiating options open.

Negotiation stage. When you become one of, say, three candidates being seriously considered, you have moved into the stage at which you are negotiating compensation and other terms of employment. Your position gets stronger as you forge toward the front. However, you can still knock yourself out by taking too tough a bargaining position.

Assume at this point that the search consultant is no more inclined toward you than toward anyone else on the short list of candidates. You're still using the recruiter as a source of information:

• How quickly will the decision be made?

• What's the process of making the decision?

• Who are involved in the process and what relative weight do they have?

• How many people are they considering?

But now you're negotiating. And while your opposite number in the negotiation is the employer, the recruiter is a factor, perhaps even a decisive factor, in the way the negotiation runs. As one consultant says, "When the client says, 'Okay, we like him,' we used to get out of the act. Now all the bells and whistles go off. The job really starts."

Negotiating with a third party involved is a special form of negotiation. You follow the principles of good negotiation: sizing up your opposite number and the overall situation; establishing your priorities; bargaining from strength; making a strategically timed concession that wins you what you want; making both parties feel good about the process. But the way in which you plan and carry out your negotiation is part of the equation.

Understand the position of the recruiter. His or her primary objective is filling the job with a highly qualified candidate. The recruiter is, obviously, working for the client, and so wants the client to like the way he or she works. The recruiter wants to close out the process as quickly as possible.

But in many negotiations involving recruiters, an important change in the dynamics of the situation takes place as the selection process draws toward its close. You become not just one of three, but the favorite candidate. At this point the recruiter's role shifts. *The client expects him to RECRUIT you.* When that point is reached, you can get a lot more help from the recruiter than just information.

Understand the nature of the third party in the negotiations. As the third party, the search professional may play a number of parts during the bargaining: facilitator; mediator, arbitrator; manipulator. You want the third party to be playing these roles in ways that are as favorable to your chances as possible.

Be active, not passive. One of the most important aspects of negotiating through an agent is *limited authority*. One party controls the agent. The other party asks for commitment or concession, and the agent can only reply, "I'll have to check that out." As Gerard I. Nierenberg observes in *Fundamentals of Negotiating* (New York: Hawthorn, 1973), "Although an agent is often desirable in one's *own* cause, it also follows that in negotiations it is best to avoid dealing with the adversary's agent."

There are points at which you will be able to say, "I think it would be better if I talk this over with the client." But by and large you will have to accept the presence of the recruiter in the process. And unless you take steps to avoid it, the recruiter may slip naturally into the role of the client's agent, talking with you about an offer but possessing limited authority to modify the offer or make a commitment. When this happens the headhunter gauges your reaction and then tells the client what he or she thinks you will go for.

You can turn the situation around to some extent by laying out, early in the process, the principles of what you see as a good arrangement: "I want a deal in the $150,000 area. This should include about $40,000 in bonus, which is payable on reasonable improvement in my unit. Also options. As for the rest of it, the title should be vice president of finance. Of course, I'd want to report directly to the CEO. . . ." You don't make it precise. You do make it high. Instead of simply reacting to what the recruiter brings to you, you are establishing a negotiating position without making specific demands.

You will have drawn up, for your eyes only, your rock-bottom list of demands, the minimum you will accept in money, status, power, and such collateral issues as protection against unwanted transfer and the signing of a formal employment agreement. Put priorities on each item; these are the keys to the concessions you will almost surely have to make. In what Howard Raiffa calls "the negotiation dance" in *The Art & Science of Negotiation* (Cambridge, Mass.: Harvard University Press, 1982), the pattern of concessions is important: "The most common pattern . . . is monotone decreasing—that is, the intervals between your decreasing offers become successively smaller, signaling that you are approaching your limit. . . ." Typically you will insist that you want a certain base salary, knowing that it is above the range of the job. (You know because you have done a thorough job of questioning the search consultant.) At a strategic moment you say, "Well, I'm willing to consider taking less on that. But I'd need firm and immediate commitment on the rest of the package" . . . including the demands you are really set on.

There is no sure way to tell—usually—that you have become a clear favorite. But when the client and recruiter are pursuing you and bargaining hard you may be able to assume that you are in that happy position and that the recruiter may be on the spot if he or she doesn't land you.

Use your advantage to bargain hard for what you want. Use it also to get counsel and help from the recruiter: "How can we get him to see that an up-front bonus is really justified?" If you make this tacit assumption of alliance too early in the process, it is likely to be ignored, but when you make it at the proper time, the recruiter will help you—because by this time his or her interest is in doing everything within reason to conclude the deal with you in the job. Remember, too, that when you are the favorite, the recruiter may be looking at you as someone who may yourself be making decisions about what executive-search firm to hire.

There are other ways in which the search consultant can be useful to you in the bargaining process. When you are really upset you can blow off steam, expressing yourself to the recruiter at the slowness of the pace or the stubbornness of the client. The headhunter has been through this and knows you're blowing off steam. (Don't try to fool him or her with a fake display of anger.) But the headhunter will act as a safety valve and shield, transmitting the feeling to the client while stripping it of the more extreme language.

Sometimes you can, with profit, talk with the recruiter about the methods by which the negotiation is being conducted. For example, some principals and agents use a counterpart of the "good guy/bad guy" routine that is a familiar feature of police interrogations. This is not unknown in job negotiation. In a three-way meeting the client hits the ceiling, proclaiming that he will never under any circumstances agree to anything more than a six-month severance arrangement, and the subject is closed, and anyone who thinks about termination at the start of the job is a wimp anyway. Outside, the recruiter says to you, "He's pretty hard-nosed about that. But I think if I went at it in just the right way I might get you nine months. Of course, there would have to be some give on the salary. . . ." You can indicate good-humoredly that you see and understand what's going on and that you won't buy it.

And there are times when you can reverse the situation almost completely and use the recruiter/mediator to sound out the client on something to which you are not willing to commit yourself just yet. In *Give & Take: The Complete Guide to Negotiating Strategies and Tactics* (New York: T. Y. Crowell, 1974), Chester L. Karrass says that mediators "can suggest compromise positions and conclusions that either party alone would be afraid to oppose for fear of weakening its bargaining position." Let's say you're at an impasse over salary. You come up with an approach that would give you a larger bonus in a shorter period, for which you'd be willing to take a lower base salary. You tell the recruiter that you feel this could be the answer—but you don't want to suggest it yourself. He floats the trial balloon.

When the bargaining reaches a certain stage, the executive-search consultant may be the person with the most by far at stake and the one who is most intensely motivated to keep the process going to success. You can take advantage of this by getting the headhunter's help in all the legitimate ways you can. But you must not take unfair advantage of the situation by bargaining in bad faith. That's shortsighted, whether you are successful or the deal falls through.

HOW HUNGRY SHOULD YOU LOOK?

Besides having to deal with occasional shortsightedness by the applicant, search consultants also have to grapple with a familiar form of client myopia: the failure to distinguish between a job *applicant* and a job *candidate*. They have commissioned the headhunter to go out and find the best candidate available. The obvious assumption is that the ideal person is already holding down an important job. If the headhunter comes up with somebody who is unemployed, the client looks upon the suggestion as a reject.

But with a lot of clients, all this changes as soon as a candidate comes in for an interview. Objectively the employer knows the candidate has been persuaded to come in, is presently employed, and has no particular reason to want to change jobs. But emotionally the employer views the candidate like an applicant. So if the manager stays cool and detached during the interview and does not display terrific eagerness for the job, the search professional is likely to be told later,

"I don't know if he wants the job enough." Headhunters are used to this and have developed ways to remind clients that the best available talent may not be salivating to join the firm.

Sometimes this is not enough. The candidate will be rejected for not being hungry enough. The client may give this as the major, or a contributing, reason for the rejection. Or other reasons may be given to mask the basic objection of lack of eagerness.

Should you play it hungry when you go in for your interview? Some candidates do this. Though they have no idea yet whether they're going to want the job, they play it safe and project a world of enthusiasm for the company and the position.

There is a risk in this. The client may have an equally illogical reaction: "He's too hungry for the job. Can he really be all he's cracked up to be?" Since gut reactions have a great tempering effect on logic in shaping employer reactions, the too-eager candidate has one or two strikes against him or her.

Some executives don't have to fake enthusiasm when they go in for an interview. They are natural-born interviewees who can psych themselves up to great heights while face-to-face with a prospective employer. Later the interviewee may let the analytical part of the brain take over and conclude that he or she does not want the job. Occasionally the client has been so carried away by the transitory enthusiasm that he or she cannot understand the candidate's refusal, and blames the search consultant for somehow mishandling the negotiation.

PLAY IT STRAIGHT/POSITIVE

What's your ideal posture in going in for the interview? You don't want to look so hungry that they will offer you less than top dollar, or even worse, reject you without thinking about what you can offer.

You don't want to turn them off through an appearance of indifference or irritation. Some candidates permit their self-confidence to translate into an attitude that seems to say, "You guys got me in here. Show me that it's worth my while to spend half an hour with you."

This can have a two-edged effect. The client resents it, but the hard-nosed coldness of the candidate who doesn't give a damn bespeaks such a wealth of self-confidence that the client figures there must be something in it. They don't like the guy, but if the job calls for a tough cookie, they may be all the more attracted.

In thinking about how eager or detached you will be on your client interviews, think beyond the bargaining stage and imagine yourself working for the company. Assume, for example, that the prevailing atmosphere in the firm is one of warmth and cordiality. They want you, they need you, and you know it. By acting as if you have no interest, even as if you dislike the whole idea of working for them, you may get them to up the ante. (You may also get them to say, "The hell with it.") When the pot has been sweetened enough, you take the job. But now you are working with the same people. You become your warm, cordial self. But they still think of you as someone who held them up and who really doesn't think that much of them or their outfit. Your job is not going to be made easier. Your life on the job may be unpleasant. And your performance will be scrutinized with great care. Any slip below the Superperson level will find people saying, "Isn't this the guy who came in here acting as if he were doing us a favor?"

Probably the best posture on the first interview is one of noncommittal agreeableness. After all, you are there; nobody held a gun on you to get you there. So it's ridiculous to imply that you have no interest at all. Let the client feel that you are used to this sort of thing. You've been sought by other firms. It is always interesting to find out about what the other guys are doing.

But you are there to *listen* and to *learn,* as well as to cooperate in responding amiably to their questions. In no way are you a job applicant yet. You're not simply sitting back and saying, "Sell me," however. Their need for executive help is a reality. Your capability is an established fact. The purpose of this meeting is exploratory—to find out if you would be interested in working there, and if the job suits you. Obviously it gives the client a chance to size you up as well, but that part doesn't worry you. Even if you are dying to have them make you an offer, it's still best to keep the first interview an arm's-length transaction in which both sides ask questions and get answers that convey attitudes as well as facts.

You want your qualifications to be judged, not your degree of eagerness for the job. Avoid the possibility that they will say, "He's too hungry," or, "He's not hungry enough." Play it down the middle.

CHAPTER 10

Negotiation II: The Money Package

WHEN THE PROCESS HAS reached the appropriate stage, the company makes a money offer. That offer is likely to come—at first—through the recruiter. It may be what some call a "Harvard offer"—an informal, nonbinding description of a *possible* arrangement. The recruiter and client want your reaction to their ideas on compensation, but they don't want a showdown. So the recruiter says to you, "How would you react if my client made you the following offer?" As A. Robert Taylor points out, the "consultant can then counsel both client and candidate before a formal offer is made."

You can be passive and just let offers be made to you. But it's better to take more firm control of the process at an early stage, using the fact that the headhunter—and to a growing extent the client—think you're good. The longer the process goes on, the greater may be the recruiter's need to be able to deliver you.

Use the leverage you acquire to work out a more favorable deal in money, status, and clout. Use it, if you wish, to get a written employment contract. And you may also want to use that leverage—but with the utmost care and candor—to get yourself a better deal in your present position.

You can use the headhunter to fill in specific areas of knowledge for you as you construct a negotiating strategy. Here are the kinds of questions on which he or she can be helpful:

• What has been the payout of the incentive plan in recent years?

• Do they have a uniform compensation plan that applies across the board? Or are there varying plans? If so, what are the differences?

• Do they offer options, junior stock plans, deferred compensation arrangements, straight bonuses, etc.? If one mode—say, options—is dominant, and you don't like it, will they listen to a proposal to replace it with some other vehicle?

• Does the company provide golden parachutes? Do they apply to just the top few executives, or is their use spread down the line? How rich are these arrangements? (Even if you are not at a level to qualify for a GP, it may be to your advantage in negotiation to know all about these deals, as we shall see.)

• What is the basic philosophy of their approach to compensation? Is incentive skewed toward short-term, bottom-line performance, or long-term criteria such as ROI? How long has the company had its present executive compensation plan? Are they considering changing it? If so, in what direction?

The executive recruiter can give you answers to questions like these—or can obtain the answers. They will be straight answers (if perhaps colored a little by the consultant's natural desire to make the position look good to you). And it is here, rather than in the broader, "What do you think?" kind of question, that he or she can be most helpful.

There are other sources of information about the company's compensation practices. The proxy statement sent to stockholders provide descriptions of the money arrangements with, typically, the top five officers.

However, a public corporation is required to file with the Securities and Exchange Commission far more information about its executive compensation plans—salaries and bonuses, stock, loans, golden parachutes, contracts, insurance, retirement arrangements, severance, consulting deals, etc. This information is contained in the following disclosure and registration documents: proxy statements, 10K reports, form 8s, 10Q reports, and 8R and 14R prospectuses. It's pretty tough to track this information down yourself, even though all of these are public documents.

There's a better way. The newsletter *Executive Compensation Reports* provides a fascinating and comprehensive service that uses the SEC data to report on executive compensation programs, policies, and practices. The newsletter is aimed at human resources departments and compensation specialists but makes vivid and interesting reading for any manager. They cover more than 1,500 companies with annual sales over $75 million. *ECR* also conducts a retrieval service. Items in the newsletter are keyed if source documents are available. So, for example, one could, in a single issue chosen at random, obtain full texts of Aetna's stock plan, Metromedia's employment agreements, Borden's multiple incentive plans, Carolina Power & Light's deferred compensation plan for directors, Goodyear's bonus plan, Coastal Corporation's executive contracts, EG&G's employment agreements, American Standard's stock plan, the retirement plan of Allied Stores, and so on. *ECR* also conducts customized searches in the SEC files.

This is a gold mine of information. The newsletter costs over $200 and may be available at your company—in the library, or in the Human Resource Department. Without making a great show of it, you may want to become familiar with it. The newsletter publishes a periodic index, so you can look up the company you're interested in. Since information is power in negotiating a compensation plan, this is a useful source. *Executive Compensation Reports* is published by DP Publications Company, P.O. Box 3141, Alexandria, VA 22302; tel., 703-370-3817.

Besides knowing about current compensation practices, you should be familiar with the discrete elements of the typical compensation package. The following pages cover the most familiar of those elements.

BONUSES AND INCENTIVES

Incentive pay in the form of bonuses has long been a staple of executive compensation. That's still the case; but for some time a considerable change has been under way. Not long ago the typical bonus was figured on the basis of a one-year bottom-line performance, with the payout keyed to annual net profit or some similar measure. The bonus would be based on overall company performance, or on the performance of the unit for which the executive was directly responsible.

The annual performance-based incentive plan has fallen into disfavor; indeed, with many, it has become notorious. Peter Drucker described this kind of compensation scheme as a license to loot the organization. In the worst-case scenario, the buccaneering executive goes all out to build up his end-of-the-year payout to the maximum level, and the hell with the consequences. He fails to maintain the plant; skips the necessary paint job; lets go of key people; guts the long-term possibilities in various markets by making short-run scores; and altogether manages in a way that allows him to extract a huge bonus while the organization begins to totter. The end result of this mismanagement is that the unit is ruined and lies belly-up in a few years, but the manager has long since pocketed his gains and gone on to something else. In many cases he has been promoted because his performance was so brilliant. He has moved to a bigger job, with a larger incentive package paid on a similar basis. He is now busy wreaking havoc in the larger entity.

This is going out of style. One firm among many that has recently decided to overhaul its compensation approach is Combustion Engineering. In October 1983, the firm's top financial officer told a senior management conference, "Like a great many other companies, CE has had an executive compensation program which has not been linked to long-term achievements and often not linked particularly to short-term results. For the farsighted manager who knows what has to be done, such a plan can be a disincentive. It penalizes you for doing the right things."

Linkage is the key word today. Companies are designing sophisticated and sometimes highly intricate plans that link compensation to performance measures, which are in turn related to strategic planning goals. The idea is to get away from industry standard as a basis for deciding compensation and to key the plan as closely as possible to what is good for the company's long-term health. The question for an increasing number of firms is not "What are the other outfits paying?" but rather "How can we structure this manager's pay so that he [or she] is of the most help to us in getting where we want to be in five years?"

The compensation plan that had existed at Combustion Engineering had based incentive on operational performance—earnings against plan, sales against plan, cash generated against plan. The new compensation arrangement, devised for Combustion Engineering by Booz, Allen & Hamilton, is keyed to growth of shareholder value. There is a higher proportion of long-term to short-term elements used in computing the payout. More bonus elements are tied to overall performance rather than group performance ("because it's important that group executives think as corporate citizens"). And the compensation plan is tied very closely to the objectives defined in the company's strategic plan.

The Combustion Engineering approach follows many of the precepts laid down by Robert H. Rock, a partner of The Hay Group, in his article in the Summer 1983 *Harvard Business Review,* "Pay for

Performance: A Concept in Search of Standards." Rock says that a plan that motivates the manager to focus on the right goals should be based on measurements that meet the following criteria:

- *Usefulness*: Does it rate the most important results?

- *Sustainability*: Can the measure forecast relevant trends?

- *Measurability*: Can the measurement be calculated from readily available data? Would different judges make the same calculation?

- *Controllability*: Are the results measured susceptible to influence by the manager?

- *Communicability*: Can the measurement be clearly explained?

- *Universality*: Can the measurement work at the operating-unit level as well as at the corporate level?

- *Timeliness*: Can the measurement apply on an annual as well as a longer-term basis?

- *Comparability*: Does the measurement gauge past performance and competitive performance?

- *Constancy*: Can the measure withstand efforts to manipulate it?

- *Volatility*: Can results vary widely from one period to the next in a way that truly reflects changes in performance?

These criteria are suggested for the company that wants to gear pay to strategic objectives. At least some of them are of use to the executive in judging a compensation plan being offered to him or her. It is important that the measurements really measure results, are based on readily available data, be easily understood, and be free from manipulation by the employer as well as by the employee.

As companies shift toward compensation plans tied to strategic plans and long-range goals, they can become more complicated. The criteria for payout are not always end-result criteria. For example, the Combustion Engineering plan rewards the manager half on the basis of his or her contribution to increased value for shareowners and half on the manager's doing the things designed to achieve that end result. Some of the payout is on results, some on conformity to a pattern of operation. The establishment of that pattern of performance is something the manager should have a full share in. If you are offered a bonus plan that designates the ways you should do your job as well as the results you should achieve, be very careful. Evaluation of your conformity to those measurements can be very subjective. You might achieve very good results and still fail, in the eyes of the employer, to do it in the way the scheme specifies, thus falling short of full bonus payout.

Shifting and nebulous criteria present a potential danger in all kinds of incentive plans, whether they are based on short- or long-range performance. The first requirement in judging the compensation plan is to understand it. That is not always easy. In *Perks and Parachutes: Negotiating Your Executive Employment Contract* (New York: Simon & Schuster, 1985), I quote a number of executive contracts, in part or in full. The section of the contract between Esquire, Inc., and Martin Winkler that covers only Mr. Winkler's compensation runs for more than a thousand words, many of them big ones. A typical excerpt:

> For purposes of this paragraph 2(s), the "applicable percentages" shall be (i) 4% of the portion of the pretax net profits for such fiscal year of Belwin in excess of $1,400,000 but not more than $1,900,000, (ii) 5% of the portion of the pretax net profits for such fiscal year of Belwin in excess of $1,900,000 but not more than $2,400,000 and (iii) 6% of the portion of the pretax net profits for such fiscal year of Belwin in excess of $2,400,000.

This is reasonably clear. But what are these percentages applied to?

> For purposes of this paragraph 2 (a), the "pretax net profits" of Belwin for any fiscal year of Belwin shall mean the consolidated earnings before provisions for taxes on income of Belwin and its consolidated subsidiaries for such fiscal year remaining after deduction from gross revenues and other income of all normal cost and expense deductions determined in accordance with generally accepted accounting principles applied on a basis consistent with the 1977 Financial Statements (as defined in the Purchase Agreement) or as contemplated by the notes thereto, including, without limitation, after deduction of (i) an amount equal to . . .

It goes on in this vein for a while. The point here is not to suggest that there is anything out of the way about the agreement quoted. It is rather to underscore that compensation plans can become pretty complicated, even when based on a simple premise—as, in the case cited, a percentage of annual net after taxes.

In negotiating an incentive arrangement, it's good first to be aware of the interesting variety of bonus setups that may be available. Procter & Gamble authorized a plan with an annual bonus fund of up to 1.5% of consolidated pretax profit. Awards might be paid in current cash, in restricted shares, or in deferred cash payable at retirement. At Genesco, Inc., the Board chairman was authorized to designate up to 60 participants in the plan in any given year, assigning each a payout cap of either 30 or 50 percent of salary.

The Genesco approach points to one question that should be considered early in the bargaining: To what extent is the size of the bonus a semisubjective judgment, made by one person or a committee? Some old-style bonus plans leave a great deal of discretion to the top brass, who are able to carry on like the capricious gods on Mount Olympus, meting out rewards and punishments without all that much regard for merit. Some plans are quite precise in spelling out the criteria for award. Some leave a great deal to discretion. Some take a middle path, laying out criteria by which one qualifies to be among those rewarded but leaving the size of the bonus to the boss. Typically, a plan adopted by the Meredith Corporation establishes a fund capped at 4 percent of consolidated net earnings each year. Bonuses are given at the discretion of the Compensation Committee. At DuPont the Compensation Committee sets bonuses.

The payment of any bonuses may be contingent on overall corporate performance. In fiscal 1984, National Service Industries passed the $1 billion sales mark, and a number of officers were rewarded with stock and cash.

Another approach can be seen in the plan set up by Baker International Corporation. Bonuses are determined each year by the Board of Directors based on how well the corporation performs against preset goals. Payouts generally range between 35 and 65 percent of base salary, depending on salary level and company performance. Plans may be individualized. General Cinema Corporation established a plan for bonuses to key executives based on meeting preset performance standards.

Sometimes bonus plans don't pay out. *Executive Compensation*

Reports told its readers that Cummins Engine Co. seemed to have made big changes in its plan after 1983 performance resulted in no awards for anyone. The plan was based on the company's attaining a threshold of 7.5 percent return on equity, which was not attained. As firms switch over to plans based on such criteria as ROE, there are apt to be years in which there is no payout.

Koppers Company's 1984 plan covered 93 key people. The incentive fund kitty accrues at the rate of 4.3 percent of the difference between a compensation base (12 percent of invested capital) and pretax income. After the fund reaches $1.6 million, the accrual rate drops to 1.5 percent.

Companies are turning toward multiple incentive plans. Inco Ltd. has plans with five-year durations, with payout in cash, shares, or "incentive units," which may be deferred or made contingent on conditions set by a Board committee. Long-term plans, like the one at Emerson Electric, frequently are keyed to five-year cycles. They offer a mix of awards in many cases. A. E. Staley Manufacturing Co. provides three basic awards: incentive shares, performance award shares, and tandem cash equivalents, interacting with each other in various ways.

When a business or an industry is flat for a considerable time, there is a tendency to seek formulas that will provide some incentive payout. For example, U. S. Steel's 1982–83 plan was based on a percentage of profits, which meant that there were no bonuses. Evidently feeling that this was the antithesis of an incentive plan, the Board of Directors substituted an approach under which the Board was able to exercise considerably more discretion.

There are all kinds of bonus plans. Companies frequently have combination approaches, with short- or long-term plans or both. It is well to understand the full range of what may be available. The recruiter should know this.

When the "package" being talked about by the recruiter contains an incentive bonus component—as is likely—there are potential pitfalls, but also good opportunities for a skillful negotiator.

One of the first questions is the proportion of the package that is contingent on factors that are partly or almost completely beyond your control. If the package is about $300,000 but if half of that is incentive bonuses, the candidate must scrutinize the provisions very carefully and calculate with a cool, objective eye the chances of making the bonuses. Companies have been known to keep salaries quite low and bonuses quite high. These days the pendulum has swung pretty far in the direction of incentive pay, but be careful that it does not swing too far. If you are relying on getting a bonus for an extremely large proportion of your compensation, you may be distracted from doing the best job you can for the corporation. Executives have been tempted to make injudicious (from the company's point of view) decisions because the bonus plan skewed their perspective. In telling the recruiter and the employer that you want a bigger percentage in straight salary, be very clear why you want it. It is by no means that you have no confidence. Most companies that go to plans heavily tilted toward incentive compensation are not trying to keep salaries low. They really feel that the plan will stimulate and reward good performance, and they suspect the commitment of one who wants more of the compensation to come in a regular salary check.

Then, too, it is worthwhile to remember that some bonus plans key the payout percentage to amount of base salary. The present plan may not be built that way, but the nature of bonus plans can be altered. The salary check has not gone out of style. There is good reason to seek a healthy bonus arrangement, but keep the salary figure well within your comfort level.

Other potential problems with bonuses are high thresholds of payout, vagueness of criteria, subjectivity, and excessive hedges masked by complicated jargon. If, for example, the bonus plan seems to mix a number of criteria—earnings, market share, and ROE, say— the failure of one of these measurements to reach the appropriate level may cancel out good performances in the other areas and excellent and deserving work by the executive. The basis for the bonus should be clear-cut, unqualified, and singular in that there is one overall standard, not several standards that could be in conflict.

You can and should be frank and thorough in expressing your feelings about the compensation package, and your desires for change, to the search professional, whose job is to find a good candidate and fill the job. The search professional is highly unlikely to be in a conspiracy with the client to get you as cheaply as possible. Bear in mind that his or her fee is usually based on first-year compensation. (This does not, of course, mean that the search professional is going to inflate the compensation package to squeeze out a few more bucks. For a headhunter that would be the most suicidal form of shortsightedness.) As you work with the recruiter, you may be able to get him or her to help you in the same way that the recruiter helps the client. A good search professional finds out where the client wants to go and shapes the assignment to fit in with long-range goals. Instead of just flatly stating a compensation mix you insist on, you may want to discuss your goals with the headhunter and listen to the recommendations. The headhunter certainly will try to be helpful—if only because you are a potential client—and with experience and savvy may be able to suggest some angles you have not thought of.

There are certain things about the bonus plan you will do well to discuss thoroughly, until you are satisfied with the answers.

What is the form of the payout? Cash? Deferred compensation? Stock? Does the company offer a variety of forms of payout? Can you select, to any degree, the mix you wish?

What kinds of plans does the company have, and who is involved in them? You may have been offered a package based in part on an off-the-shelf approach used for a great many executives. There may well be one or more plans restricted to the elite. Johnson Controls, Inc., has a performance unit plan applying to a range of executives. It also has a long-range plan with just two participants: the president-CEO and vice president. You may not be able to get everything in the most desirable (from your point of view) plan, but when you know other deals exist you are better equipped to bargain.

Does the plan depend on company performance? If the bonus is keyed to overall company criteria, how good a chance do you have of getting a good payout? If, for example, you have a lot of confidence in the profit center with which you will be concerned, but not all that much faith in the ability of others, you may want to try for a scheme more attuned to your own efforts. In another case, like that of an executive being given the responsibility of a new division of a profitable company, the more desirable criterion is apt to be geared to overall performance.

Who decides on the bonus? How subjective is the scheme? Is it pretty much entirely up to the Compensation Committee to distribute the amount in the bonus fund? How do they decide? Or are there hard, objective standards? Is the plan a combination, with a committee making allocations within a certain range?

What triggers the payout? If bonuses cannot be paid until a certain point is reached—say, in pretax income—how likely is it that the trigger will indeed be pulled? On this point, as on others with regard to the bonus plan, you will want to consider a number of factors relating to the industry as well as to the company.

Does the bonus percentage depend on salary? If it does, you have additional reason to make your base salary as high as possible. Obviously base salary is a yardstick of great importance in determining overall compensation, and it probably is indicative of the pecking order in the firm. A higher salary means greater status.

What's the track record? What have awards been like in recent years? Have bonuses dropped off, or even been nonexistent during any period? How many people collect? How big are their bonuses?

Full and realistic discussion of the bonus element of the compensation package is essential. Try for the maximum in information and guidance from the search consultant.

STOCK OPTIONS

Nowadays stock options are part of the package offered by almost every public company. The search consultant should be able to answer some basic questions about the nature of the offer of options, allowing you to assess the real value to you of this part of the package. If you are not satisfied with the option part of the package, it's best to start negotiating about it early.

The basic distinction in stock options is between "qualified" and "nonqualified" plans. "Qualified" means that the options meet the criteria established by the Tax Reform Act of 1981 and that the holder of the options is therefore entitled to certain advantages. The big advantage is that under a "qualified" plan, you can sell the stock and treat the money you receive as capital gains, thus significantly reducing your tax bill. Another advantage is that you pay no taxes until the stock has actually been sold.

To qualify, you must wait two years after receiving the option before you exercise it, then hold the stocks for one year after you buy them.

Under a "nonqualified" plan you don't have to be bothered about the restriction in the Tax Reform Act of 1981. The down side is that the proceeds are taxed as ordinary income.

Incentive Stock Options (ISOs)—qualified options—have become the options of choice for thinking executives. (A fundamental change in the federal tax structure might alter this situation considerably.) From the employer's point of view, ISOs are more expensive than nonqualified options. With the nonqualified variety, the company gets a tax break, being able to deduct an amount equal to the amount the holder of the options makes when the option is exercised. With ISOs no such deduction is possible. But companies find that they are obliged to offer the more valuable kind of option as an incentive to executives and professionals they want to attract and keep.

One basic point to think about in considering the option part of the package is that it constitutes a set of golden handcuffs as well as an incentive, a reward, and a piece of the action. If you are concerned about being tied down, you may want to bargain to shift the option portion into something more immediately tangible. After all, options are definitely deferred compensation. There's no payout for a good length of time.

Not only is the payout deferred, but it also can be a lot less than was hoped for. While it would seem rudimentary, many people forget that the stock has to go up for one to realize the profit hoped for when the options are granted. As the market climbed steeply through the last quarter of 1985, ISOs took on a brighter golden glow than ever before. But some remembered those periods a few years back when stocks lagged badly and people were forced to contemplate their once-valued options dangling uselessly from their hands.

A lot of companies offer more than one kind of option plan. Others can be persuaded to give you the plan you like. The newsletter *Executive Compensation Reports* (a publication primarily for compensation specialists but very useful for all executives; it is described elsewhere in this book) is a good source of information about the specific nature of the plans offered by specific companies. For example, Tyco Laboratories has two plans; vesting in one takes five years, vesting in the other takes 10 years. McKesson Corporation authorizes qualified and nonqualified options, along with tandem Stock Appreciation Rights (SARs), a recent creation that enables the holder to profit from an increase in the value of stock without actually buying it. The executive has the right to receive in stock or cash the market value of the stock. AT&T has a plan including ISOs, nonqualified options, and SARs. And so on.

Find out from the sources available to you, including the headhunter, the variety of option plans the company has in effect. In some cases the company may not be publicizing the fact that it has made certain kinds of arrangements with certain executives. Figure out your general strategic approach with respect to stock options. At one end of the spectrum, you may not want options at all, because you don't know whether you'll stick around, or because you are unsure of the stock market, or for some other reason. At the other end of the spectrum, you may be eager for all the option participation you can get, willing to trade other compensation elements for options if you can.

A thorough rejection of options in cases where they are commonplace will not exactly endear you to senior management, who are likely to say, with some justification, "If this guy doesn't want shares in the company, he [or she] isn't really committed." As in other areas of the prehiring negotiation, purely monetary considerations must be balanced against less tangible but highly important considerations, such as evidence of commitment and goodwill.

If there is one kind of option—nonqualified, for example—you will absolutely not consider, let the search consultant know that early. It saves trouble, misunderstanding, and hard feelings. It also keeps the employer from gaining an advantage in the bargaining by exacting concessions from you as the price for changing the option mix.

You may be less than thrilled about some of the aspects of the company's option plans but be willing to accept them. It may still be to your advantage to make your reservations known so that you may possibly get some negotiating advantage from agreeing to the plan later. Misdirection is one of the elements of negotiation. If the other party thinks you are adamantly against something, and you then give in, the adversary feels he has won a point, which justifies his or her giving in to you on a point of more importance to you.

Make yourself more of an expert on options in general and the company's plan in particular than is the recruiter. Tell him or her what you want and don't want; don't passively accept what is offered if you don't find it satisfactory.

CHAPTER 11

Negotiation III: Bargaining for Position, Protection, and Power

THERE'S MORE TO THE negotiation than money. You want the right kind of job. You want the best possible shot at better jobs in the future. You want the maximum in protection against sudden firing, unwanted transfer, or harmful treatment.

And while you're negotiating through the recruiter, you will be comparing your present job to the possible new job and considering ways in which you might make your present situation better.

So let's look at the nonmonetary aspects of the bargaining process.

RESHAPING THE JOB

Search consultants often feel that the specification provided by the client does not precisely meet the company's needs. A good recruiter will discuss the matchup between spec and needs and may get the client to modify its requirements. Frequently the basis for this discussion is the recruiter's feeling that the company is overspecifying, putting in so many qualifications, some of marginal importance, that it will be more difficult to recruit the best executive for the position. Another reaction felt by search consultants is that the client may be searching for someone at too low a level and that the real need is for a manager who carries more weight.

The spec may be modified and the scope broadened to some extent, but the consultant still may feel it is not altogether descriptive of the person the company really needs. In such a case he may, in looking for candidates, push against the upper limits of the specification, hoping to find someone perhaps a little overqualified according to the instructions but who will so impress the decision-makers that they go for what the consultant thought they needed all along.

The job the recruiter talks to you about may not be big enough to interest you. But if the company is one you would consider joining, and if other considerations—location, company position in the industry, etc.—suit you, there may be a chance of broadening the scope of the job. Find out what the search professional thinks. Ask where the company hopes to go in the next few years and how the job function fits into those plans. Then ask if the qualifications required in the specification really fit those aspirations. The recruiter, overtly or tacitly, may indicate a belief that maybe the firm really needs someone who draws a little more water.

Explore the possibilities. Don't make your primary aim in bargaining more money. Begin to negotiate for greater power. Say, "I'm interested, but the way it's structured now I would be too cramped. To achieve these goals, the guy on the job needs more authority."

You are likely to be encouraged to expand on your ideas. (In the unlikely case that the headhunter responds, "Oh, no, this is exactly the way it should be structured, and there's no point talking about it," your interest may be dampened, and with good reason.) Of course, your observations are keyed to the achievement of goals and the necessity to have sufficient means for achieving those goals. Everybody wants a bigger job, more resounding title, more money. That's no news to the recruiter. What is useful to him or her is a cogent argument for giving you the scope you need. The recruiter can go to the client and use your points in making a renewed pitch for upgrading the job.

Begin with your campaign to enlarge the job—if you feel it should be enlarged—as soon as you know enough about the situation. Tell the headhunter exactly how you feel. Do not wait until you are talking to the potential employer to make your case. To begin with, it makes the recruiter look bad if the candidate walks in and, without warning, begins to insist that he or she wants to draw more water or else cannot come on board. Moreover, the recruiter can be an effective ally. The arguments of a candidate, no matter how well reasoned, will be perceived as self-serving. (Of course, they are self-serving, and they have every right to be; but as we have mentioned, a lot of senior managers expect manifestations of selfless objectivity from the candidate right from the start.)

Often the client is unwilling to make a job as big as it should be not because there is no logic to the move but because of a political situation. Well-entrenched veterans would be upset if a newcomer is brought in on their own level. A highly influential manager opposes the proposition because the manager would see the incumbent of the job as a threat to his or her turf and future. A division that has traditionally been the most important in the company hierarchy would feel diminished.

Find out as much as you can from the recruiter about the nature of the opposition, its strength, the individuals who are most opposed, and their reasons. If one particular member of management is the center of the opposition, why? Rivalry? A sincere feeling that all the company needs is the lower-powered candidate called for in the spec? His own candidate for advancement?

Asking questions of this kind can not only help in your campaign to land a good job but also tell you a lot of things you need to know to function smoothly and effectively after you take the job. The profiles and positions of the people who are deciding on the nature of the job are major elements of the atmosphere in which you'll be working. And the more you know about the person who opposed the enhancement of the job, the more you may be forearmed about a potential adversary in corporate politics.

Let's say you have gotten to the point of serious negotiations with the company. Obviously you are one of the top candidates, if not the leader. The stumbling block is your feeling that the job isn't big enough. The employer still will want you. In fact, your objection may make you more desirable. Without necessarily looking at the merits of your position, some will applaud the ambition it shows and declare that you are the right stuff, someone to be landed if at all possible.

But that doesn't mean they'll give you what you want. It's likely that they will try to buy your acquiescence with money, perks, and relatively empty emblems of status. If you feel strongly that the position must have more scope, you will not allow yourself to be bought. Make your position clear to the headhunter.

When asked what precisely you do want, be ready to articulate it in meaningful terms. Importance and authority have various measures. One is reporting level; if you report directly to the CEO rather than to the COO or executive vice president, you may have all the additional clout you need. Another criterion of clout is the crowd around you or lack of it: How many others are there at your level? Then there is the size of the budget you dispose of, or the number of people you boss, or the sources of information you control.

These are the realities of power. A bigger compensation package, a grander office, even a more resounding title—these can be the facsimiles of power. Go for the real power. Set up a full-scale presentation to those making the decisions. Make sure the search consultant is in on it. Prepare your pitch carefully. It *is* a pitch, and an important one. Use graphics and props as necessary. Proceed to give as powerful a sales talk for your viewpoint as you can. Pull no punches. Argue hard for the position you want.

This brings you to the point of no return. If they decide that they don't want to enlarge the scope of the job, then they are likely to turn their attention away from you; albeit reluctantly. They won't want you in a job you think is too small. Of course, you don't want that job, either. Just be sure this is your position before going all out to seek more authority.

Even if you are unsuccessful in winning the job you want, you will have made a powerful impression on the would-be employer; on the recruiter; and on others who will, through the ripple effect, undoubtedly hear about it. Your self-confidence, and the cogency and force with which you have put your position, will help your career considerably.

POWER, POSITION, AND PARTICIPATION

One of the most pivotal career points comes when you make the transition from paid employee—however high that pay might be—to having a piece of the action. A prime opportunity to make that transition comes when you are the target of a search. The very fact that a search consultant has singled you out as a leading candidate bestows an aura of desirability. You are on your way to having a strong bargaining power that can be used to make a decisive career move.

But being on the way to possessing leverage is not the same as possessing it. Timing is of the essence in any negotiation, and it is particularly the case when you are negotiating with a potential employer. While you are still just a good possibility—one among, say, three or four—your ability to bargain hard for difficult-to-get concessions is limited. A power move at this point can simply knock you out of contention. The search consultant may feel that you have an edge on the other contenders but that the cost of getting you may be too high. The recruiter has not yet tilted markedly toward you in discussions with the client, and the client has not seen enough of you to say, "That's the person we want." So no matter how many potential advantages you have in your bid for power, they have not yet become actual advantages. Your timing for a bold move is premature. If you make it at this point you are likely to eliminate yourself from the picture.

How do you know when to make the move?

The relationship between a recruiter and a strong candidate progresses from the screening or "knockout" stage to the stage in which the recruiter embraces the candidate and starts a wooing process. The candidate should not be fooled into thinking that he or she is the sole target of the courtship. The headhunter is apt to have narrowed the field to a handful of lively possibilities and wants to keep them all interested while firming up his or her own judgment and getting a better sense of which one the client likes best.

During this stage the candidate will, of course, be talking with one or more people at the client company. It's important to know how many people are involved in the decision, who they are, how much relative weight they carry, and how strongly they are likely to express their opinions. The amount of decision-making weight cannot be gauged solely by place in the organization. For example, a 35-year-old marketing executive was approached by a search consultant on behalf of a large New England hi-tech company in search of a vice president for marketing. The money was very good; the recruiter assured the executive that the package would amount to well over $200,000, almost double what the candidate was earning at the time.

The executive felt that this was his chance to make a big move. He liked the company's chances to succeed in a previously untried market. He felt he could be of great importance in achieving that success. He decided he wanted equity—a great deal of it, enough to bring him several million in five years if everything went well. He was willing to take a lot less in assured income as a trade-off for the equity.

The executive had studied the firm thoroughly, reading everything he could get his hands on, including some exceptionally revealing information about special compensation plans devised for two of the company's senior managers. (This information, not publicized by the company, had been filed with the SEC according to legal requirement and was subsequently printed in *Executive Compensation Reports*.) He had progressed smoothly through the process, including several satisfactory meetings with the president and chairman. Now, he felt, was the time to make his move.

The executive sat down with the chairman and president and unveiled his ideas about compensation. They were taken aback at the sweeping nature of his ideas. He was willing to be paid significantly less than the two other managers at his level, but he was asking for a large chunk of equity, based on the assumption that the part of the operation under his control would surge ahead. While the senior managers were surprised at the audacity of the request, they applauded the man's spirit and his willingness to risk so much on the company's success. The candidate came away feeling that he would get most of what he wanted—and that, furthermore, he would have it in a written employment contract, another of his demands.

The candidate had not disclosed his plan to the search consultant. That individual learned of it from the president of the company, who was startled to find that the recruiter was unaware of such a major factor in the negotiation. The recruiter felt he had been treated like a pawn and made to look bad. The next time he talked with the candidate, the candidate observed without apology that he had felt his bid had the greatest chance of success if it came as a complete surprise to the people who would make the decision. He could see that the headhunter resented being bypassed, but what difference did that make? He had brought it off.

Failing to be candid with the search professional usually is a mistake. In this case it turned the recruiter off. He was not willing to go an extra mile to help this candidate, although he had to acknowledge that the guy could do a lot for the company and certainly had made a big hit with the top two officers of the firm.

However, contrary to the marketing man's confident assumptions, the deal was not sewed up. His timing, which had looked perfect, was premature. True, he had forged ahead in the opinions of the chairman and the president, but there was another person he had not yet seen— the firm's executive vice president, who was on an extended trip abroad. This had not seemed to loom very large; after all, the executive vice president was an engineer and production man, not a marketer, and he ranked below the top two on the chart. So the candidate had assumed this was a pro forma matter.

It was not. The executive vice president had decisive influence on filling this job. He did not have the power to pick the candidate, but he did have the power to reject a candidate. One reason for this was his solid value as a senior manager. The second was a hidden factor. There was a possibility that the president would leave the company— amicably—in three to five years. This had been discussed among the top brass but kept very quiet. The executive vice president had received a pledge of very strong consideration for the job. This had been made to him, via a handshake agreement, a year before, when he had been tempted by an offer of a lot more money by another company.

The recruiter, although he didn't know of the agreement, had a very strong sense that the executive vice president was a vital factor in the decision. He had told the candidate this, but it had not registered to the degree that it should have.

When the executive vice president heard about the requirements advanced by the marketing manager, he had an immediate negative reaction. He did not want the company to commit that much potential compensation to someone else. He reasoned that such an arrangement would of necessity create a dangerous rival. This was not what the marketing man had in mind; if he had brought off the coup he would have been more likely to start his own company. If he had presented his ideas to the executive vice president he might well have been able to reassure him.

But he had not presented his ideas to this person. He had not even met him. The timing was wrong. He subsided out of consideration for the job, which ultimately went to another candidate, perhaps less qualified but more conventional in his ideas about compensation. When the original candidate learned what had happened, he felt with some bitterness that the recruiter could have given him firmer guidance. The recruiter pointed out that he had been kept in the dark.

When you intend to up the ante considerably, or to put forth conditions that will make the decision-makers at the client company swallow hard, you must time it well. It's important that you have progressed beyond the stage at which you still are being screened. You probably should be past, or nearly past, the stage at which you are one of a handful of good candidates. The time when you have maximum leverage is when you feel you are the favored candidate.

You are not in this position until you have talked with all of the decision-makers, including those who constitute the kinds of hazards that hidden reefs constitute for mariners. It is unwise to assume that the decision-making clout always is apportioned by title. In fact, while you can't always find out for sure, it's well to assume that there are people involved in the hiring decision of whom you as yet know little.

Sometimes the recruiter will be unaware of these behind-the-scenes actors but usually should have a pretty good sense of who they are. One way to get a better sense of what the recruiter knows is to ask about the meetings he or she had with the client. Who was there? What was said? If there are any whom you have not yet met, are you going to meet them? Should you meet them? How influential will they be? What might they be looking for in the candidate?

–

Until you feel you are looked upon with some degree of approval by most if not all of the key people, you cannot assume you have arrived at a position of really powerful leverage.

One way to test the extent to which you are regarded highly by the client is to imply to the recruiter that you might be cooling off in your enthusiasm for the job. If this is greeted with the equivalent of a polite yawn, or just a perfunctory pep talk, you're not in the catbird's seat—at least not yet. If you get a fairly intense concentration of efforts to boost your interest, it's reasonable to conclude that they think of you as an active possibility. When you get to this point, you can make your move. If you do this carefully, you can also strengthen your position.

By declaring that you want to participate to a greater extent than usual in the company's success or failure, you manifest commitment, which makes you an attractive commodity. That doesn't mean you will find it easy to get a piece of the action. Chances are that the firm will attempt to deflect you from that aim by sweetening the pot. For this they will put on the table the additional money that was being held in reserve as a bargaining chip. So even if your bid for equity is not successful, you may win a bigger compensation package.

But if you have decided that this is your chance to participate extensively, and if this is an important objective, don't back off too quickly. It's not a demand that diminishes your value in the eyes of the employer—*if your timing is right, and if you have made it at a point when you have achieved a high degree of acceptance.*

Negotiating for equity is one possible strategy. In other cases, the executive is not interested in greater equity so much as in changing the nature of the position for which he or she is being considered.

POSITIONING YOURSELF FOR POWER

Another important consideration in the deliberations of the candidate is the present-day tide that will lead to the future ebb and flow of power. You want to know where the company is going. You want to know what is in store for the particular segment of the company you are being asked to join. You may be very interested in the firm, but you must be careful to assure yourself a spot in the mainstream of progress toward the future, rather than a backwater.

To position yourself for maximum future power you must learn as much as you can about plans, not all of which are going to be revealed to you. Here the search consultant may be of great help. Why is the company looking for someone? Is the job—whether it is a new one or one that has been previously occupied—open because the person who fills it figures importantly in the future of the enterprise?

Ask the recruiter how the specification compares with the job description previously applied to the post. If the spec carries increased responsibility and scope, does this mean top management is looking toward the new executive to play an important role in a developing plan? If the spec is about the same as before, you may wonder if you are getting into a static situation. Certainly you are likely to have a chance to enlarge your importance in the firm once you have proven yourself, but it's easier to assume that you're headed for bigger things if the specification says so. If, by the way, you develop a feeling that the job is somewhat more restricted in scope than before, consider the implications. There may be many reasons why you would want the job and would be effective and happy in it, but it may not be where the principal action is tomorrow. In fact, diminution of the authority and status implicit in the position may be the reason it is open.

Maybe the client company has recently retained a general management consultant to study the organization, with the present search partly a result of that study. Indeed, the search might be being conducted by the same consulting firm that did the study. You should certainly be aware if the search professional talking with you works for a firm that also does management consulting, and if this assignment is connected with something else they have done for the client.

Whether or not he or she works for the same company, the recruiter is practically certain to know about a relevant consulting report if one exists. Ask the recruiter if there is such a study. You'll probably be told. Ask about its conclusions. Be particularly attentive to the implications with respect to the future of the job you may be asked to fill. (You may even be able to look at a copy of the consultant's report. There is no harm in asking.)

Consultant's report or not, learn all you can about the directions in which the firm intends to move, and about industry trends that will crest in the future. If the position appears to be going nowhere, you may want to forget it, whatever the near-term rewards. If you spot what seems to be a prime opportunity for the company, negotiate to shift the focus of the position so you will be more involved in that area.

You cannot get guarantees of future power. But you can be given assurances that unless something happens to intervene, you will be given a substantially greater opportunity—let us say the chance to run your own strategic business unit in a promising area—at a point in the future. Pin this down as precisely as possible. Put a time frame on it—say, five years. Then, when you're in the job, you can shape your moves toward preparation for that goal. And you can monitor your progress toward it, reminding the top brass of the agreement if there seems to be some inclination to shift you to another track.

To bargain for power you must know as much as possible about where the power levers of the enterprise will be located tomorrow. The recruiter has some knowledge of that. Let him or her tell you what you need to know.

GETTING IT IN WRITING

While looking at the attractions of the job you're being recruited for, you should not ignore the problems and potential dangers.

Sometimes the immediate attractions can be so great that they blind one to what may happen tomorrow. In an extreme case, an editor was recruited from a Boston publishing house and persuaded to join a Philadelphia firm at a very high salary. The editor was given a division to run. As an additional assignment, he was asked to set up a new enterprise within the firm, putting it into a new area of publishing in which he had some experience.

The editor took over his established division and immediately began to set up the new venture. When he had the new operation in good shape, he was summarily fired. Evidently the employer had wanted his expertise in establishing the new department, which was then taken over by someone with tight family connections. The job for which the editor had ostensibly been recruited was as head of a division that was soon to be dead in the water.

In the vast majority of cases the employer is dealing from absolute good faith. Nevertheless, there may be problems ahead, undetected now, that would put you in jeopardy. Think about protecting yourself, by means of a contract, against sudden firing or another form of mishandling.

Today executives are getting employment contracts in greater numbers than ever before. The prevalence of mergers and take-overs is one reason; people think that a contract is a prudent form of protection. Another reason is the increasing complexity of compensation arrangements. You really have to have it in writing. And then there are the "life-style" considerations that have become important to a lot of managers. They are bargaining for agreements that provide up-front

126 / STALKING THE HEADHUNTER

bonuses and cost-of-living adjustments, protection against unwanted transfer, maternity (or paternity) leave, special arrangements for time off, and so on. It's no longer the case that executives who think about such things can be dismissed as not having their hearts in their work (though some of the older generation of senior management still hold that view). Today's younger executives are willing to put immense energy into their jobs, but they are not willing to devote every fiber of their beings to it. Things have changed in a great many ways. For example, the marriage or partnership in which both parties pursue careers is now commonplace. The partners look at a written employment agreement as a sensible precaution in protecting them against the threat of unwelcome transfer, as well as termination without adequate severance pay.

So the employment contract is no longer just for entertainers, athletes, and supersenior-level executives. It's possible to have a good shot at getting one if you really want it. Many firms that never used to offer contracts are now doing so, not because they enjoy it but because they must to recruit the caliber of talent they want. Furthermore, the company may want a written contract for its own protection—against the executive going into competition or disclosing secrets. Another reason for the increasing willingness of employers to consider contracts is the ground swell of court decisions declaring that there is an implicit contract between employer and employee, even when there is nothing in writing, and that the employer has no unlimited right to fire. Suits for wrongful dismissal are challenging the assumption, taken for granted in American business, of employment at will (of the employer). When one adds to this the restriction imposed by laws against discrimination because of age, sex, or race, one sees a narrowing of the old management privilege of firing because the "chemistry is wrong" or to straighten out a glitch in the organizational chart. Given this situation, some companies are saying, "Since the courts are finding an implicit contractual relationship anyway, we might as well have a written agreement over which we will have some control."

You can't always get a contract. But you're in a good position to get one when an employer really wants to hire you. So when the process moves along to the stage at which you're actively being wooed, you should think about the advantages of a written agreement, and if you want one, work through the executive recruiter to enhance your chances of getting one.

Work *through*, not *with*. Recruiters don't like contracts; the idea of a written agreement complicates the deal. Clients have, in many cases, a deep-seated if illogical feeling that the candidate should be absolutely salivating for the job. Learning that the candidate is talking about getting it in writing, the reaction may be, "What's the matter? Doesn't he [or she] trust us?" So the search consultant may try to guide you away from the contract area.

However, if the notion of a written agreement is attractive to you, don't back off without thoroughly investigating the possibilities. If the employer wants you and is willing to put together an attractive package to get you, why shouldn't the employer be willing to put it in writing?

As I discussed in *Perks and Parachutes: Negotiating Your Executive Employment Contract*, the resistance to a written agreement is often based more on habit and emotion than on logic. The vast majority of employers do not make oral commitments with the intent of reneging on them. They just "don't want to be tied down" to a contract; or they resist because it's a change ("We've never had contracts"); or they take the candidate's desire for a binding agreement as excessive self-absorption or mistrust.

The employer does not have any intention of reneging—at the time they are trying to recruit you. But things may change, and they may want to be free to get rid of you, or treat you cavalierly, not because you're not doing a good job but because you don't fit in with some change of circumstance.

Women executives are finding the concept of written agreements particularly useful. As they move into the senior ranks, they often find it's still a man's world and that merit doesn't count as much as it did before. When a crunch comes, they may confront a solid front of male bonding. As a result, the female manager becomes vulnerable.

If you're interested in getting a contract, it's best not just to inform the headhunter of that fact, unless you are so determined to get it in writing that you want to make it a major bargaining issue. There's another approach. Work through each of the elements of your employment arrangement—money, title, perks, etc.—in turn, indicating what you want. Write your conditions down, and keep revising them as you talk with the search consultant and the employer. You're producing a draft of your contract, although you don't tell the consultant that. He or she cannot agree to give you a contract; only the client can do that.

If the client has delegated to the recruiter a considerable part of the negotiation, you will ultimately cover all the salient points. Then you close. You have, in writing, what the client agrees to give you for joining the company. You say, "Okay. Now, since we agree on this, and the guts of it is already written down, let's get it in proper form so we can both sign it and put it in the bottom drawer."

There will be resistance. Be prepared by being willing to make concessions in one or two areas that are not of paramount importance to you. This gives the consultant a chance to go back to the client and say, "He's pretty hard-nosed about the contract, but I think I can get him to go easy on the demand for junior options."

A contract may be a very useful piece of paper. You may have to bargain hard to get it, but it can be mighty worthwhile.

TODAY'S REALITY VS. TOMORROW'S POSSIBILITIES

A signed contract, a good benefits package, and other perks are all important, but not as important as deciding if the job is really right for you. To do that, compare your present job, with its possibilities, against all the aspects of the job you're being recruited for. The money may be better than you're getting now. But what about other vital career considerations?

Look at the job specification with an eye toward the "irrelevant" requirement. For example, the spec may call for some consumer-goods experience in a marketing manager ostensibly concerned with industrial sales. Or familiarity with overseas trade practices in what would seem to be a strictly domestic division. Such things may signal possibilities you want to know about.

The job with the new company may imply a certain amount of potential you *don't* want. Let's say the would-be employer is offering you the chance to run your own operation, a chance that seems, on the surface, to be exactly what you've been looking for with your present company but that does not appear to be materializing fast enough. You know how it would work in your present firm; you're familiar with the company's resources, culture, products, and markets. But what looks like a similar operation in another enterprise may be wildly different. The project may be moving faster than you like. It may not have the degree of support you are used to enjoying.

So if the new employer is offering a job with big responsibility and a great deal of autonomy, press for quantification. Get it as precise as possible: budgets, areas of operation, and, particularly, expected results.

Beyond the quantifiable there are the intangibles. Here the search consultant can help. Ask him or her about the company's track record with similar ventures. Discuss the internal competition: who in the firm would not be too unhappy if you fall on your face, and how much those persons could do about helping you to fall on your face. Ask particularly about those executives within the firm who might have been eligible for the job they are offering to you.

To sum up, in assessing the potential of your current situation against that of the new one, potential—where you're going and how soon you can get there—is of paramount importance. It's probably to your advantage to focus on the power and importance of the job, today and tomorrow, rather than just on the money. If you don't have a well-defined *power goal,* think it through: How much scope and responsibility are you comfortable with?

Potential power is easier to assess in your present firm than in another. The position being dangled in front of you may seem to offer unlimited sea room, while in actuality there can be dangerous currents and hidden shoals. Get the facts about the new job to the extent that you can get them. Talk with the search professional about the intangibles that might inhibit what looks like very broad powers, or might on the other hand offer the semblance of power without the resources to back it up.

If you get to this point and decide that the job is not right for you, say so, but be up front about it and explain why. Otherwise you could make things very awkward for yourself.

Without deliberately trying to use the situation, some executives go all the way through to the point of getting a firm offer—then allow themselves to be wooed back by more money, a bigger title, etc.

It's a wonderful feeling to have another job offer in your pocket. You're in a position to negotiate with your present employer from a position of total strength. If you don't get what you want, you can threaten to leave—and you have another job to step into.

But—don't expect that you can parlay the approach of a headhunter into a situation in which you are absolutely sure of another position before you risk leaving your present one. You may very well decide to bargain with your present employer, but while the possibility of another offer may be very strong, don't count on its being a certainty.

There are executives who play out the whole string with the head-hunter. They go through the interview process, give every indication (to the point of lying about it) that they will take the new job if offered—and then, when the offer comes, they use it to get a better deal. The would-be employer is frustrated. The headhunter is embarrassed and made to look bad.

This is one of the headhunter's major nightmares. It's not just that the whole process turns out to have been a waste of time. Nor is it merely a matter of placating a client who expected that the search professional had the whole thing set. When a candidate pulls out after an offer has been made (or when it is about to be made), the other candidates who have been available at the same time are apt to be knocked out of the box as well. The jilted employer is unwilling to settle for "second-best"—even though one of the alternates may be just as good. So the client tells the headhunter to go out and find another "Mr. (or Ms.) Right." (Occasionally, to the profound distress of the search firm, the employer may decide that another matchmaker should be called in on the case.)

Obviously headhunters have become sensitized to this possibility. So they will do everything possible to make sure that the favored candidate will really take the job if his or her requirements are met. So if you seem to be pushing your nose ahead of the rest of the field, you are going to be asked to commit yourself.

You don't have to give the search person a guarantee. But if it looks as if you're going to be offered the job, play it on the level. If you are really interested in the job, say so, and commit yourself to taking it if your demands are met in substance. Don't figure that you can change your mind at the last second and give an excuse like, "My wife decided she couldn't cope with the move," or, "They weren't willing to give me a sabbatical two years from now" (or some other demand that has been dragged in at the last second or magnified out of proportion). You will be welshing on your tacit agreement.

Well, why not? What do you care if the would-be employer is disappointed and the headhunter looks bad? If you've been able to use the whole thing to get what you want in your present spot, isn't that the sole consideration?

It's not. Apart from the cynicism of using other people and the abandonment of honesty in lying to them, there are considerable dangers in this kind of power play.

You may be marked down as a moral deadbeat and an untrustworthy person, not only by the headhunter whom you have betrayed, but also by others. This sort of thing gets around. You may lose out on some important opportunities because people don't want to take a chance with you.

There is, moreover, a perilous temptation implicit in such a situation. The executive, armed with an iron-clad offer, walks into his employer and really applies the screws. This may be the worst possible time for the employer even to consider letting a key person get away. So the boss feels over a barrel. You get everything you demand.

And then what? You've still got to work in the place. The employer may be thoroughly resentful, resolving to line up a replacement for you so you can ultimately be told to go to hell. Your subsequent career with the company may be bogged down in difficulties, and while you were able to get the money and promotion you were bargaining for this time, you are not a good bet to keep moving up.

And your colleagues in the firm, when they find out what you did (and they probably will), are likely to be resentful. That's not what they'll tell you; they'll congratulate you on being a smart cookie. But you should not count on their friendship or their cooperation. People may work, consciously or unconsciously, to make you look bad.

So you've got to decide to pull out or go for it. If you don't feel you're likely to take the job, discuss it with the headhunter. He or she won't give you a hard sell but may point out things that make it look better to you.

This doesn't mean you should not use the *possibility* of another offer to bargain with your boss. Bargain to the hilt. But play it straight. Give the search professional (and perhaps the potential employer) the message that you have *not* made up your mind. Be clear with them on this, even if it means that your chances of getting the other offer are diminished. And if you conclude that you're highly unlikely to leave, take yourself out of the running. But make sure that's really what you want to do.

In comparing your present situation with the possible new job, there are intangibles as well as tangibles to consider. The "old shoe" comfort of an existing situation can mask its drawbacks. The promise of a new situation may be exaggerated out of all relationship to reality. And there are the realities of life in the present situation after you've used the leverage to get yourself a better deal. For example, one of the things you should consider, when you are negotiating from strength, is a written employment contract that will protect you in case things turn sour, or in case the employer's festering resentment impels them to want revenge.

You need to compare the advantages of the new job with the advantages of staying. There is no method of doing this to a mathematical certainty. The equation has more variables than fixed quantities. Nevertheless, it is possible to make a reasoned assessment of the situation. Here are some of the principal factors to consider:

Potential: Where are you going in your present job? You should have a specific goal to be attained within, say, five years. Now, most of us have, more or less, a "goal" in the sense that we hope to have a bigger job with more money. Your objective should be a lot more specific than that. Have a definite job in mind in terms of responsibility, scope, compensation, and power. Bring that goal up to date. Since the objective should be realistic, the job you want must be attainable within a reasonable time under conditions that apply now and are likely to apply tomorrow.

Are you closer to where you want to be than you were a year ago? If you cannot answer with a loud *yes*, maybe your career is not at flank speed, and a change would be good. If you're really making progress toward where you want to be, and if bargaining from strength can speed your progress, staying put may be the best bet.

Power: Make the most of your leverage by bargaining not for money or status, but for power. Managers who use this kind of situation to extract a bigger base salary or bonus often miss the point. When your continued employment can be bought just with money, you are, in a way, diminished. Furthermore, if the employer resents your use of an advantage, it's not that hard for them to retaliate later if all you've done is obtain more money.

However, if you decide that your chances of getting another job are favorable enough to warrant an all-out effort, go for power. For example, if your objective is to run your own division or strategic business unit, ask for it. You can't get it immediately, but if you bargain hard enough, you may be able to get a definite commitment (in writing), accompanied by the initial steps that will turn it into a reality by an agreed-on date. If the boss insists that under no circumstances can any such commitment be made to you, well, that may make the other company look better.

But remember that it can be relatively easy for a potential employer to talk about the big things in store for you. You can be misled in a way that would not be the case with reference to your present company, about which you know a great deal more.

Explore the real potential in the new company thoroughly with the headhunter. If this person has done the right job, he or she will have talked intensively with top management about where the enterprise is headed and how the candidate fits in. The headhunter is unlikely to have volunteered everything he or she knows to you, but will tend to be selective. Milk the headhunter not only of facts about the company's plans but also of his or her opinions and hunches.

CHAPTER 12

Negotiation IV: Moving the Process to a Successful Conclusion

WHEN YOU UNDERSTAND THE position of the recruiter, you are better able to handle the bargaining process. Try to take control of the negotiation process as early and as firmly as you can so that you are initiating rather than reacting. You can begin to take control even before the bargaining over the deal begins. You can use the headhunter to speed up the process of getting an offer.

One of the most disheartening things for a search consultant is to bring the candidate to the point of receptivity and the client to the point of making an offer, only to have the client hem and haw for no good reason. The search professional is well aware of the danger. The candidate may have been moved from a posture of being happy where he or she is to a posture of being ready to move. Thus the candidate is ripe for another offer. Another offer comes along while the first client is still thinking it over. The search consultant learns about this, rushes to the client, there is a mad scramble to put together a package, but it comes too late. The candidate takes the other job.

As we have observed, this is a rotten situation for the recruiter because it is likely to move everything back to square one. Logically the spotlight should now shift to the other two people who were under consideration, but because human nature is what it is, the client is apt to think this would mean second-best and wants a whole new deal. And, even worse, the client blames the recruiter for the whole imbroglio.

A. Robert Taylor observes, "When a candidate's interest in the open position has been brought to a point at which he is willing to consider an offer, time is of the essence. There should be no delay in presenting the proposed conditions of employment to him." You can heighten the headhunter's uneasiness at delay by indicating your receptivity while hinting that you might not be able to wait forever.

This does *not* mean to fake another offer. That's an old ploy, the dishonesty of which usually is matched by its ineffectiveness. Rather it means being open about your feelings.

One tactic is to say, "I'm starting to cool off. I thought they were as interested in me as I am in them. But evidently they've got somebody else's name ahead of mine." The headhunter may try to reassure you that this is not the case, that they are just tying up all the loose ends, etc., but you refuse to be convinced. Since the recruiter definitely does not want to have you cool off on the deal, he or she may do what is possible to nudge the client to make an offer.

Another tactic is more indirect. It is not exactly "playing hard to get," but it is a series of manifestations of waning interest—being too busy to talk, calling off a meeting, not being able to make lunch until the end of the following week. When you are sure you are a prime candidate and that it is the nature of the package, not your qualifications that still is being debated, signals of this sort can reach the sensitive antennae of the search professional and set off an alarm.

It's perhaps best just to say, "Look, a great many things about the job are attractive. And I'm not actively looking at anything else. But I think that, when all the discussion is over, it's time to act. If they can't make up their minds, then it could be that the company is not as decisive as I thought. Or it could be that they are not as sold on me as I thought. Either way, I have to reexamine my own situation in the light of what I know. And what I know now is that nothing is happening at a time when something should happen."

When you move to expedite the offer, you are also positioning yourself positively for subsequent negotiation.

As you begin to look more and more like the winner, the headhunter's stake in you gets heavier.

So bargain hard, but bargain in good faith. It's one thing to negotiate with—and through—people. It's another thing to try to deceive or exploit them. Even the most illustrious candidate can lose a fine deal by maladroit handling of the negotiation.

A CASE OF POOR NEGOTIATING

Here's the story of how one deal fell apart.

The candidate—call him Freeland—had moved into a position where he was clearly favored over the other two candidates who had been put forward by the executive search professional, whom we'll call Danbury. The CEO—Rudd—of the client firm was looking for a senior vice president for finance. The job would be very important within the next few years as the company began to move in new directions and engaged in some innovative financing.

Freeland was vice president for finance at a smaller firm in a city about 700 miles distant. Danbury, the recruiter, felt that Freeland was the best bet in all important respects. His credentials made a good fit. But beyond that, Freeland offered youthful vigor, innovation, and drive—qualities needed by the client firm. There had been the obvious question of whether the personal chemistry between candidate and client might be altogether wrong, but the client's top people had, with a few reservations, liked Freeland. And Freeland, though he was breezily caustic about the "squares" who inhabited the client firm, had gotten along with them well enough.

For a while the negotiations were tough but reasonably free from problems. Freeland was making $85,000 a year. The new job would pay $100,000 base salary, with a bonus that probably would bring the total to about $125,000. Freeland had bargained the bonus possibility up by about $10,000. The rest of the package, including a substantial but not lavish program of stock options, seemed acceptable. The discussions moved to another track. Freeland wanted a freer hand on some decisions than Rudd was at first willing to allow. Danbury argued hard for Freeland's point of view. "Tom," he said to Rudd, "guys who come in and just cut the coats to fit your cloth are easy to get. This company's headed for change. The man is going to help you get where you want to go. And he will help you avoid the problems on the way. He wants to participate. Give him a share of the success everybody wants. After all, if he doesn't deliver, there's no bonus." Rudd agreed to up the ante. Freeland was, in his opinion, asking for a hell of a lot but probably was worth it. Rudd was tougher to convince about the degree of autonomy Freeland demanded: "Money is one thing. But he wants us to turn over to him a huge chunk of policy-making. He's not on board yet. It's all right about the compensation—if he doesn't work out, it's just gone—but if he makes some really bad decisions he could take the whole outfit down, and then he's gone, but we have to live with it."

Danbury talked frankly to Freeland: "There are two things here. The authority you want, and the symbol. Maybe it's logical for you to get all the power you want going in. But it's almost impossible for them to accept, all in one bite. But why do we have to go through all this?

Once you're there, you're going to call the shots on financing, no question about that. Your job will be harder if you push them too hard before they're ready, or at least I think it might be. Think it over. Do you really need that sort of mandate on paper?"

Freeland made some concessions on the scope of his authority, at least in terms of the formal job description. He gave every indication, as he talked with Rudd, that he expected to exert the desired authority in fact, whatever the formal arrangement. Rudd was not thrilled about this but was willing to live with it.

The deal seemed to be ready for consummation. But then Freeland had another demand. The cost differential between locations, and the hardship of moving his family, were greater than he had thought. The employer's willingness to pay all expenses and to provide a cost-of-living adjustment was not sufficient. Freeland wanted an up-front bonus.

This was not a shock to Danbury. Indeed, he had been surprised that Freeland had not already asked for it. As the search consultant explained to the client, relocating executives often underestimated, at first, the amount of disruption involved in the move. The executive himself is, after all, "plugged in" at the new location. But the kids have to make new friends, go to new schools; the spouse has to get used to a whole new way of life without being caught up in an important new job. When all of the problems become more apparent, the executive feels he or she needs to be compensated for the intangible sacrifices. The best way to do this is often through an up-front, one-shot payment.

Rudd said, "We've never done that before." Danbury made the case that a reasonable bonus was well worth the cost if it helped to free the new arrival's mind from concerns about the hardship of relocation and the suspicion that he had, in some way, been taken advantage of. Rudd could see the point in the argument. The amount—$25,000—was not, in his view, worth making a fuss about. By this time the CEO was convinced that Freeland was the right manager for the job, and it was pointless to endanger the deal or to make him unhappy. So the up-front bonus was agreed to.

There was another issue that had been simmering throughout the negotiation. Freeland had mentioned several times that he would like a written contract. He had never pushed the idea hard. Rudd had ignored the oblique reference to an employment agreement—to him, a handshake was enough. Danbury didn't care about the contract one way or another.

Now Freeland said he wanted it in writing. Rudd was disagreeably surprised. Candidate, consultant, and client had lunch. Danbury had been afraid that Freeland would use the issue of a contract to up the ante on the compensation package and that this might upset the deal. But Freeland was not asking for anything more than what he had already gotten agreement to. But he did want a piece of paper. "Why not get it in writing? That way we can both put the thing in the bottom drawer and forget about it, and I can do the best damn job I can for you." Rudd responded, "Why do we need it? We trust each other. Nobody's ever questioned my word. My handshake has always been good enough. That's the way we do business here."

Danbury's role now was to mediate the discussion while steering it away from tricky areas. He didn't want the candidate even to seem to be questioning the employer's good faith. Nor did he want to get into an argument about what might happen if Rudd should get sick or die, or if the company happened to be taken over, or any of the other unpleasant implications the client might draw from the demand for a contract. The recruiter observed that as a matter of course, the compensation arrangement would be put in writing, anyway. Freeland was not trying to pull a fast one. He was just doing what more and more executives are doing: asking for a written contract as a matter of course. Why not give it to him?

Rudd at last acknowledged that his objections were largely based on the fact that the idea of a written agreement was new, rather than on substance. All right, he could see Freeland's point. A contract could be drawn up.

How long should the contract run? Freeland said he thought the term really should be five years, but he was willing to take four. Danbury said this would never fly. Freeland dug in his heels: "Why the hell not? I'll tell Rudd why I want it. If he can't see the point, well, he isn't thinking clearly. . . ." The recruiter did not feel a head-to-head session over this issue would be helpful at this time. With some trepidation he informed his client about the demand for a four-year contract. And how Rudd blew up. "What's he trying to do, make a monkey out of me? I won't consider anything beyond one year, and that's that!"

Back and forth they went over the latest stumbling block. One year seemed too short to Danbury, and he said so: "The minimum on most employment contracts is two years; anything less doesn't have much meaning." But Rudd was truly annoyed and would not commit himself even to consider two years.

On his next talk with the candidate, Danbury was candid and

urgent: "You can't get four years. It's stretching things for them even to give you a contract at all. Now, look. You're right for the job, you think it's right for you. Do you really want to jeopardize the deal over this?" After some thought, Freeland said that, well, though he was reluctant, he was willing to bend on this issue. To Danbury's surprise the candidate bent enough to agree to an 18-month term.

At this, Danbury thought the thing was wrapped up. Eighteen months had been quite a compromise. To the search consultant, this meant that Freeland was indeed serious and that he was willing to make a big concession to get the job. Rudd, calmed down, said 18 months would be acceptable. All that was left was the meeting at which they would shake hands on the arrangement.

Before the meeting, Danbury talked with Freeland. "Are we all set now? Let's review the package. It's all okay with you? There shouldn't be any surprises in there." The candidate assured the recruiter that there would be no surprises.

They met. The conversation was positive. The arrangement was reviewed. The CEO told Freeland how glad they were to have him aboard. Freeland talked about how glad he was to be joining the organization. There was some talk of office arrangements, staff, etc. Everything was fine. Then Freeland said, "Oh, by the way . . ."

And Danbury's blood ran cold. The candidate was raising what he called a "pro forma" matter. His title. From the beginning, there had been no discussion of this point. The title referred to by the client was senior vice president for finance. Freeland observed that this was not descriptive anymore, that their discussions had framed a broader job, and that the title should be more in line with the reality. How about "executive vice president"?

That did it. Danbury watched Rudd's eyes narrow and his lips tighten. No, he said, he could not consider changing the title on the job. And since that seemed so important to Freeland, perhaps it would be best if they rethought the whole thing. It didn't seem to him that Freeland would be happy with the firm after all, and that would not be a good situation for anybody. Rudd's response was measured—he did not blow up—but it came from the heart. Freeland began to marshal his arguments, but they fell on deaf ears. Danbury, consumed with frustration and fury, tried to manage the dispute, but it was no use. Even when Freeland indicated that, with a little negotiation, he was probably willing to back off from this demand, Rudd remained adamant: "You would always feel cramped, like you didn't have enough room to swing in. We made a lot of concessions to get you on board, but now I can see that it wouldn't be a comfortable arrangement. You certainly have a lot to offer any company, and I've learned a lot just talking with you. . . ."

And that was it. The deal was blown. Months of work went down the drain.

The recruiter found, as he had anticipated, that the client was not interested in reconsidering the other two candidates who had been unearthed at the same time as Freeland. The search would have to start again, from the beginning.

This "back to square one" effect came as no surprise to the search professional. This was often what happened. Danbury felt lucky that the client did not blame him for the whole fiasco.

But the recruiter did have a surprise in store. The candidate said to him, "What went wrong? Why should he react like that? After all, I was just negotiating. Okay, I'll drop the title stuff. When he calms down, we'll tell him I accept the deal, and we'll finalize the whole thing, huh?" Danbury realized with amazement that Freeland really wanted the job and did not see that it was almost certainly over. Danbury did his best, but had to tell the candidate, "Sorry. He won't reconsider." Freeland got angry. *He* blamed the recruiter. It was useless for Danbury to point out that he had shepherded the deal through all of Freeland's escalating demands, that he had helped the client to swallow things he did not want to accept, and that Freeland had assured him there would be no surprises at the last meeting.

This episode underscores some important points about the three-sided negotiation that so often takes place in the latter stages of a search. Of course, the most obvious fact is that the candidate pushed it too far. His "Chinese water torture" method of adding one demand to another was thoroughly unsuited to the situation.

Some people think of the bargaining process as if it were just fun and games, although with real money instead of counters. They push as hard as they can push, for the sheer exhilaration of adding one more victory. As in the case of Freeland, whose name here is fictionalized but whose words and actions are only too real, the prizes to be won by further bargaining got smaller and smaller as the process went on. He gave little thought to the reaction of the adversary in negotiating, assuming that the employer would feel the same way about the "game," playing hard but then shaking hands after the game was over.

People resent being outbargained by a tough negotiator. They may not show it, but it stings. In most negotiations over an employment package, the toughness of the candidate usually is forgotten soon after he or she starts the job, especially if the subject of the bargaining is more money, whatever the form in which it is given. But when the candidate pushes for nonmonetary gains—power and status—the situation is intensified. Manifestations of status—title, for example—may remain as a visible irritant long after the deal is done and the candidate is on board.

This does not mean an executive should not push hard for power and status. On the contrary, these are the areas in which the bargaining may be most meaningful. But it's important to understand the effect the negotiation may have on the other party, today and tomorrow.

In the case just described, even if the employer had not gotten fed up and canceled the deal, there probably would have been considerable difficulties for the new executive, stemming back to the way in which he handled himself. The boss would have resented the piecemeal nature of the negotiation rather than the toughness with which it was conducted. Rudd probably would have thought that Freeland was just jerking him around to show off his muscles.

And to a great degree the employer would have been right. Here was a case in which the candidate bargained just to chalk up marginal victories rather than to gain things of real meaning.

The fact that there are such candidates is one reason why recruiters want to stay solidly in the middle of the negotiation process—in fact, to orchestrate the process all the way. The recruiter wants to decide at any given point whether it's best to act as intermediary, to have a three-way meeting, or to let the candidate and client go one-on-one. The search consultant cannot always control this, of course. Sometimes the client wants to do his or her own thing. Candidates frequently are willing to take their lead from the headhunter, responding to his or her direction more and more as the process goes on. This is not the best way to bargain. The ideal approach is to plan and run the negotiation process that will get you what you want, using (*not* manipulating) the search consultant to help you.

That the consultant can be a big help is another point made by the case. Headhunter Danbury was really, on more than one occasion, acting as the candidate's agent, pleading his case more skillfully and less abrasively than the candidate was able to do himself. To some extent the search professional does this to wrap up the deal and get the rest of his or her fee. That's only natural. To some extent the headhunter does it because he or she feels the candidate is truly the best bet for the job, and the headhunter wants to overcome the client's objections for the client's own good. Another reason for the intercession is that the headhunter is thinking about what happens down the road. One leading recruiter puts it this way: "If I think the demand is legitimate but will be hard to get, I want to do the asking. When a candidate overplays his hand, is too brash, too cocky, pushes too hard, the kind of atmosphere created can make for tough times in the future. Sometimes worse than tough. Disastrous. The guy really sticks it to the CEO, almost laughs in his face, practically saying, 'You're going to give me what I want because you need me.' He does need him, so he goes along. For now. The guy is hired, moves his family, cuts all his old ties, is committed to the new job. *Then* the CEO calls him in and says, 'Joe? All that stuff we talked about? Now I'm going to tell you how it's *really* going to be.' You'll say that's illogical, that the CEO is biting off his nose to spite his face, that he is lousing up his relationship with a man he went out of his way to get. That's right. But who says logic always controls these situations? The CEO felt like he had been screwed. At the time he papered it over. But later the feeling came out, and he acted on it."

THE THIRD-PARTY NEGOTIATOR

The availability of the recruiter as a counselor and an advocate in the bargaining process should be taken advantage of to the fullest extent. The recruiter is an experienced hand and can be a great help. The recruiter's wish to close the deal and avoid future repercussions motivates him or her to do whatever has to be done to get you hired— *after* you have emerged as the leading candidate. Here timing is everything. If you start to make a lot of demands while you are still neck-and-neck, you can simply eliminate yourself from the field.

But perhaps the most fundamental point here is that raised by Robert G. Cox, president of the large international firm of PA Executive Search. Cox says, "What drives the negotiating process is *faith*." Each party has faith in himself or herself. Each party must have faith in the other parties. And each party wants the other party to have faith in him or her. The client wants an executive with faith in the firm. When the candidate seems to be asking for too much security, the employer feels this indicates a lack of faith in the firm.

Meanwhile the candidate is saying, "I'm the one who is taking the really big risks. They want me to leave my job and come with them. I want them to act as if they understand the risk I'm taking, not as if they were doing me a favor." The elements over which the bargaining is taking place are things of value in themselves, but they may loom even larger as symbols of the intangibles that are the real stakes in the game.

Egos are involved. Emotions become heated. This is one great reason that the search consultant wants to be in the middle, to act as lightning rod. Cox observes, "A danger point may come well along in the process. One side thinks the other side is getting too much, or pushing too hard. We work with both parties for the good of the process. I've seen an executive miss out on a job because he wanted $110,000 instead of $100,000. He was perfect for the job, and in two years he would have been making $400,000."

So, says Cox, "We warn both parties beforehand. We lay out the scenario, saying, this thing may fall apart, and here's how that might happen. What's more important to you: winning on this point, or making this whole thing a success?"

One of the useful moves a candidate can make is to ask the consultant for a candid assessment of the state of the process, and for a scenario describing the problem points that might cause the deal to fall through. While this scenario may not be laid out with total objectivity—after all, everyone is acting out of self-interest—the candidate can and should listen carefully to what the recruiter has to say, and judge its validity and applicability. It's a way to keep from becoming so immersed in the nitty-gritty of negotiation that you blow the deal.

THE ANATOMY OF A SUCCESSFUL NEGOTIATION

There are some basic elements in negotiating successfully with a recruiter as part of the process.

Learn all you can about the company. Rely on the recruiter as an information resource, right from the first. Get the facts on the company—what their compensation practices are, what exceptions they make to their established ranges, etc. At the same time, avail yourself of the recruiter's impressions of the client—how far he or she thinks they will bend on a certain point, who makes the final decisions, how the decisions are made, etc.

Draw up your wish list. Write down what you would like to have in each aspect of the employment arrangement—salary, bonus, stock, severance, status, title, perks, authority, reporting relationship, contract. Have a specific goal for each category.

Set priorities. Having compiled your wish list, classify your objectives into "musts" and "desirables." You may desire a written contract and a two-year severance arrangement, but you may insist upon having a bonus deal based on gross sales.

Bargain hard on all fronts. Having made your requirements known to the headhunter early—thus giving yourself an active rather than reactive posture—seek your objectives calmly but firmly. Don't indicate too early your willingness to give way on any point.

Time your trade-offs. The key to a successful negotiation can lie in the timely giving of concessions. Whenever you feel you can win one of your "must" points, be ready to give way on one of your "desirable" objectives.

Save one concession to close the deal. The final moment approaches. You still haven't got a deal, but the differences have narrowed. The recruiter sets up a meeting. Go to the meeting prepared to make one more trade-off, even a minor one. You may not have to. The client may finally meet your demands. But at this stage face-saving is important, too. The client will find it much easier to accede if you give on some point. In that way all parties can come away feeling like winners.

And even if you feel you can push it through without giving another inch, consider giving that inch anyway. You're going to have to live with the employer and the job. Your chances of success are enhanced if there is no lingering resentment. You'll have won respect as a tough negotiator, but at the same time you will have shown yourself as less than greedy, as willing to cooperate and compromise. A good send-off into the new job is well worth a small trade-off.

A FINAL WORD

The executive-search industry is not in business to get you a job. Nor, as recruiter Robert Dingman observes, is it a career-change medium. When the recruiting process is conducted properly, it is to meet the needs of clients by finding good people to fill jobs. "Recruiters" who imply that they are primarily interested in placing you are not real recruiters.

So no career plan can rest primarily on getting places through search consultants. But by the same token, no sound strategy can omit the recruiter. If you don't achieve visibility, you have less of a chance of coming to the attention of the search professional. If you don't know how recruiters work, you may not handle the contact with optimum adroitness. If you are not prepared for the kind of three-cornered negotiation that is often intrinsic to the search process, you may not get the best deal available to you.

You want to be the target of a search that will place a good offer in front of you. This is an area in which a *moving target* is the best kind— moving *ahead,* that is. As you grow in accomplishment, your head becomes a more likely prize for the hunter. Make it as easy as possible for him or her to find you. And be ready to handle yourself skillfully when the headhunter does find you.

APPENDIX I:
DIRECTORY OF INDEPENDENT RESEARCHERS

Here is a listing of independent researchers throughout the United States. This listing, with expert observations, has been compiled by Kenneth J. Cole, publisher of *The Recruiting & Search Report,* P.O. Box 9433, Panama City Beach, FL 32407; tel., 904-235-3733. Ken Cole is a primary source of information and intelligence about all phases of the recruiting industry.

EAST

Barbara Caroll Research
994 Beachwood Place
Warminster, PA 18974
215-674-8935
Contact: Barbara Caroll

On her own one year. Previously, four years with Christenson & Montgomery. Generalist. All search firm clients, no corporate. Also does reference checks.

Rates: $40 per hour plus expenses.

Kevin Browne Associates Research Services
160 West 85th Street
New York, NY 10024
212-595-3846
Contact: Kevin Browne

Works most fields nationally, strong at international/overseas work. Will provide names, titles, reporting relationships in organizational chart form. Produces miniresumes.

Rates: $25 per hour plus telephone expenses.

Margie Dunn
2426 Marbury Road
Pittsburgh, PA 15221
412-241-3729

Formerly with Boyden Associates as director of research in the
Pittsburgh office. Strong on sales/marketing and basic industries. Not
fond of EDP.

Rates: $50 per hour.

Robert Lawrence Associates
Judy Bowers
142 High Street, Suite 320
Portland, ME 04101
207-773-1888

Eight years in research, seven researchers on staff. Generalists, no
EDP assignments unless top-level. Produces organizational charts,
miniresumes. Splits work between corporate/search firm clients.
Also does reference checking.

Rates: $75 per hour plus expenses.

Jay Mettler, Inc.
45 West 60th Street
New York, NY 10023
212-765-6800
Contact: Jay Mettler

Sixteen years as a researcher. Mettler is the only purely *corporate*
researcher encountered on this project; he also had the longest story.
Briefly (his words): (1) search research to identify all potential
candidates in all organizations that the corporation selects—before
anyone is contacted; (2) miniresumes to provide current background
information on most probable candidates before anyone is contacted;
(3) telephone qualification to persuade candidates selected to
consider the position or opportunity.

Rates: $100 per hour plus expenses.

N. Donald Nierenberg, Inc.
R.D. 1, P.O. Box 167C
Jackson, NJ 08527

201-928-1420
Contact: Don Nierenberg

Generalist, also strong internationally. Seven years as a researcher, spun off from Gil Simon. Minor amount of corporate work; will consider additional corporate accounts.

Rates: $50 per hour plus expenses. More complex assignments additional.

G.E. Price & Associates
3900 Galt Ocean Drive, No. 510
Fort Lauderdale, FL 33308
305-566-4788
Contact: Gail Price

Thirteen years in research with the CIA. Particular expertise in sales/marketing, hi-tech; pharmaceuticals.

Rates: $35 per hour.

Hamilton Wenham Associates
105 Chestnut Street
Needham, MA 02192
617-444-8503
Contact: Kathy Barber

Eight years' experience with two major Boston search firms. Prefers banking, finance/accounting, retail, hospitality.

Rates: $100 per hour.

Arch S. Whitehead Associates, Inc.
845 West End Avenue
New York, NY 10025
212-316-1400
Contact: Arch Whitehead

Unique approach to research, prefers corporate clients. In business since 1959. Produces extensive research "products"—like book of all personnel/HR people in headquarters of *Fortune* 500 companies—12,000 people classified. Also has consumer packaged goods, finance/accounting books.

Does custom research as well. Extensive repeat/referral business, but will discuss new assignments/new clients.

Fees: variable.

MIDWEST

Barton Business Research
400 East Randolph Drive
Chicago, IL 60601
312-861-0495
Contact: Mary Jo Barton

Barton is ex-Billington, Fox & Ellis, Inc., has 11 years' experience, and is quite credible. Generalist; works for search firms and corporations, midlevel and up. Also performs marketing surveys and compensation studies.

Rates: $35 per hour and up plus expenses. Typical assignment: 20 to 25 hours for candidate locating and research; interviewing/screening (variable rate/additional). Retained only.

Joan Fee Associates
1157 East 56th Street
Chicago, IL 60637
312-955-5351
Contact: Joan Fee

Fee has 15 years as a researcher (12 years as director of research for Peat, Marwick and Korn/Ferry; three years on own). Works for corporate clients and search firms but prefers search firms. Assembles preliminary candidate lists, prepares miniresumes. Generalist with lots of mid- to upper-level financial experience: banks, thrifts, insurance, CFOs for manufacturers, etc. "Nonlibrary" approach—direct sourcing. Also does reference checking.

Rates: $50 per hour plus expenses. Retained only.

S. A. Jaeger & Company, Inc.
2001 Spring Road, Suite 665
Oak Brook, IL 60521
312-986-1390
Contact: Sue Jaeger

Six years as a researcher. Generalist (no low-level EDP assignments). Performs work for corporate and search-firm clients. Is very persuasive and professional (good follow-up); helpful for this research project.

Rates: $60 per hour plus expenses. Retained only.

M/E Research Associates
300 Golf Road
Algonquin, IL 60102
312-658-6330
Contact: Diane Masse

Masse has nine years' experience, five with Ward Howell. Splits work between search firms and corporate clients; prefers search firms. Describes herself as a generalist but doesn't like to work on insurance projects.

Rates: $35 per hour plus expenses. Retained only.

J. A. Neurauter & Company
115 South Wilke Road, #206A
Arlington Height, IL 60005
312-577-1760
Contact: Jackie Neurauter

In research two years; was previously a recruiter. Splits work evenly between search firms and corporate clients. Will take most assignments but not EDP; generalist.

Rates: $60 per hour plus expenses; $1,000 minimum for a given project. Retained only.

Personal Power Potential, Inc.
Woodfield Corporate Center, 300 North Martingale Road, #500
Schaumburg, IL 60194
312-426-6979
Contact: Karen Ross

Generalist, handling all of the usual functional areas and most industries.

Rates: $50 per hour plus expenses. Retained only.

Phalen Business Research
9603 Nieman Place
Shawnee Mission, KS 66214

913-492-5810
Contact: Peg Phalen

Phalen spent 17 years with Heidrick & Struggles, and started their Research Department; on own seven years. Worked in President Reagan's transition team office (with Pendleton James). Generalist; prefers senior-level and director assignments.

Variable hourly rate plus expenses. Prefers referrals but will discuss assignments with new clients. Retained only.

Research
3501 North 56th Street
Omaha, NE 68104
402-553-7053
Contact: Michelle Gorman

Two years' research experience. Extensive database review capability. Strong in journeyman-level technical work: engineering, aerospace, defense, electronics.

Rates variable depending on assignment complexity; $25 per hour plus expenses typical. Will work for contingency-basis firms but only on retainer basis.

RLM and Associates
22140 Euclid Avenue
Euclid, OH 44177
216-531-0422
Contact: Jerome R. LaManna

Eight years as a researcher. Nontechnical generalist; likes sales/marketing, especially foods, HBA, consumer durables. Splits work evenly between corporate and search firms.

Rates: $30 per hour, retainer basis; will negotiate for share of total fee on contingency assignments.

Joan Robbins Mirsky & Company, Inc.
728 Fox Hunt Trail
Deerfield, IL 60015
312-940-0728
Contact: Joan Robbins

Robbins has six years in the business, three with Kearney. Works nationally; splits work between corporate clients (20 percent) and search firms (80 percent). A generalist, but (like many Kearney "alumni") strong and well connected in health-care areas.

Rates: $55 per hour plus expenses. Will work for contingency-basis firms if her fee is guaranteed.

Regional Office:
4 Bedford Road
Katonah, NY 10536
914-232-7187
Contact: Pamela Martin

Source Enterprises, Inc.
336 Clearwater Lane
Schaumburg, IL 60194
312-882-0192
Contacts: Lamont C. Sanders, Melinda Mellecker

Four years' research experience. Specialty areas are engineering (electrical, electromechanical, mechanical, industrial), sales (technical areas similar to engineering, plus consumer packaged goods), marketing (consumer packaged goods plus the transportation industry), and manufacturing (plastics, consumer packaged goods, and electronics).

Several variable billing procedures: a package price of $2,500 to produce a minimum of 30 to 50 preliminary candidates, payable in advance, or $65 per hour, including expenses.

Willis & Associates
5122 Spencer Road
Lyndhurst, OH 44124
216-461-3709
Contact: Francille S. Willis

Ten years as a researcher (Booz, Allen; director of research, Spencer Stuart). Works for corporate and search-firm clients. Generalist; will take no EDP assignments.

Rates: variable. Start at $20 an hour. Retained only.

Annas/Clancy Associates
110 LaBolsa Road
Walnut Creek, CA 94598
415-932-7612
Contact: Lillian Clancy

Clancy has six years' research experience with Tholke/Interdatum, plus two years on her own. Generalist, prefers top management. Special contacts in hi-tech, venture capital, and start-ups. Splits 50/50 between corporate and search firms.

Rates: $65 per hour plus expenses. Retained only.

Renny Mintz
13835 Riverside Drive
Sherman Oaks, CA 91423
213-872-0422

Twenty years in search and research; own firm since 1979. Splits work evenly between corporate and search firms. Does mostly top-level assignments requiring specialized skills, primarily through referrals; will discuss unusual assignments.

Rates: $75 per hour plus expenses. Retained only.

Resources Management
45 Possum Lane
Portola Valley, CA 94025
415-851-0192
Contact: Leon Bernard Davis

Company offers national and international sourcing, screening, and referencing services to companies and executive-search firms in all industries and functional areas. Specializes in searches at the management level. Also specializes in providing recruitment strategy planning, recruitment training, and systems development.

Rates: from $50 per hour plus expenses.

RG Associates
6740 Springpark Avenue
Los Angeles, CA 90056
213-670-4015
Contact: Rebecca Gates

Two years at Korn/Ferry as senior associate; on own for two years as an independent researcher. Generalist; strong in hi-tech/financial-management areas. No corporate clients, works strictly for search firms.

Rates: $50 per hour plus expenses. Retained only

Janis Roche
1104 Goodman Avenue
Redondo Beach, CA 90278
213-374-3051

On her own 3½ years; previously, three years at Eastman & Beaudine and at Korn/Ferry as a researcher. Generalist; not wild about EDP assignments but will take them. Splits work evenly between corporate and search firms. Works primarily through referrals but will discuss assignments with new clients.

Rates: $35 per hour plus expenses. Retained only.

Elaine R. Shepherd Company
The Marketplace Tower II
3025 South Parker Road, Suite 941
Aurora, CO 80014
303-745-5055
Contact: Elaine Shepherd

Shepherd (along with her four assistants) has a strong reputation for quality work. Her research mix—80 percent corporate, 20 percent search community—is a little unusual but speaks well about her firm. Performs "first half of search"—locating likely sources, then candidates, preliminary interviews, and resumes. Eleven years as researcher. Described as "generalists" but cites strong background in hi-tech areas, banking, insurance, and energy.

Rates: $75 per hour plus expenses; additional charge for written report preparation. Most assignments are at midlevel up; prefers $60,000 salaries and above. Typical assignment requires 15 to 20 hours of research work. Retained only.

Shireman and Shireman Research
2055 Sacramento Street, Suite 201
San Francisco, CA 94109
415-441-3922
Contacts: Judy and Richard Shireman

Judy started five years ago and recruited her husband later. Judy is ex-Foster Associates, San Francisco. Prefers search-firm work but will consider corporate assignments. Generalists; very strong in sales, marketing, financial management. Will not do nonmanagement assignments.

Rates: $60 per hour plus telephone. Retained only.

APPENDIX II: A SAMPLING OF SEARCHERS

Here is a sampling of profiles of executive-search firms based in the United States and Canada. The information in the profiles is based on what the recruiters have written in response to a survey conducted to gather information for this book and from almost 40 other sources. It is not an exhaustive listing—there are thousands of recruiting companies, of all types.

The profiles included here give a sense of the diversity of the search field. In the sampling you'll find profiles of the biggest firms and some of the smallest; general recruiters and specialists; firms from all over the United States, along with some in Canada; firms that recruit worldwide and firms that confine their efforts to particular areas. Most of the recruiters listed work on a retainer basis, being paid a specified fee, some of it in advance, for conducting the search. As covered elsewhere, this is the method of doing business of most of the leading search firms. However, there are some very active contingency firms, who are paid only if their candidates are hired. Many of these contingency searchers are smaller, more specialized units, focusing on functional areas such as C.P.A.'s, or specific industries such as aerospace or advertising.

The profiles cover the functional and industry areas in which the firms have described themselves as most and least active. Where significant, the specialties of key members of the firm are indicated, along with the name of the director of research where available. The great majority of these search companies are willing to look at unsolicited resumes and to have executives who are seeking positions get in touch with them.

Some firms indicate that they make "special efforts" to recruit women and members of minority groups. It should be absolutely clear that *all* recruiters carry out searches without any prejudice whatever. They recruit those whom they consider best for the job, without reference to gender, race, or other such criteria. In this context, "special efforts" usually means that besides going to the regular sources for information about candidates, the search firm will attempt to tap in on the organizations and networks that might provide the names of people who would not be turned up through the ordinary methods. Some years ago, when the advance of women and members of minorities into management positions was new, recruiters felt it was necessary to make such special efforts. Today, to a considerable extent, they find that they can identify good candidates of all races and sexes without the special apparatus.

Firms have indicated in the survey the compensation levels within which they usually recruit. Many will recruit for jobs at lower compensation levels, particularly for good clients.

Abbott Smith Associates
Franklin Avenue, P.O. Box 318
Millbrook, NY 12545
914-677-5051

SALARY RANGE—$35,000 to $150,000

CHARACTERISTICS—Specialists in the human resources area—personnel/training. In business 20 years. They work worldwide. No special efforts to recruit women or minorities. They look at resumes and may be contacted by people in the HRD field. Gross revenues, $500,000. Contingency basis.

KEY PEOPLE
David W. Brinkerhoff, president
David D. Dalenberg, vice president
Howard Frankel, vice president

❧

Accounting Resources International
30101 Town Center Drive, Suite 202C
Laguna Niguel, CA 92677
714-495-3730

SALARY RANGE—$30,000 to over $200,000

CHARACTERISTICS—Specialists in the recruitment and placement of C.P.A.'s; operate throughout the United States and worldwide. In business 10 years. Branches in Denver, Dallas, Houston, and New York. Their clients include many international C.P.A. firms, from the Big Eight to small regionals: "We are the nation's largest firm in placement of C.P.A.'s into public accounting firms, particularly at partner and manager level; we place professional consultants into 70 percent of all major consulting firms, both Big Eight C.P.A. firms and nonaccounting national consulting firms." They make special efforts to recruit women and members of minority groups: "Women and minority professionals (who) are C.P.A.'s are in demand." They look at resumes and may be contacted by those in their field. Contingency basis.

KEY PERSON
T. Robert Storevik, C.P.A., founder and managing partner

∾

Alexander Edward Associates, Inc.
1218 Chestnut Street, Suite 510
Philadelphia, PA 19107
215-923-2102

SALARY RANGE—$30,000 to $250,000

CHARACTERISTICS—Data communications specialists, in business seven years. While they operate worldwide, greatest emphasis is on the U.S. East Coast, Massachusetts to Florida. They recruit for positions involving data communications sales, marketing, engineering, software, manufacturing, and administration. They do the least in financial. No special efforts to recruit women and minorities. They look at resumes; will talk only with executives in the data communications field. Contingency basis.

KEY PEOPLE	AREAS OF SPECIALIZATION
R. Edwin Alexander, president	Marketing
Edward L. Ralph, vice president	Data communications sales and marketing
Carl York, manager	Data communications engineering
William Garrity, manager	Data communications sales

∾

Allerton, Heinze & Associates, Inc.
208 South LaSalle Street, Suite 766
Chicago, IL 60604
312-263-1075

SALARY RANGE—over $50,000

CHARACTERISTICS—Their principal areas of concentration include health care, hi-tech, and marketing. They work primarily in the United States, with some Canadian recruiting. They will make special efforts to seek women and minorities. They look at resumes and may be contacted. Eight years in business. Annual gross, $450,000. Retainer basis.

KEY PEOPLE
Donald T. Allerton, president
Darryl Zupancic, vice president

❧

Amansco, Inc.
Amansco Building, 103 Smithfield Street
Pittsburgh, PA 15222
412-765-3710

SALARY RANGE—over $40,000

CHARACTERISTICS—A general management firm, 35 years old, operating in the United States. Annual gross, about $500,000. No special recruiting efforts to recruit women or minorities. They look at resumes and may be contacted. Retainer basis.

KEY PEOPLE
Ralph W. Young, president
Carl Wolter, vice president
Dr. Robert Fitzpatrick, psychologist
Claude Buckley, consultant

❧

American Executive Management, Inc.
30 Federal Street
Salem, MA 01970
617-744-5923

SALARY RANGE—$70,000 to $300,000

CHARACTERISTICS—A large, general-line recruiting firm, in business 10 years. They have working relationships in France, England, and Japan. They do 80 percent of their business in the United States, 20 percent in the rest of the world. Greatest areas of expertise in marketing and sales management and general management of technology-related industrial and consumer services and products. They do the least in legal and finance. They look at resumes and may be contacted; no special efforts for women and minorities. Annual gross, over $1 million. They state that they maintain one of the largest databases of executives in the following industries: software, industrial and factory automation, computer control, and the engineering-construction industry. Retainer basis.

KEY PEOPLE	AREAS OF SPECIALIZATION
S. K. Okun, senior vice president	General management and finance
J. E. Buckley, vice president	Marketing/sales/manufacturing
E. J. Cloutier, senior vice president	Marketing/sales/technical management
R. Holmes, vice president	Marketing/sales

❧

American Executive Search Services, Inc.
3350 Scott Boulevard, No. 24
Santa Clara, CA 95054
408-496-6872

SALARY RANGE—$50,000 to $150,000

CHARACTERISTICS—They recruit in areas such as finance, general management, marketing, manufacturing, engineering in hi-tech industries, flexible packaging, and printing. Least activity in banking, consumer, and retail industries. Operate throughout the United States. Working relationship with firm in Copenhagen. Annual gross, $300,000 to $400,000. They file unsolicited resumes. Executives may get in touch with them. No special efforts to recruit women and minority members. Retainer basis.

KEY PEOPLE	AREAS OF SPECIALIZATION
Donald Tischer, president	Management, marketing, administration, finance, human resources
David Mayer, associate	Manufacturing, engineering
Bub Gregory, associate	Marketing, sales, R&D

❧

Ames Associates, Inc.
6935 Wisconsin Avenue
Chevy Chase, MD 20815
301-656-5222

SALARY RANGE—$30,000 to $100,000

CHARACTERISTICS—A specialized company focusing on corporate real estate, commercial and residential, financial and executive management; corporate construction, mortgage banking and S&L, support and executive personnel. In business 18 years. They operate in the United States and the Middle East. They have an affiliate in England. They make special efforts to recruit women and minorities. They look at resumes and will talk with executives within their field of expertise. Contingency basis.

KEY PEOPLE
Michael J. Ames, president
Mildred S. Ames, vice president
Mary Jo Daugherty, associate
Pat Cibel, associate

❧

Amory Associates, Inc.
60 Arch Street
Greenwich, CT 06830
203-625-0294

SALARY RANGE—$90,000 to $300,000

CHARACTERISTICS—Working in the United States and Canada, they do the most in venture capital, asset-base lending, corporate finance, biotechnology, bionutrition, telecommunications, and specialty chemicals, with the functional areas concentrated most heavily in general management, marketing, finance, and strategic planning. Least work in manufacturing, engineering, purchasing, service functions other than financial, smokestack and basic materials industries, automotive, energy-related. In business 29 years. They make special efforts to recruit minority candidates. They may be contacted (within their salary range), and they look at resumes. Retainer basis.

KEY PEOPLE	AREAS OF SPECIALIZATION
Harcourt Amory, Jr., president	Financial services and biotechnology
Domenica Maimone, vice president and associate	All industries
E. A. Hammerle, associate	Office equipment, consumer packaged goods, pharmaceuticals

❧

Andre Group, Inc.
2000 Valley Forge Towers
King of Prussia, PA 19406
215-783-5100

SALARY RANGE—$50,000 to $100,000

CHARACTERISTICS—Specialty is personnel/human resources. Special efforts to recruit women but not minorities. They look at resumes and may be contacted. In business 17 years. Nationwide. "Currently service 85 percent of the *Fortune* 500 companies." Retainer basis.

KEY PERSON
Richard Andre, president

ॐ

Bartholdi Partners
One Devonshire Place, Suite 901
Boston, MA 02109
617-227-8118

SALARY RANGE—$60,000 to $200,000

CHARACTERISTICS—Branches in Vail, Colorado, and San Mateo, California. They recruit for most functional areas, with special emphasis on hi-tech, financial services, and consumer packaged goods. Least work in manufacturing management. They make special efforts to recruit minorities and women. They look at resumes and may be contacted. In business 15 years. Retainer basis.

KEY PEOPLE	AREAS OF SPECIALIZATION
T. G. Bartholdi, president	Hi-tech, financial services
Dave Mazza, vice president	Consumer and packaged goods
Dee A. Soder, vice president	Financial services
Brian Webb, vice president	Hi-tech
Nancy Markham-Bugbee, consultant	

ॐ

Bason Associates, Inc.
401 Crescent Avenue
Cincinnati, OH 45215
513-761-9881

SALARY RANGE—not provided

CHARACTERISTICS—A generalist firm, in business more than 10 years, working throughout North America. They maintain "an outstanding record with smaller business units ($10MM–$150MM sales, many privately held)." No special efforts to recruit women and minorities. They "rarely" look at unsolicited resumes. They may be contacted by mail only. Least work in retailing, banking, and wholesale. Retainer basis.

KEY PEOPLE
Maurice L. Bason, president, CEO
Robert L. Fancher, vice president
Jane Gross, chairman of the Board

∾

Battalia & Associates, Inc.
275 Madison Avenue
New York, NY 10016
212-683-9440

SALARY RANGE—$75,000 to $300,000

CHARACTERISTICS—A generalist firm in business 22 years, with particular expertise in telecommunications and electronics, pharmaceuticals, chemicals, financial services, paper and packaging, consumer products, and computer manufacturing. Special efforts on women and minorities: "We always include all qualified candidates in our universe of candidates to be considered without regard to race or sex." Branches/affiliates in Glasgow, London, Wiesbaden, Madrid, and Toronto. Least work in airlines, automotive, oil, and gas. Revenue, $500,000 to $1 million. Retainer basis. They may be contacted, and they look at resumes.

KEY PEOPLE	AREAS OF SPECIALIZATION
O. William Battalia, president	General management, senior vice-presidential level
Dale Winston, executive vice president	Marketing, senior vice-presidential level
Everett Peterson, senior associate	Manufacturing and personnel
Laurie Atkins, senior associate	Legal and finance
Alexandra Sternberg, director of research	

❧

Rick Beedle Associates, Inc.
5301 Laurel Canyon Boulevard, No. 219
North Hollywood, CA 91607
818-506-8611

SALARY RANGE—$35,000 to $200,000

CHARACTERISTICS—In business 24 years, operating worldwide. Their areas of greatest focus are accounting/finance, marketing, corporate legal, EDP, and engineering. They do the least in human resources, retail, hospitality, sales, and production control. "We are asexual and colorblind. All we look for are *good* candidates." Their gross revenues are about $500,000. They may be approached by executives seeking new positions; they look at resumes. Contingency basis.

KEY PEOPLE
Richard E. Beedle, president
William G. Allen, vice president

❧

Bentley & Evans, International
One Penn Plaza
New York, NY 10119
212-371-1212

SALARY RANGE—$75,000 to $300,000 (not below $60,000)

CHARACTERISTICS—They recruit for positions in general management, law, finance, telecommunications, and biomedical. Branches in Los Angeles, Hartford, and Tampa. Areas of operation are America, Europe, and Asia. Annual gross revenues, approximately $1 million.

They may be contacted; they look at resumes. No special recruiting efforts on women and minorities. In business 14 years. Retainer basis.

KEY PEOPLE
Charles E. Evans, chairman
Robert H. Horton, president
Robert D. Bentley, executive vice president
Tucker H. Warner, senior vice president

❧

Billington, Fox & Ellis, Inc.
20 North Wacker Drive
Chicago, IL 60606
312-236-5000

SALARY RANGE—$60,000 to $90,000

CHARACTERISTICS—Branches in New York and San Francisco. They work throughout the United States, with greatest emphasis on general management, sales and marketing, and financial, least on engineering. No special efforts to recruit women or minorities. Executives may get in touch with them through resume only. Annual gross, $2 million. In business 22 years. They charge on a retainer basis.

KEY PEOPLE
William H. Billington, Jr., chairman
Ferderic C. Carr, senior vice president
Robert A. Proctor, senior vice president
Malcolm L. Baas, vice president

❧

Blackshaw & Olmstead, Inc.
134 Peachtree Street, N.W., Suite 400
Atlanta, GA 30303
404-525-6700

SALARY RANGE—$30,000 to $125,000

CHARACTERISTICS—Their greatest area of expertise is in real estate, construction, and human resources development. In business 10 years. They operate throughout the United States. Annual gross, $400,000 to $500,000. No special efforts to seek women and minorities. They may be contacted, and they look at resumes. Retainer basis.

KEY PEOPLE
Brian M. Blackshaw, partner
George T. Olmstead, partner
John M. Lupton III, partner

❧

Blau Kaptain & Associates
3073A Route 27
Franklin Park, NJ 08823
201-821-7900

SALARY RANGE—over $70,000

CHARACTERISTICS—Specialists in medical/health care only. They work worldwide. In business 16 years. No special efforts to recruit women and minorities. They look at resumes and may be contacted. Annual gross, $500,000. Retainer basis.

KEY PEOPLE
John Kaptain, president
Ted Blau, vice president

❧

Bowden & Co., Inc.
5000 Rockside Road, Suite 120
Cleveland, OH 44131
216-447-1800

SALARY RANGE—$50,000 to $500,000

CHARACTERISTICS—Greatest areas of expertise: general management, venture capital, hi-tech, manufacturing, marketing, and finance. Least activity in hospital/health. Working relationships with recruiters in Europe. They work throughout the United States and in Europe. In business 14 years. No special efforts to recruit women or minorities, but of course "we do not undertake discriminatory searches." They look at resumes and may be contacted. In business 14 years. Retainer basis.

KEY PEOPLE	AREAS OF SPECIALIZATION
Otis H. Bowden II, president	General management, venture capital
Harrison R. Magee, vice president	Manufacturing, marketing
Jane E. Pinkas, associate	Finance, venture capital

☙

Bowersox & Associates, Incorporated
1025 Margret Street
Des Plaines, IL 60016
312-296-3302

SALARY RANGE—over $50,000

CHARACTERISTICS—With branches in Venice, Florida, and La Jolla, California, this firm operates in the United States. Some clients have international operations. They recruit for general management, marketing, finance, and other functions. Least emphasis on hi-tech. "No discrimination, but we make no 'special' efforts to recruit minorities or women." They look at resumes and may be contacted. Annual gross, $250,000 to $350,000. In business 17 years. Retainer basis.

KEY PEOPLE
Thomas L. Bowersox, president
Jeanette E. Bowersox, vice president

∿

Boyden Associates, Inc.
260 Madison Avenue
New York, NY 10016
212-685-3400

SALARY RANGE—$60,000 to $500,000

CHARACTERISTICS—One of the largest and longest-established of search firms, operating worldwide in all industries, with annual gross of about $20 million. Branches in Atlanta; Chicago; Dallas; Fort Lauderdale; Houston; Los Angeles; Menlo Park, California; Morristown, New Jersey; Pittsburgh; San Francisco; Stamford, Connecticut; Washington, D.C.; and Wellesley, Massachusetts. Foreign branches in Bangkok; Bad Homburg, Germany; Brussels; Geneva; Hong Kong; Seoul, Korea; London, England; Toronto; Madrid; Mexico City; Milan; Neuilly/Cedex, France; Rome; São Paulo; Singapore; Johannesburg; Stockholm; Sydney; Valencia, Spain; Tokyo; Taipei, Taiwan; Barcelona; and Melbourne. In business 40 years. They make special efforts to find women and minorities. They may be contacted, and they look at resumes. Retainer basis.

KEY PEOPLE
Putney Westerfield, president
John M. Foster, director
Paul C. Richardson, director
Peter R. Schmidt, director

∿

Heath C. Boyer Co.
101 Marietta Tower, Suite 3608
Atlanta, GA 30303
404-588-0550

SALARY RANGE—over $50,000

CHARACTERISTICS—Greatest focus on general management, marketing, finance, manufacturing/operations, and professional. Least on engineering and R&D. They may be contacted, and they read resumes. Annual gross over $1 million. They cover the United States and have working relationships in Western Europe. Retainer basis.

KEY PERSON
Heath C. Boyer, president

❧

The Brand Company, Inc.
12740 North River Road
Mequon, WI 53092
414-242-6203

SALARY RANGE—$40,000 to $150,000

CHARACTERISTICS—A Milwaukee-area firm operating worldwide. Their greatest areas of expertise: general management plus major functional areas, particularly in manufacturing and education. They do the least in data processing/information systems. In business 12 years. They do not make special efforts regarding members of minority groups. They do make such efforts to recruit women: We "have a female division for full-time executives and board assignments." Retainer basis. Annual gross, about $500,000. They look at resumes and may be contacted.

KEY PEOPLE
J. Brand Spangenberg, president
Gerald W. Mullins, vice president

❧

Brissenden, McFarland & Wagoner, Inc.
1111 Summer Street
Stamford, CT 06905
203-324-1598

SALARY RANGE—$75,000 to $400,000

CHARACTERISTICS—A five-year-old firm operating in the United States. They have a branch in Somerset, New Jersey. They are a general recruiting firm focusing on upper- and middle-level positions. They make special efforts regarding members of minority groups but not regarding women: "We are color- and sex-blind. We respond to our clients' needs. Recently we have carried out assignments to find experienced minority managers for *Fortune* 500 companies." Revenue is about $1.75 million. They work on a retainer basis. They may be approached and look at resumes.

KEY PEOPLE	AREAS OF SPECIALIZATION
Hoke Brissenden	Health care
Richard M. McFarland	Process industries
Robert E. Wagoner	Electronics/manufacturing
Carl J. Fuccella	Financial services

Bryant Associates, Inc.
875 North Michigan Avenue, Suite 1524
Chicago, IL 60611
312-649-0700

SALARY RANGE—$30,000 to $85,000

CHARACTERISTICS—They work throughout the United States. Greatest area of expertise in marketing, least is clerical/administrative. They make special efforts to recruit women and minorities: "We recruit in these areas to satisfy specific client requests." They prefer that those who want to get in touch mail their resumes. In business 23 years. Annual gross, about $300,000. Contingency basis.

KEY PEOPLE
Richard D. Bryant, president
Jack Farrell, associate
Stanley Bakewell, associate

~

Buell Associates
20 North Wacker Drive, Suite 544
Chicago, IL 60606
312-332-5478

SALARY RANGE—$50,000 to $150,000

CHARACTERISTICS—They work in the United States, with particular emphasis on the Northeast and the Midwest. Heaviest in human resources, law, MIS, finance, and marketing. Branch in Ridgefield, Connecticut. They make special efforts to recruit women, and they seek minorities. They look at resumes. Executives may get in touch with them. Gross is somewhat over $300,000. In business five years. Retainer basis.

KEY PEOPLE	AREAS OF SPECIALIZATION
Stanleigh B. McDonald, managing principal	HR, finance
Scott A. McDonald, partner	HR
William H. Hrabak, partner	HR, marketing

~

Robert J. Bushée
1370 Washington Pike
Bridgeville, PA 15017 (Pittsburgh area)
412-257-2300

SALARY RANGE—$30,000 to $100,000

CHARACTERISTICS—They work worldwide, with working relationships in England and France. In business 29 years. Greatest expertise in manufacturing/operations/engineering. They do the least in insurance/administration. They make special efforts to recruit women and minorities. They look at resumes and may be contacted. Contingency basis.

KEY PEOPLE
Robert J. Bushée, senior vice president
Robert B. Georgia, executive vice president
Donald A. Levenson, vice president
Dorothea R. Ross, vice president

❧

Byrnes Mirtz Morice, Inc.
1 Dock Street
Stamford, CT 06902
203-964-9266

SALARY RANGE—over $70,000

CHARACTERISTICS—Generalists, operating worldwide, in business four years. They make special efforts to recruit women and minorities. They look at resumes and may be contacted. Retainer basis.

KEY PEOPLE
Thomas A. Byrnes, partner
P. John Mirtz, partner
James L. Morice, partner

❧

Canny, Bowen, Inc.
425 Park Avenue
New York, NY 10022
212-758-3400

SALARY RANGE—$80,000 to over $1 million

CHARACTERISTICS—One of the major search firms, working worldwide in all general management areas. They do the least in the academic area. They have branches/affiliates in Boston and London and working relationships with firms in Australia, Belgium, Brazil, Canada, Denmark, France, Germany, Holland, Italy, South Africa, and Switzerland. In business more than 30 years. They do make special efforts in the area of women and minorities: "Attempt to promote women and minority candidates in all assignments, maintaining close contact with such organizations as Catalyst, for example." Executives may get in touch, and they look at resumes. Gross volume is over $3 million. They work on a retainer basis.

KEY PEOPLE
Carl W. Menk, chairman
Robert A. Howard, managing director
George W. Peck IV, vice president/treasurer
John P. Carroll, vice president/secretary
Nelson O. Bell, Jr., vice president
David O. Bailey, vice president
Waldo Newcomer, vice president
Rosslyn A. Lyell, vice president
Robert L. Trowbridge, vice president

✺

Andrew B. Carr & Associates
P.O. Box 5631
San Angelo, TX 76902
915-942-9109; 942-9036

SALARY RANGE—over $25,000

CHARACTERISTICS—A one-person operation specializing in aerospace and general aviation industries, filling management and technical positions. Special efforts to recruit women and members of minorities, utilizing minority organizations, university placement organizations, networking, etc. "Many clients request minority and female recruiting." Annual gross revenues, $180,000. They look at resumes and may be contacted. In business four years. Contingency basis.

KEY PERSON
Andrew B. Caracciolo, president

❧

Carre, Orban & Partners International
230 Park Avenue, Suite 1624
New York, NY 10169
212-953-7722

SALARY RANGE—$75,000 to $300,000

CHARACTERISTICS—They work in the United States and Europe. Greatest emphasis is on staffing U.S. subsidiaries of European companies. Least work in legal. They recruit for most functional areas. Branches in Paris, Belgium, Geneva, Dusseldorf, Milan, and London. They "make every effort to recruit women and minorities." Executives seeking positions may get in touch with them. They read resumes. Retainer basis.

KEY PEOPLE
Tener Eckelberry, president
Raymond DuBois, Jr., consultant
Ann Jordan, junior consultant
Annegret Ruge, special assistant

❧

Chaloner Associates
P.O. Box 1097, Back Bay Station
Boston, MA 02117
617-451-5170

SALARY RANGE—$25,000 to $75,000

CHARACTERISTICS—A small firm that works primarily in public relations, advertising, and corporate communications. In business seven years. Chaloner makes special efforts to recruit members of minorities, but not women. ("The communications field is predominantly female and I have not encountered resistance to women executives.") The firm works in the New England area. They look at resumes and may be approached. Gross revenues, about $150,000. Contingency basis.

KEY PERSON
Edward H. (Ted) Chaloner, president

❧

Christopher Drew & Associates, Inc.
28790 Chagrin Boulevard, Suite 200
Cleveland, OH 44122
216-831-7722

SALARY RANGE—$60,000 to over $300,000

CHARACTERISTICS—They operate worldwide. Greatest area of expertise in aerospace-hi-tech electronics-automotive, least in retail. Annual gross, $3.5 million. They look at resumes but do not wish executives to get in touch. They make special efforts to recruit women and minorities. In business seven years. Branch in Sarasota planned for 1986. Retainer basis.

KEY PEOPLE	AREAS OF SPECIALIZATION
John R. Donnelly, president	Aerospace/hi-tech electronics
Robert Zeltner, executive vice president	Automotive/consumer products
Terry Trimmer, consultant	General practice
Robert Manzer, consultant	Automotive/hi-tech electronics
Frank Zamataro, associate	General practice
Mary O'Brien, director of research	

❧

Clemo Evans & Co.
33 River Street
Chagrin Falls, OH 44022
216-247-2030

SALARY RANGE—$70,000 to $150,000

CHARACTERISTICS—This company has been in business 12 years, with a branch in Tampa, Florida. Affiliate in London. Area of operation is "mostly U.S. except for affiliate relationship." Most functional areas; least emphasis on technical. Approximate gross revenue, $500,000; professional fee range; three professional staff members; $100,000 expenses. They make special efforts to recruit women and minorities when client specifies. They read resumes but prefer that executives not contact them. They place heavy emphasis on service companies, nonprofit organizations, and fine-arts organizations. Retainer basis.

KEY PEOPLE
Roland Orr, principal

❧

Robert Clifton Associates, Inc.
200 Fleet Street, Suite 5045
Pittsburgh, PA 15220
412-922-1900

SALARY RANGE—$30,000 to $75,000

CHARACTERISTICS—A 17-year-old firm working in the United States. Heaviest in engineering, data processing, legal, and finance. Lightest in administration. They look at resumes and may be contacted. Gross revenues, $600,000 to $1.2 million. Contingency basis.

KEY PEOPLE	AREAS OF SPECIALIZATION
Robert Gerbe, president	Sales, marketing, engineering
Gary Rocco, executive vice president	Finance, personnel, law
Frank Coda, associate	Engineering
Karen Coda, associate	Engineering
Denise McClure, associate	Data processing
Stan Hamlin, associate	Data processing

∾

Cole International
1400 Shattuck Avenue, Suite 8
Berkeley, CA 94709
415-540-0213

SALARY RANGE—$25,000 to over $100,000

CHARACTERISTICS—Specialists in biotechnology, pharmaceuticals, medical instrumentation. In business five years. Primarily in the United States, but some international. They rarely look at unsolicited resumes. Executives seeking positions may get in touch with them. They make special efforts to recruit women and members of minorities: "We seek out women and minority candidates, though the number is limited in our specialty." They do the least in nontechnical areas, except for finance. Retainer basis. They have a branch in Sacramento and working relationships in England and Belgium.

KEY PEOPLE
Natasha Cole, president
Ann Price, vice president
Herman Thal-Larsen, executive vice president

∾

Cole, Warren & Long, Inc.
2 Penn Center, Suite 1020
Philadelphia, PA 19102
215-563-0701

SALARY RANGE—$60,000 to $175,000

CHARACTERISTICS—Greatest area of expertise includes general management, insurance, data processing, and health care. They do the least in engineering and retail. They do make special efforts to recruit women and minorities: "We have conducted many searches where this is not only highly preferred—but is a 'must' requirement." They have been in business 16 years. They look at resumes and may be contacted. Worldwide: We "recently completed two assignments in Japan." Also two recent assignments for the Reagan administration, in the office of Donald Regan and for OMB. Retainer basis.

KEY PEOPLE	AREAS OF SPECIALIZATION
Ronald Cole, president	General management
Richard Warren, executive vice president	Health care and insurance
Lloyd Spangler, senior vice president	Manufacturing and data processing
Leonard Stevens	Insurance and finance

❧

W. Hoyt Colton Associates, Inc.
67 Wall Street
New York, NY 10005
212-509-1800

SALARY RANGE—$60,000 to $250,000

CHARACTERISTICS—They recruit for the financial community in all management areas: investment banking, commercial banking. In business seven years. Annual gross, about $1 million. No special efforts to recruit women or minorities. They look at resumes, but do not wish to be contacted by executives seeking positions. Areas of operation are financial centers in the United States. They work on a retainer basis.

KEY PEOPLE
W. Hoyt Colton, president
Joseph M. Sinopoli, executive vice president
Lynn Halbfinger, senior vice president

❧

Colton Bernard, Inc.
417 Spruce Street
San Francisco, CA 94118
415-386-7400

SALARY RANGE—$50,000 to $300,000

CHARACTERISTICS—A specialized firm working in the apparel and textile industry exclusively. Sixteen years old. Worldwide. They recruit for all management and professional areas, but exclusively within the apparel/textile wholesale industry. No special efforts on women or minorities. They have an affiliate in New York City. They look at resumes. Executives may contact them—but only those in the apparel/textile industry. Retainer basis.

KEY PEOPLE
Roy C. Colton, president
Harry Bernard, executive vice president
Richard Bilski, vice president, recruiting
Jerard Less, vice president, marketing
Barbara Gleason, director, market research

❧

Robert Connelly and Associates, Inc.
P.O. Box 24028
Minneapolis, MN 55424
612-925-3039

SALARY RANGE—$40,000 to $110,000

CHARACTERISTICS—A general recruiter, in business 10 years, with least emphasis on data processing. They work nationwide. They make special efforts to recruit women and minorities, look at resumes, and may be contacted by executives seeking positions. Annual gross, $500,000. Retainer basis. Branch in Chicago.

KEY PEOPLE
Robert F. Olsen, president (Minneapolis)
Sandra R. Henoch, vice president (Chicago)

❧

Consulting Associates, Inc.
5525 Twin Knolls Road, Suite 326
Columbia, MD 21045
301-997-5800

SALARY RANGE—$50,000 to $135,000

CHARACTERISTICS—They work throughout the United States, with greatest emphasis on general management, financial services, manufacturing, and marketing; least on human resources. Branch in New York City. In business more than 10 years. Annual gross, about $2 million. They may be contacted, and they read resumes. No special efforts to recruit minorities and women; they recruit the best person for the position. Retainer basis.

KEY PEOPLE
Lawrence J. Holmes, president
Robert Gauthier, senior vice president
Fred Siegel, senior vice president
Scott Price, senior vice president

❧

Corporate Staffing Group, Inc.
Barn Office Center—Two Village Road, Suite 6
Horsham, PA 19044
215-659-7600

SALARY RANGE—$50,000 to $150,000

CHARACTERISTICS—A Philadelphia area firm operating throughout the United States. In business 18 years. Specialists in telecommunications and process control; lightest in financial. They have a branch in Largo, Florida. They look at resumes and may be contacted. No special recruiting efforts on minorities and women. Annual gross, above $1 million. Retainer basis.

KEY PEOPLE
C. D. Baker, C.P.C., principal
Laurie B. Carey, C.P.C., principal

❧

The Corson Group
641 Lexington Avenue
New York, NY 10022
212-371-3090

SALARY RANGE—$60,000 to $500,000

CHARACTERISTICS—Specialists in health care: "We believe we are the highest quality search firm for physicians in the country." They make special efforts to recruit women and minorities: "A disproportionately large share of our final candidates are women members of the minority groups." They may be contacted but "rarely" look at unsolicited resumes. Revenues between $1 million and $2 million. In business 14 years, working in the United States and Canada. Retainer basis.

KEY PERSON
Ralph Herz, Jr., M.D., medical director

❦

Counsel Search Co.
Kort Industry Square (124 North Summit)
Toledo, OH 43604
419-242-8696

SALARY RANGE—$45,000 to $200,000

CHARACTERISTICS—Specialists: legal only, conducting, for example, searches for general counsels for corporations. They look at resumes but do not want to be contacted. In business 11 years. Retainer basis.

KEY PERSON
William Falvey, president

❦

Creative Search Affiliates
1385 York Avenue
New York, NY 10021
212-734-5323

SALARY RANGE—$50,000 to $100,000

CHARACTERISTICS—Their greatest concentration is in recruiting Wall Street executives. They do the least work in industry. In business 20 years, with an affiliate in Palm Beach, Florida. They make special efforts to recruit women. They may be contacted, and they look at resumes. Reported revenues, $500,000. They work on contingency.

KEY PEOPLE
A. Allan Resnick, senior partner
Michael Resnick, Sr., senior vice president

❧

Curry Telleri Ziegler, Inc.
At the Castle, 433 River Road
Highland Park, NJ 08904
201-828-3883

SALARY RANGE—$30,000 to $150,000

CHARACTERISTICS—They conduct searches for the chemical, plastic, pharmaceutical, electronic materials, and related industries throughout the United States. In business 13 years. They normally do the least work in financial. They make special efforts to seek women and minorities: "Our research director is a Ph.D. candidate in women's studies. . . . One of our account executives is black and does considerable work with minorities." They look at resumes but do not wish to be contacted by executives seeking positions: "We would prefer getting in touch with them for an appropriate search." Annual gross, $200,000 to $500,000. They charge on a retainer basis.

KEY PEOPLE
Frank C. Telleri, president
Michael J. Curry, secretary/treasurer

❧

Daniel Associates
575 Madison Avenue, Suite 1006
New York, NY 10022
212-605-0490

SALARY RANGE—$40,000 to $150,000

CHARACTERISTICS—In business four years, covering the United States. Annual gross, over $500,000. Greatest expertise in management science, market research, strategic planning, and MIS management. No special efforts on women or minorities. May not be contacted; do not look at resumes. Retainer basis.

KEY PERSON
Beverly Daniel, principal

❧

Deane, Howard & Simon, Inc.
630 Oakwood Avenue
West Hartford, CT 06110
203-727-0721

SALARY RANGE—$50,000 to $250,000

CHARACTERISTICS—They recruit for most industries. Least work in medical industry. Revenues, $500,000. In business eight years. They work throughout the United States. Retainer basis. Working relationship in Great Britain. They look at resumes and may be contacted.

KEY PEOPLE	AREAS OF SPECIALIZATION
Howard D. Nitchke, president	General management and marketing
Robert A. Simon, vice president	Technical management and research

❧

Thorndike Deland Associates
1440 Broadway
New York, NY 10018
212-840-8100

SALARY RANGE—$50,000 to $400,000

CHARACTERISTICS—They are proud of being the oldest search firm; in business since 1926. A particular area of expertise is retailing and consumer marketing; they do the least in hi-tech, professional. Working relationship with firm in Canada. They look at resumes and may be contacted. They make special efforts to recruit women and minorities. Their range is worldwide. Retainer basis.

KEY PEOPLE	AREAS OF SPECIALIZATION
E. A. Raisbeck, partner	Retailing
T. Deland, Jr., partner	Retailing
R. Deland, partner	Food retailing, finance, personnel
J. Carideo, partner	Retailing apparel
H. Bratches, partner	Consumer

☙

Deven Associates, Inc.
1 Clairidge Drive
Verona, NJ 07044
201-239-5500

SALARY RANGE—$60,000 to $250,000

CHARACTERISTICS—In business nine years, they work throughout the United States. Branches/affiliates in New York City and Irvine, California. Greatest expertise in financial services, manufacturing, and finance. Least work in R&D, scientific, and aerospace. Annual gross reported as $1 million. No special efforts to find women or minorities. They look at resumes and may be approached. Retainer basis.

KEY PEOPLE
John P. DiVenuto, chairman
Peter T. Maher, president, eastern operations
Ray Schwartz, principal
James Wilson, principal

❧

Dieckmann & Associates, Ltd.
75 East Wacker Drive
Chicago, IL 60601
312-372-4949

SALARY RANGE—$60,000 to $250,000

CHARACTERISTICS—Generalists in business five years, operating throughout the United States. Gross revenues $650,000. They do the least in technical engineering and actuarial. They make special efforts to recruit women and minorities. They look at resumes; may be contacted by letter only. Retainer basis.

KEY PEOPLE	AREAS OF SPECIALIZATION
Ralph E. Dieckmann, principal	General management
James P. O'Neill, principal	Financial institutions
James F. McSherry, principal	Marketing management

❧

Diversified Search, Inc.
2600 Two Mellon Bank Center
Philadelphia, PA 19102
215-732-6666

SALARY RANGE—$50,000 to $500,000

CHARACTERISTICS—They work throughout the United States. Greatest area of expertise in finance and banking. Least work in sales. They look at resumes and may be contacted. No special efforts to recruit women or minorities. In business 16 years. Their annual gross is about $2 million. They work on a retainer basis. A very young staff.

KEY PEOPLE	AREAS OF SPECIALIZATION
Judith M. von Seldeneck, president	General executive
Kendall A. Elsom, Jr., executive vice president	General executive
Edward R. Howe, Jr., executive vice president	Manufacturing
Marta C. Riemer, vice president	Banking
James C. Hess, vice president	Health, financial
Leslie P. Mazza, vice president	General executive
Laurada B. Byers, vice president	General executive

ઌ

Earley Kielty and Associates, Inc.
Two Pennsylvania Plaza, Suite 1990
New York, NY 10001
212-736-5626

SALARY RANGE—$40,000 to $300,000

CHARACTERISTICS—A majority of the staff are C.P.A.'s. Their greatest expertise is in accounting, tax, finance, data processing searches for controllers, treasurers, CFOs. They look at resumes and may be contacted. No special efforts to recruit women and minorities. In business six years. They operate throughout the United States. Branch in Stamford, Connecticut. Retainer basis.

KEY PEOPLE
Jack Kielty, chairman
Martin R. Levine, president
Francis E. Jones, executive vice president

ઌ

Executive Recruiters
630 Oakwood Avenue, Suite 127
West Hartford, CT 06110
203-527-3875

SALARY RANGE—$30,000 to $75,000

CHARACTERISTICS—They do the most in accounting, finance, and all areas of EDP, least in sales and marketing. No special efforts to recruit minorities or women. In business nine years, working in the United States, with particular coverage in New England. They look at resumes and may be contacted. Contingency basis.

KEY PEOPLE
Kevin J. Rita, vice president
Peter J. Travers, vice president

❧

Executive Recruiting Group of Robert Heller Associates
522 East Putnam Avenue
Greenwich, CT 06830
203-869-1666

SALARY RANGE—$60,000 and up

CHARACTERISTICS—Robert Heller Associates is a consulting company that has been in business for more than 65 years, operating in the United States only. The firm is particularly involved in the energy field—utilities, gas and electric, nuclear, and fossil. They place presidents, senior managers, and operating and engineering executives among others. Gross revenues, about $2 million. No special efforts to recruit women and minorities. They will look at resumes, and executives may get in touch with them. They charge on a retainer basis.

KEY PEOPLE
John Hart, president
H. McKeever, vice president
R. Schultz, vice president
R. Riess, president, consulting group

❧

Leon A. Farley Associates
468 Jackson Street
San Francisco, CA 94111
415-989-0989

SALARY RANGE—$100,000 to $500,000

CHARACTERISTICS—Leon A. Farley Associates is an all-around search firm operating in the United States, Australia, the United Kingdom, and Continental Europe. The firm has offices in Washington and Dallas and is affiliated with firms in London and Melbourne. In business 10 years. Areas of greatest expertise include financial services, hi-tech, professional services, energy, and real estate. They do the least in consumer products and heavy industry. They make special efforts to recruit women and minorities: "We believe our clients are best served by being afforded the widest range of choice. Accordingly, we encourage them to consider candidates without regard to sex, race, or age." They will look at resumes sent by executives earning over $75,000. Retainer basis.

KEY PEOPLE	AREAS OF SPECIALIZATION
Leon A. Farley, managing partner	Financial, hi-tech
Richard T. Bergsund, Sr., vice president	Insurance
C. E. Barton, chief financial officer	Financial, hi-tech
Robert O. Brudno, vice president, Washington office	Financial, hi-tech, consulting
Marshall L. Anderson, vice president, Dallas office	Hi-tech, real estate

～

Fenvessy & Schwab, Inc.
645 Madison Avenue
New York, NY 10022
212-758-6800

SALARY RANGE—$50,000 to $500,000

CHARACTERISTICS—Particular areas of expertise in recruiting for all jobs in minerals (coal, oil, and gas), direct marketing, and distribution. Least in manufacturing, R&D, and not-for-profit. This is a general management consulting firm with two divisions, one specializing in resource industries and the other in distribution and direct marketing industries. The Recruiting Division is one of several divisions within the firm. In business 20 years. They work worldwide, with concentration on the United States. Firm's annual gross is between $2 million and $3 million. No special efforts devoted to women or minorities: "We try to recruit the most appropriate individual for the job regardless of age, ethnic background, or gender." They may be contacted and sent resumes. Working relationship in Sweden. Retainer basis.

KEY PEOPLE	AREAS OF SPECIALIZATION
Stanley J. Fenvessy, chairman	Direct marketing
Violet Opalka, vice president	Direct marketing
Frank Schwab, Jr., president	Resource industries and all major staff functions
Brian Todes, vice president	Resource industries and all major staff functions

～

Jerry Fields Associates
515 Madison Avenue
New York, NY 10022
212-319-7600

SALARY RANGE—$20,000 to $250,000

CHARACTERISTICS—A byword in advertising. In business 38 years. They specialize in advertising-creative-marketing (any area to be found in an advertising agency or an advertising or marketing department of a corporation). They work throughout the United States. Annual gross, $1.5 million. They look at resumes and may be contacted. They make special efforts to recruit members of minority groups. "Not necessary to make a 'special effort' to recruit women. If they are in our area of specialization, they come to us on their own." They have a wholly owned subsidiary, Jerry Fields—Group II, specializing in art direction, graphic and corporate design, and print production-traffic. Contingency basis.

KEY PEOPLE	AREAS OF SPECIALIZATION
Jerry Fields, president/CEO	Senior ad agency, creative, mergers and acquisitions
Janou Pakter, vice president	Graphic design
Beth Lawrence, vice president	Copywriters
Jack Tauss, vice president	Ad agency art directors
Corinne Darby, vice president	Account management
Roger Bumstead, vice president	Media/media sales

❧

Fleming Associates
1428 Franklin Street, P.O. Box 604
Columbus, IN 47202
812-376-9061

SALARY RANGE—$45,000 to $200,000

CHARACTERISTICS—Though they have offices in New York, Miami, Atlanta, Houston, and New Orleans, Fleming Associates continue to serve primarily the "heartland" of the United States. They have offices in Columbus, Ohio; Louisville; and Memphis. Fleming Associates has been in business for 18 years. They maintain working relationships with recruiters in London, Paris, Munich, Brussels, and Berne. Annual gross, $5 million. They recruit for positions in general management, marketing, manufacturing, and a full range of line and staff jobs. They do the least amount of work in advertising and health care. They make no special effort to recruit women or minorities, commenting, "It is estimated that less than 1 percent of former searches have specifically called for female executives and the same holds true for other minority group members." Fleming looks at unsolicited resumes and is willing to hear from executives seeking jobs. Retainer basis.

KEY PEOPLE
Dick Fleming, president
Norm Mitchell, managing partner
Robert Piers, managing partner
John Mestepey, managing partner

∾

George W. Fotis & Associates, Inc.
170 Mason Street
Greenwich, CT 06830
203-661-1081

SALARY RANGE—$50,000 to $200,000

CHARACTERISTICS—Basically they are general management consultants, although they have carried out executive searches for more than 25 years of their 33-year existence. Usually their search assignments grow out of other assignments, such as management development or audit. They have senior associates in Tucson; Phoenix; and Hendersonville, North Carolina, and have an affiliate in the United Kingdom. George W. Fotis & Associates' greatest areas of expertise lie in senior-level management, including manufacturing, and engineering in hi-tech, electronic data, and telecommunications; forest products and petrochemicals. Many of their clients are multinationals. They charge on a retainer basis. They work worldwide, with emphasis on the United

States and Western Europe. They employ 12 to 15 people. They do the least work in consumer-oriented industries. No special efforts to recruit women or minorities: "Our efforts in these directions are largely dictated by a number of factors beyond our control, such as type of position, experience, academic requirements, etc., as stipulated by the client. However, we have no policy of exclusion in this regard. Our aim is to make the 'best fit for both sides.'" They will look at resumes; they will talk to executives only if there is an active search that fits.

KEY PEOPLE	AREAS OF SPECIALIZATION
George W. Fotis, president	General management
George F. Dappert, vice president	Chemical engineering
Donald Gately, vice president	Manufacturing operations
Dr. J. Myron Johnson, vice president	Organizational development

∾

Garofolo, Curtiss & Kaplan
326 West Lancaster Avenue
Ardmore, PA 19003
215-896-5080

SALARY RANGE—$50,000 to $80,000

CHARACTERISTICS—Heaviest concentration in health care, insurance, financial services, hi-tech, and entertainment; least in manufacturing. They may be contacted, and they look at resumes. In business 14 years. "We make no special efforts to include or exclude members of any minority group, male or female." They operate throughout the United States, recruiting for all functional areas. Annual gross, $2.75 million. Retainer basis.

KEY PEOPLE	AREAS OF SPECIALIZATION
Gary Kaplan, executive vice president/partner	Financial, entertainment, hi-tech
Joseph A. Ryan, senior vice president/partner	Generalist

David H. Lambert, senior vice
    president/partner   Development
Frank A. Garofolo, president   Generalist/health care
Joel Shear, vice president/partner   Finance/hi-tech
William F. Wilson, vice president/   Utilities/banking
    partner

❧

N. W. Gibson International
5900 Wilshire Boulevard, Suite 760
Los Angeles, CA 90036
213-930-1100

SALARY RANGE—over $75,000

CHARACTERISTICS—They recruit for all functions in aerospace and other hi-tech industries. Annual gross revenues, over $2 million. They operate in the United States and Europe; affiliate in New York, working relationships with firms in London, Zurich, and Dusseldorf. In business 15 years. They look at resumes and may be contacted. They charge on a retainer basis.

KEY PERSON
N. W. Gibson, president

❧

J. B. Gilbert Associates, Inc.
420 Lexington Avenue
New York, NY 10170
212-661-2122

SALARY RANGE—$60,000 to $300,000

CHARACTERISTICS—A general management recruiter, more than 30 years in business, operating worldwide. Gross is over $1 million. They make special efforts to recruit women and minorities. They look at resumes and may be contacted. They do the least in government. Working relationships with recruiters in Europe and South America. Retainer basis.

KEY PEOPLE
J. B. Gilbert, partner
Steve Van Campen, partner
Daniel Pitchon, partner

❧

Gilbert Lane Associates
2840 Mount Wilkinson Parkway
Atlanta, GA 30339
404-434-2300

SALARY RANGE—$40,000 to $85,000

CHARACTERISTICS—They operate nationwide. In business nine years. No special efforts to recruit women or minorities. They look at resumes but do not want executives seeking positions to get in touch with them. Gross is over $1 million. Retainer basis.

KEY PEOPLE	**AREAS OF SPECIALIZATION**
William Handler, president	General
Harold Massey, vice president	Boiler and power industry
Charles Shoecraft, senior consultant	Chemicals and plastics industries
Tom MacMullan, senior consultant	General

❧

Gilbert Tweed Associates, Inc.
630 Third Avenue
New York, NY 10017
212-697-4260

SALARY RANGE—$60,000 to over $300,000

CHARACTERISTICS—One of the few search firms that are female-owned and -operated. Approximately 15 percent of their searches are for women. They make special efforts to recruit members of minority groups. Their greatest areas of strength are in general management, hi-tech, sales/marketing, engineering/manufacturing/research, finance, and human resources. They do the least in retail and advertising. Gilbert Tweed has branches/affiliates in Boston; Chicago; Washington; and Winterport, Maine. They have one overseas branch, Gilbert Tweed/International, in Paris. In business 14 years, their annual gross is about $2 million. Gilbert Tweed offers programs called *InSearch, ReloSearch,* and *SpouseSearch* "to include the internal candidate in the search process. To anticipate a candidate's objections to relocation and deal with them. To provide assistance, information, support, and counsel to the entire family. To relieve the anxiety and ease the trauma associated with career relocation in the dual-income family." Retainer basis.

KEY PEOPLE
Lynn Tendler Gilbert, principal
Janet Tweed Arkush, principal

∾

Glynn, Brooks & Company, Inc.
2175 Lemoine Avenue
Fort Lee, NJ 07024
201-947-7307

SALARY RANGE—over $50,000

CHARACTERISTICS—A general line recruiting firm, operating throughout the United States. In business six years. They make special efforts on women and minorities if requested by the client. They may be contacted, and they look at resumes. Annual gross, about $1 million. Retainer basis.

KEY PEOPLE	AREAS OF SPECIALIZATION
Thomas J. Glynn, president	Marketing, general management, finance
Harvey Brooks, vice president	MIS, technical
Harold Grill, vice president	Manufacturing, marketing, general management
Ray Harrison, Jr., vice president	Financial, technical

❧

The Goodrich & Sherwood Company
521 Fifth Avenue
New York, NY 10017
212-697-4131

SALARY RANGE—$50,000 to $400,000

CHARACTERISTICS—A large firm recruiting for all functional areas, primarily in the United States. In business 15 years. Branches in Greenwich, Connecticut, and Morristown, New Jersey. Annual gross is "confidential—should be in top ten in billings." They look at resumes. Executives seeking jobs may contact them. They "work hard to develop the best candidates possible and do not exclude females or minorities nor single them out." Heaviest in marketing and sales, lightest in legal. Retainer basis.

KEY PEOPLE
Andrew Sherwood, CEO
Stanley C. Johnson, COO
Richard A. Miners, partner
Linford E. Stiles, partner
James F. Blair, partner
L. Marshall Stellfox, partner
Walter O. Sonyi, partner

❧

Grant Cooper & Associates
680 Craig Road, Suite 301
St. Louis, MO 63141
314-567-4690

SALARY RANGE—$45,000 to $200,000

CHARACTERISTICS—A general management recruiting firm, 28 years old, working in the United States and Canada. They work least in the medical area (but this involvement is growing). No special efforts to recruit women. They do make special efforts to recruit members of minority groups: "Minority searches are not a high percentage of our business but we have had a very high success ratio in the ones that we have undertaken." Revenues are reported at over $1.5 million. They look at resumes and may be contacted. They work on a retainer basis.

KEY PEOPLE
H. Evan Roberts, chairman
Byron J. Johnston, president
J. Dale Meier, vice president
Joseph H. Danklef, vice president
Charles Luntz, vice president
Ronald W. Jones, vice president

❧

Growth Placement Associates, Inc.
900 Creek Road, P.O. Box 38
Downingtown, PA 19335
215-269-5791

SALARY RANGE—$50,000 to over $100,000

CHARACTERISTICS—Their greatest area of expertise lies in principal levels for architectural, engineering, and design firms. Least work in manufacturing. No special efforts to recruit minorities or women. They look at resumes but do not wish to be contacted. Approximate annual gross is $450,000. In business 10 years, working with architectural and engineering firms that range in size from 30 to 100 professional employees. Retainer basis.

KEY PEOPLE
Daniel N. Kanouse, president
Rosaria Taraschi, senior consultant
Philomena D. Warihay, CEO

Haley Associates, Inc.
375 Park Avenue
New York, NY 10152
212-421-7860

SALARY RANGE—over $60,000

CHARACTERISTICS—A general management recruiting firm, in business 22 years, operating worldwide. No special efforts to recruit women or minorities: "Should a minority be most qualified, he or she would be recommended." They do the least in technical. They may be contacted, and they read resumes. Retainer basis. They have a subsidiary, Haley International, at the same address.

KEY PEOPLE
George H. Haley, chairman
James K. Makrianes, Jr., president
Thomas H. Ogdon, executive vice president

❧

Handy Associates, Inc.
245 Park Avenue
New York, NY 10017
212-867-8444

SALARY RANGE—$100,000 to $300,000

CHARACTERISTICS—They recruit for most functional areas. Special emphasis on information processing, consumer goods, and financial services. Least work in nonprofit, transportation, government. They do make special efforts to recruit women and minorities. They may be contacted, and they read resumes. Handy has been in existence in consulting for more than 40 years. Scope of operations, the United States. Retainer basis.

KEY PEOPLE	AREAS OF SPECIALIZATION
Norm Sanders, vice president	Information processing
Frank Shields, vice president	Consumer goods
William Davidson, vice president	Financial services

❧

W. Hanley & Associates
230 Park Avenue
New York, NY 10169
212-661-6060

SALARY RANGE—$50,000 to $150,000

CHARACTERISTICS—Their greatest area of expertise lies in recruiting chief financial officers and those who report to them. They make special efforts to find women and minorities. They look at resumes and may be contacted. In business 32 years. They operate worldwide and have working relationships with firms in London and Paris. Retainer basis.

KEY PEOPLE	AREAS OF SPECIALIZATION
Richard T. Hanley	Financial
J. Patrick Hanley	Financial
Layrene Kofalt	Tax
John Conaghan	General management

∾

Haskell & Stern Associates, Inc.
529 Fifth Avenue
New York, NY 10017
212-687-7292

SALARY RANGE—over $60,000

CHARACTERISTICS—An established general line recruiting firm, in business 19 years. Greatest strengths in financial services, consumer products, energy, marketing, manufacturing, and financial. Least in R&D and technical. They were among the first firms to have a principal in charge of recruiting women executives. They look at resumes but prefer that executives seeking employment not contact them. Branches in Fort Worth and Westport, Connecticut. Working relationships in London and Australia. They work in the United States, the United Kingdom, Continental Europe, and Australia. Retainer basis.

KEY PEOPLE	AREAS OF SPECIALIZATION
Allan D. R. Stern, chairman	General management and financial services
John A. Coleman, president	General management and investment banking
Edward F. Walsh, executive vice president	General management and consumer products
Gretchen Long, managing director	General management and financial services

John Laguzza, senior vice president

Financial functions

Peter Ambler, managing director

General management, energy, and manufacturing

~

Health Industry Consultants, Inc.
7353 South Alton Way
Englewood, CO 80112
303-850-7611

SALARY RANGE—over $25,000 (health care provider); $45,000 to $100,000 (medical product manufacturer)

CHARACTERISTICS—They focus on the health care field: health care device manufacturers and health care providers; professionals specializing in the health care field. They cover the United States, with occasional European assignments. In business 10 years. Annual gross, about $1 million. They look at resumes and may be contacted. Special efforts to recruit women and minorities: "The nature of health care field requires females and/or minorities in certain positions—provides a higher level of suitability for the candidate and client in certain cases." Least work in accounting, data processing. Retainer basis.

KEY PEOPLE

Jon K. Fitzgerald, president

Michael J. Turnock, senior vice president

Thomas C. Miller, senior vice president

AREAS OF SPECIALIZATION

Medical product manufacturers/ general management

Health care providers/general management

Biotechnology/clinical/technical

~

The Heidrick Partners, Inc.
20 North Wacker Drive, Suite 4000
Chicago, IL 60606
312-845-9700

SALARY RANGE—$60,000 to $350,000

CHARACTERISTICS—They work nationwide, with the greatest area of expertise on senior-level management in most functional areas and Boards of Directors. They look at resumes and may be contacted. In business four years. Retainer basis.

KEY PEOPLE
Robert L. Heidrick, president
Gardner W. Heidrick, chairman
Stewart C. Fiordalis, vice president

∾

Heidrick & Struggles, Inc.
245 Park Avenue
New York, NY 10167
212-876-9876

SALARY RANGE—$75,000 to $500,000

CHARACTERISTICS—A giant of the industry, third in most recent rankings. Branches and affiliates in Atlanta; Boston; Chicago; Cleveland; Greenwich, Connecticut; Houston; Los Angeles; Palo Alto; San Francisco; Brussels; Dusseldorf; London; and Paris. They recruit for senior executives in all industries. They look at resumes and may be contacted. In business more than 32 years. Like other very large recruiting firms, they include women and minorities in their searches as a matter of course. Retainer basis.

KEY PEOPLE
Gerard R. Roche, chairman
David R. Peasback, president/CEO

William J. Bowen, vice chairman
Richard D. Nelson, chief financial and administrative officer and counsel

❧

Hodge-Cronin & Associates, Inc.
9575 West Higgins Road
Rosemont, IL 60018
312-692-2041

SALARY RANGE—$50,000 to $500,000

CHARACTERISTICS—A worldwide firm in business 23 years, pursuing all aspects of executive search, including international. They have a working relationship with a firm in Dublin, Ireland. No special efforts to recruit women or minorities unless specified by the client. They look at resumes and may be contacted. They do the least in banking/financial services. Retainer basis.

KEY PEOPLE
Richard J. Cronin, A.P.D., president
Kathleen A. Cronin, vice president

❧

Houck, Meng & Co.
4010 Palos Verdes Drive North, Suite 204
Rolling Hills, CA 90274
213-544-3212

SALARY RANGE—over $45,000

CHARACTERISTICS—They conduct a general practice covering most professional areas. In business 15 years. Annual gross, about $500,000. No special efforts to recruit women or minorities. They may be contacted, and they look at resumes. Retainer basis.

KEY PEOPLE
Charles M. Meng, president
Linda L. Ziach, research consultant
Marlene M. Rafferty, vice president
Carl L. Finseth, vice president

❧

Houser, Martin, Morris & Associates
1940 116th Avenue, N.E.
Bellevue, WA 98004
206-453-2700

SALARY RANGE—$30,000 to $100,000

CHARACTERISTICS—They operate throughout the western United States, particularly the Northwest. They have affiliates across the United States. Greatest areas of expertise are in data processing, accounting/finance, banking, technical management, and insurance. They do the least in marketing. They make special efforts to recruit women and members of minority groups. In business since 1974. They invite resumes from executives looking for jobs. Gross revenues exceed $2 million. They bill on a contingency basis.

KEY PEOPLE	**AREAS OF SPECIALIZATION**
H. James Morris, chairman	Management information services
David V. Martin, president	Banking
Robert H. Holert, vice president	Data processing
Douglas E. Arnold, associate	Accounting/finance

❧

Ward Howell International, Inc.
99 Park Avenue
New York, NY 10016
212-697-3730

SALARY RANGE—$60,000 to over $300,000

CHARACTERISTICS—Ward Howell International is one of the oldest and largest executive-search firms. They have been in business for 35 years. They work around the world for large and small clients. Ward Howell International claims expertise in practically every industrial and nonprofit area and in all management disciplines. There are more than 80 professionals working for the firm, equally split between the United States and international. They are the only major search firm owned equally by the partners. Worldwide gross is about $20 million. They charge on a retainer basis. The company has branches/affiliates in Chicago; Dallas; Houston; Los Angeles; San Francisco; and Greenwich, Connecticut; and in Amsterdam, Brussels, Dusseldorf, London, Melbourne, Mexico City, Milan, Munich, Paris, Sydney, Zurich, Toronto, Tokyo, and Singapore. They look at unsolicited resumes. Executives looking for new jobs may get in touch with them.

KEY PEOPLE
Max Ulrich, president/chairman, CEO
And the managers of the offices throughout the United States and the world.

❧

The Hunt Co.
274 Madison Avenue, Suite 1500
New York, NY 10016
212-889-2020

SALARY RANGE—$60,000 to $500,000

CHARACTERISTICS—An across-the-board management recruiter in business for more than 20 years, operating in the United States and Europe. They make no special efforts to recruit women and minorities. They may be contacted, and they look at resumes. Working relationship with a firm in London. Retainer basis.

KEY PEOPLE
Bridgford Hunt, principal
Martyn Little, principal

∾

Huntress Real Estate Executive Search, Inc.
P.O. Box 8667
Kansas City, MO 64114
913-451-0464

SALARY RANGE—over $30,000

CHARACTERISTICS—Specialists in commercial real estate and related industries. In business 15 years, covering North America. Revenues, over $2 million. They search for executives with expertise in the areas of shopping centers, office buildings, industrial/office parks, hotels-motels, multifamily apartments, single-family residences, and medical facilities. They look at resumes and may be contacted. No special efforts to recruit minorities, but they do make such efforts with women: "Women constitute almost 20 percent of searches completed and are becoming increasingly visible in commercial real estate." Retainer basis.

KEY PEOPLE	AREAS OF SPECIALIZATION
Sandford I. Gadient, president	
Arlene L. Davis, vice president	Office buildings, industrial
Donald S. Peterson, vice president	Corporate real estate
Deborah E. Hecht, assoc. consultant	Syndication
Dr. Ralph Hook, senior consultant	Research/compensation and organization studies
Stan Stanton, senior consultant	Real-estate brokerage

∾

Inside Management Associates
24 East 38th Street
New York, NY 10016
212-683-7200

SALARY RANGE—$50,000 to "high six figures"

CHARACTERISTICS—Generalists, working worldwide. In business 15 years. No special efforts to recruit women and minorities. They look at resumes and may be contacted. Retainer basis.

KEY PEOPLE	AREAS OF SPECIALIZATION
Paul D. Steinberg, president	Generalist/soft goods, package goods, retail
Charles Seitz, senior associate	Retail, soft goods, general
Neail Behringer, senior associate	Soft goods, Wall Street, retail
W. Michael Healy, senior associate	Soft goods, consumer products, retail

~

International Management Advisors, Inc.
767 Third Avenue
New York, NY 10017
212-758-7770

SALARY RANGE—over $50,000

CHARACTERISTICS—They recruit in all areas of management and in most industries. Worldwide operation, with emphasis on the United States and Europe. Working relationship with firm in England. "We present the best qualified people to our clients without regard to race, creed, color, national origin, or sex." They look at resumes but do not encourage executives to get in touch with them. Least work in the hotel and advertising fields. Retainer basis.

KEY PEOPLE
R. James Lotz, Jr., president
Constance W. Klages, executive vice president

Donald P. Close, vice president
William C. Parker, vice president
Robert A. Raidt, vice president

❧

Charles Irish Company, Inc.
420 Lexington Avenue
New York, NY 10170
212-490-0040

SALARY RANGE—$50,000 to $200,000

CHARACTERISTICS—Their emphasis is on "serving *Fortune* 500 manufacturing companies and their divisions; recruitment of professionals for venture capitalists." Least on financial services, government, and banking. No special efforts to recruit women or minorities "unless emphasized by client." They look at resumes; executives may get in touch "by mail, *not* by telephone." In business 12 years. Annual gross over $300,000. They work throughout the United States. Branch in Raleigh, North Carolina. Retainer basis.

KEY PEOPLE
Charles W. Irish, chairman
Joan S. Irish, president

AREAS OF SPECIALIZATION
Generalist
Venture capital

❧

Pendleton James and Associates, Inc.
200 Park Avenue, Suite 3706
New York, NY 10166
212-557-1599

SALARY RANGE—over $100,000

CHARACTERISTICS—Pendleton James was formerly assistant to the president for presidential personnel in the Reagan administration. He founded his present company four years ago. Mr. James runs what amounts to a one-man operation. Gross revenue is reported as about $500,000. Area of operation is the United States. Mr. James says that his "close association with Reagan administration . . . coupled with years of experience with two major search firms and my own business on west coast has given me an almost inexhaustible base of contacts at the top level of the country's major corporations plus a close association with present and former government leaders." Greatest expertise in general management positions at the CEO, COO, and chairman levels. Least amount of work in marketing, sales, and the process industry. No special effort to recruit women or minorities. Retainer basis. He is interested in receiving resumes from senior-level executives.

KEY PERSON
E. P. James, chairman

❧

Johnson & Genrich
5481 North Milwaukee Avenue
Chicago, IL 60630
312-792-2323

SALARY RANGE—$35,000 to $90,000

CHARACTERISTICS—In business 16 years. Greatest focus on hi-tech, durable goods, marketing, and manufacturing, least on international. No special efforts to recruit women and minorities. They look at resumes and may be contacted. Reported gross revenues, $200,000. They work on a retainer basis.

KEY PEOPLE	AREAS OF SPECIALIZATION
Eugene Johnson, president	General management, technical, marketing
Allan E. Crabb, vice president	Financial and MIS
Jim Ekwall, senior executive recruiter	Human resources, manufacturing

∾

Kearney Executive Search
222 South Riverside Plaza
Chicago, IL 60606
312-648-0111

SALARY RANGE—$50,000 to $200,000

CHARACTERISTICS—In business more than 40 years, with greatest expertise in general management, manufacturing, marketing, finance, engineering, health care, and transportation/distribution. They make special efforts to recruit women and minorities: "Our research department utilizes various resources which would provide names of minority executives. We present any candidates who are qualified for positions, regardless of sex, race, or age." They work worldwide. Annual gross, $3 million to $5 million. They look at resumes and may be contacted. Retainer basis.

KEY PEOPLE
James R. Arnold, president
Charles W. Sweet, vice president, North America
Patrick McGrath, vice president, transportation
Bonnie Wiseman, vice president, health care

∾

Kenny, Kindler & Hunt
780 Third Avenue, Suite 2202
New York, NY 10017
212-355-5560

SALARY RANGE—over $100,000

CHARACTERISTICS—An across-the-board recruiting firm, in business four years. They look at resumes. They make special efforts to recruit women and members of minority groups. Retainer basis.

KEY PEOPLE
Roger M. Kenny, partner
Peter A. Kindler, partner
James E. Hunt, partner

&

Kensington Management Consultants, Inc.
25 Third Street
Stamford, CT 06905
203-327-9860

SALARY RANGE—$40,000 to $300,000

CHARACTERISTICS—Their area of operation is primarily the United States (although they have a working relationship with Technox International in Israel). In business since 1972, they "have yet to fail to fill a position nor have we ever had to refund a fee or replace a candidate." Kensington conducts searches for all kinds of companies and financial institutions and nonprofit organizations, including various disciplines, such as maintenance engineers, executive vice presidents of finance, publishers, chemists, and technical writers. They make special efforts to recruit women and members of minority groups. They report annual gross revenues of $1 million. They charge on a retainer basis. Kensington looks at unsolicited resumes and will talk with executives who get in touch with them.

KEY PEOPLE	AREAS OF SPECIALIZATION
Ann F. Fimmano, president and CEO	Finance, general management, electronics, marketing, training, and development
E. G. Campbell, vice chairman	All industries and disciplines
S. J. Sindeband, CEO	Hi-tech, engineering, directorships

❧

Kiley Owen Associates, Inc.
1218 Chestnut Street, Suite 510
Philadelphia, PA 19107
215-923-0740

SALARY RANGE—$30,000 to $200,000

CHARACTERISTICS—A general line recruiter in business more than 20 years. They work throughout the United States. They do the least in insurance and nonprofit. They make special efforts to find women and minorities: "advertise in women's publications, etc." They do not wish to be contacted and do not look at unsolicited resumes. Retainer basis.

KEY PEOPLE
Ralph E. Owen, president
Michael A. Kiley, vice president
Sheila M. McGovern, secretary-treasurer

❧

Kline-McKay, Inc.
3 East 48th Street
New York, NY 10017
212-371-2077

SALARY RANGE—$40,000 to over $150,000

CHARACTERISTICS—Greatest expertise in finance, marketing, EDP, and human resources. Least work in PR, sales promotion, legal, and medical (M.D.'s). They look at resumes—"some we put in our data bank, some we throw out." They do *not* wish to be contacted. They make special efforts to recruit women ("always have") and minority members: "We're on the NYC/NYS list of firms with specialty expertise in EEO. Also on federal D.O.D. list for EEO related matters." Annual volume, $600,000. In business eight years. Retainer basis.

KEY PEOPLE
Linda Kline, president
Joseph A. McKay, vice president
Lynda Michaels, director of research and recruitment

❧

Korn/Ferry International
237 Park Avenue
New York, NY 10017
212-687-1834

SALARY RANGE—over $75,000

CHARACTERISTICS—The biggest executive search firm. They recruit worldwide, in all functional areas for all industries. Korn/Ferry has a Financial Services Division, High Technology Division, and divisions devoted to energy, fashion/retail, real estate, hospitality/leisure, entertainment, health care, government/not-for-profit/education, and Board services. Founded in 1969. Offices in Los Angeles; Houston; Atlanta; Chicago; San Francisco; Dallas; Cleveland; Stamford, Connecticut; Washington, D.C.; Palo Alto, California; Denver; Newport Beach, California; and Boston, as well as 18 money-market centers in Europe, Latin America, Australia, and the Far East. Annual gross, about $60 million. They look at resumes and may be contacted. They recruit women and members of minority groups as a matter of course, without mounting special efforts. Retainer basis.

KEY PEOPLE
Lester B. Korn, chairman
Richard M. Ferry, president
Jean-Michel Beigbeder, managing partner
Morgan H. Harris, Jr., managing partner
Windle B. Priem, managing partner
David F. Smith, managing partner

❧

Kunzer Associates, Ltd.
208 South LaSalle Street
Chicago, IL 60604
312-641-0010

SALARY RANGE—over $40,000

CHARACTERISTICS—Greatest area of expertise in energy, hi-tech, instrumentation, financial services, health care, pharmaceuticals, consumer products, machinery and equipment, and chemicals. They work primarily in the United States. In business seven years. They look at resumes and may be contacted. No special efforts to recruit women and minorities. Retainer basis.

KEY PEOPLE
William J. Kunzer, president
Diane S. Kunzer, vice president

❧

Lamalie Associates, Inc.
101 Park Avenue
New York, NY 10178
212-953-7900

SALARY RANGE—$100,000 to $1,000,000 (the ordinary range; they may go lower, but never below $60,000)

CHARACTERISTICS—Lamalie Associates, with annual fees of nearly $7 million, is rated as the sixth-largest search firm in the United States. The firm has offices in Atlanta, Chicago, Cleveland, Dallas, and Tampa. They have 24 full-time consultants and a 35-member research and administrative staff. Founded in 1967. The firm is best known for expertise in senior-level searches, including manufacturing, electronics, hi-tech, and consumer goods. Nearly 100 clients are *Fortune* 500 companies. They rely on a sophisticated research setup: "Lamalie Associates monitors the real qualifications and experience of nearly 25,000 executives via its proprietary database system." The firm makes no special efforts to recruit women or members of minority groups. They charge on a retainer basis. They look at unsolicited resumes and suggest that executives seeking jobs get in touch with them.

KEY PEOPLE
Robert E. Lamalie, chairman and CEO
John F. Johnson, president

◈

Lauer, Sbarbaro Associates
1 North LaSalle Street
Chicago, IL 60602
312-372-7050

SALARY RANGE—$40,000 to $500,000

CHARACTERISTICS—They operate in the United States and Europe. In business 15 years. They have the greatest focus on marketing, finance, and manufacturing, the least on advertising. They have an affiliate in Zurich. No special efforts to recruit women or minorities. Revenues are about $1.5 million. Retainer basis. They look at resumes and may be contacted.

KEY PEOPLE
P. H. Lauer, chairman
Richard Sbarbaro, president
William Yacullo, senior vice president
Jean Trela, vice president

❧

Lawrence-Leiter & Company
427 West 12th Street
Kansas City, MO 64105
816-474-8340

SALARY RANGE—$35,000 to $125,000

CHARACTERISTICS—At their Kansas City office they handle general business recruiting for middle and top management. They recruit physicians and health care professionals in their St. Louis office, at 135 North Meramec, St. Louis, MO 63105; 314-726-1630. Least work in hi-tech. No special efforts to recruit women or minorities: "We recruit based on qualifications, neither favoring nor disfavoring based on sex or minority status." In business 35 years. They work most in the midwestern United States, though they have recruited in South America and Africa. They may be contacted, and they read unsolicited resumes. Retainer basis.

KEY PEOPLE	AREAS OF SPECIALIZATION
Wm. B. Beeson, vice president	General
Katey Tryon, senior consultant	Retailing
Ronald V. Raine, vice president	General
Sue Ceska, president (St. Louis)	Physicians

❧

Locke & Associates
2160 Charlotte Plaza
Charlotte, NC 28244
704-372-6600

SALARY RANGE—$50,000 to $100,000

CHARACTERISTICS—A smaller firm with greatest emphasis on construction, engineering, manufacturing, financial, and service. Least work in not-for-profit. In business 16 years. They look at resumes and may be contacted. They make special efforts to recruit women and minorities. Area of operations, the United States. Retainer basis.

KEY PERSON
M. Fred Locke, Jr., president

❧

Robert Lowell International
12221 Merit Drive, No. 1510
Dallas, TX 75251
214-233-2270

SALARY RANGE—$35,000 to over $1 million

CHARACTERISTICS—Worldwide, with working relationships in England, Mexico, and Belgium. Greatest focus in marketing, sales, finance, and human resources. Least in hospitality. They look at resumes. Executives may get in touch with them. They make special efforts to recruit women and members of minority groups. Gross revenues, $4 million to $7 million. In business over 20 years. Retainer basis.

KEY PEOPLE
Robert M. Bryza, president
Mark Moore, vice president
Lowell Foster, vice president
Emanuel Perlman, vice president

❧

James H. Lowry & Associates
303 East Wacker Drive, Suite 1340
Chicago, IL 60601
312-861-1800

SALARY RANGE—over $50,000

CHARACTERISTICS—Lowry is a consulting firm operating throughout the United States, with a special focus on the recruitment of minorities: "We are first and foremost a minority-oriented organization, capable of helping both major corporations and government agencies develop programs that involve interaction with the minority community." Their recruiting arm works as a full-service operation, with a specialty in recruiting women and members of minority groups. In business 10 years. Annual gross, $5 million. Executives may get in touch with them, but they do not look at unsolicited resumes. Retainer basis.

KEY PEOPLE
Olivet Ames, director, executive search
Lois White, senior associate
Marilyn Riegel, vice president

❧

The John Lucht Consultancy, Inc.
The Olympic Tower, 645 Fifth Avenue
New York, NY 10022
212-935-4660

SALARY RANGE—$100,000 to $500,000

CHARACTERISTICS—A worldwide, upscale firm, with affiliates in England, France, and West Germany. They recruit for CEOs, presidents, and general managers, and officer-level heads of function—vice presidents of finance, marketing, manufacturing, R&D, administration, MIS, and law. They do not work much in the lower- and middle-management areas. Special efforts to recruit women and minorities: "We present all women and minority candidates who are appropriately qualified in every search. Beyond that, we have been very successful in filling upper-management positions with women and minority candidates when that is the client's specific objective." They accept resumes only by mail and reply only by mail. Unsolicited phone calls are politely turned away, and interviews are not granted at candidate request. In business nine years. Retainer basis.

KEY PEOPLE
John Lucht, president
George Range, research director

❧

Management Recruiters International, Inc.
1015 Euclid Avenue
Cleveland, OH 44115
216-696-1122

SALARY RANGE—$25,000 to $75,000

CHARACTERISTICS—A nationwide franchise network combining functions of employment agencies with certain recruiting functions. Management Recruiters (with its allied division, Sales Consultants International) claims 400 offices, 90 percent of which are run by franchiseholders. When given an assignment, they obtain names from lists, then screen potential candidates by phone, after which they turn over names to the client without meeting the candidate face-to-face. In business 28 years. They look at resumes: "If we get a resume from a 'water-walker' we'll try to place him." They maintain, though, that no one's name is given out to potential employers without getting the candidate's permission first. Franchiseholders usually have little or no background in search; the company trains them. They work on a contingency basis.

KEY PEOPLE
Alan R. Schonberg, president
Louis R. Scott, vice president
Michael F. DiDomenico, vice president
Stephen W. Fogelgren, director of field operations

❧

Management Search Associates, Inc.
10 Bay Street
Westport, CT 06880
203-227-3524

SALARY RANGE—$50,000 to $125,000

CHARACTERISTICS—A generalist firm, with the greatest expertise in general management and technical positions, the least in manufacturing. They have an affiliate in New York. They work in the United States and Japan. In business five years. They make special efforts to recruit women and minorities; they look at resumes and may be contacted. They charge on a retainer basis.

KEY PEOPLE
Stephen Dean, president
Mattie Jourdan, vice president

❧

Management Search, Inc.
664 North Michigan Avenue, Suite 1010
Chicago, IL 60611
312-426-7700

SALARY RANGE—$20,000 to $100,000

CHARACTERISTICS—They do the most in accounting/finance, data processing, engineering, general management, hospitality, insurance, medical, and marketing, least in general office. They have associates in Denver; Omaha; Washington, D.C.; Dallas; Buffalo; Crete, Illinois; Marina del Rey, California; Charleston, South Carolina; Birmingham,

Michigan; and Georgetown, Texas. In business 20 years, they work throughout the United States. Annual gross reported as over $2 million. "We recruit people on the basis of qualifications matching job specifications. Special efforts to recruit women or minority executives are made if clients so request." They look at resumes and may be contacted. Retainer basis.

KEY PEOPLE	AREAS OF SPECIALIZATION
R. Stephan Levy, president	Management search
Richard Nasatir, president	Management search/data search
Bobbi Hansen, manager	
Pam Maxwell, interoffice network consultant (database)	

&

Marshall Consultants, Inc.
360 East 65th Street
New York, NY 10021
212-628-8400

SALARY RANGE—$25,000 to $300,000

CHARACTERISTICS—Their greatest area of expertise is in communications: public relations and advertising. They do the least in general management. They have a branch in Seattle. "We belong to minority group professional associations; also, most of our executive staff are women recruiters." In business 19 years. Yes on contacts and resumes. Revenues reported at $500,000. They work on a contingency basis.

KEY PEOPLE	AREAS OF SPECIALIZATION
Larry Marshall, president	Corporate communications/public relations/advertising (senior level)
Judith Cushman, executive vice president	Manager, Seattle branch (all levels)
Sandra Charet, vice president	Corporate communications, public relations (mid/to junior level)

Susan Elion, vice president   Corporate communications, pub-
                                lic relations (mid/to
                                junior level)

❧

Massey Charbonneau, Inc.
20 Prince Arthur Avenue, Suite 16G
Toronto, Ont. M5R 1B1 Canada
416-968-0438

SALARY RANGE—over $100,000

CHARACTERISTICS—A large Canadian firm in business 12 years, operating worldwide. Their greatest focus is on the CEO level, least in upper-middle management. They recruit for a broad range of business and functional areas. They do not look at unsolicited resumes, nor do they wish executives to get in touch with them. Annual gross, over $1 million. Working relationships in the United States, Australia, Belgium, Brazil, France, Germany, Italy, Singapore, South Africa, Switzerland, and the United Kingdom. Branch in Montreal. Retainer basis.

KEY PEOPLE
R. Bruce Massey, president
Paul Bourbeau, partner
Ron Drennan
Alan H. Burns

❧

Matté & Company, Inc.
60 State Street
Boston, MA 02109
617-742-5130

SALARY RANGE—$60,000 to $300,000

CHARACTERISTICS—Greatest areas of expertise: banking, financial services, hi-tech, and manufacturing. They do the least in retail. In business 16 years. They look at unsolicited resumes "as a courtesy." Executives may get in touch with them—"but we are retained exclusively by the company to search for very specific talent." They have branches and affiliates in New York; Greenwich, Connecticut; and London. They cover the United States, Europe, the Middle East, and Latin America. Annual gross, $250,000 to $600,000. Special efforts to recruit women and minorities: "On every executive search we encourage our clients to consider women and minorities, as well as actively sourcing for these categories." Retainer basis.

KEY PEOPLE
Norman E. Matté, president
Tracy S. Hollis, senior consultant
R. William Faville, senior consultant

෴

McBride Associates, Inc.
1511 K Street, N.W.
Washington, DC 20005
202-638-1150

SALARY RANGE—over $100,000

CHARACTERISTICS—Mr. McBride works in the United States, mostly east of the Mississippi. Most functional areas. Least work in technical/engineering. No special efforts to recruit women and minorities: "Don't discriminate on any direction." In business seven years. Looks at resumes. Executives may get in touch—"probably won't do them a lot of good." This is a firm run by a sole proprietor "with clear objective of being alter ego to . . . CEOs, each of whom would like to use my services . . . where they think a one-man, thorough, professional if obscure search firm is more appropriate/suitable than a large search firm." Retainer basis.

KEY PERSON
Jonathan E. McBride, president

❧

McManners Associates, Inc.
555 Madison Avenue
New York, NY 10022
212-980-7140

SALARY RANGE—over $80,000

CHARACTERISTICS—In business seven years, with a particular focus on hi-tech. No special efforts to recruit women or minorities. They may be contacted, and they look at resumes. Least work in the financial area. Revenues, $500,000 to $1 million. Retainer basis.

KEY PEOPLE
Donald E. McManners, president
Richard Perry, vice president
Susan Kelly, director, client services
Edmund Brodie, director of research

❧

MD Resources, Inc.
7385 Galloway Road, Suite 200
Miami, FL 33173
305-271-9213

SALARY RANGE—$80,000 to $250,000+

CHARACTERISTICS—Specialists in health care, working in the United States, Canada, and some areas of Europe. They make special efforts to recruit women: "We are in the process of recruiting women physicians for women's ambulatory care clinics, as well as women for multi-specialty groups in sub-specialty areas." In business seven years.

Annual gross, about $2.5 million. Branches/affiliates in Herndon, Virginia, and Newport, California. They look at resumes and may be contacted. Retainer basis.

KEY PEOPLE
Judith E. Berger, president
Stephen G. Schoen, executive director
Michael E. Kurtz, vice president

❧

Harold A. Miller Associates
P.O. Box 9006
Winnetka, IL 60093
312-446-7900

SALARY RANGE—$80,000 to $200,000

CHARACTERISTICS—This firm's greatest focus is on the "top ¾ executive positions in smaller, growing companies." Least work in technical and R&D. No special efforts to recruit women or minorities. They look at resumes, and executives may get in touch with them. In business 27 years. Area of operation is the United States. Annual gross, about $200,000. Retainer basis.

KEY PERSON
Harold A. Miller, owner

❧

Marion Mills Associates
875 North Michigan Avenue, Suite 1524
Chicago, IL 60611
312-649-0703

SALARY RANGE—over $25,000

CHARACTERISTICS—Greatest expertise in marketing, sales, EDP, and finance. In business 24 years, operating in the United States. They do make special efforts to recruit women and minorities. They read resumes and may be contacted. Retainer basis.

KEY PERSON
Walter T. Coonan, Ph.D., executive vice president

☙

Morgan/Webber, Inc.
Townhouse 24, Union Wharf
Boston, MA 02109
617-227-1155

SALARY RANGE—$45,000 to $150,000

CHARACTERISTICS—They work mainly in the United States, though they have done some international work. Greatest expertise in technical, marketing and sales, and data processing, least in finance. They make special efforts to recruit women and minorities. They look at resumes and may be contacted. In business five years. Annual gross, about $1 million. Retainer basis.

KEY PEOPLE	AREAS OF SPECIALIZATION
Steven M. Lavender, president	Hi-tech, precious metals
Michael P. Lombardo, partner	Rubber plastics,
Sibyl Masquelier, vice president	Human resource, graphics

☙

Moriarty/Fox, Inc.
20 North Wacker Drive, Suite 2604
Chicago, IL 60606
312-332-4600

SALARY RANGE—over $60,000

CHARACTERISTICS—They recruit for senior management in all functions and all industries. In business 13 years. They work throughout the United States and handle international assignments for companies based in the United States. They look at resumes and may be contacted. Annual gross, $750,000 to $1 million. Retainer basis.

KEY PERSON
Philip S. J. Moriarty, president

~

MSL International, Ltd.
1110 Vermont Avenue, N.W., No. 710
Washington, DC 20005
202-467-6407

SALARY RANGE—$45,000 and up

CHARACTERISTICS—A very large recruiting firm; in business since 1955 worldwide, since 1977 in the United States. Branches and affiliates in Atlanta, Los Angeles, San Francisco, New York, Chicago, Philadelphia, and Dallas. Working relationships in Australia, Belgium, Germany, Italy, Switzerland, the United Kingdom, Ireland, Japan, Hong Kong, France, Mexico, Argentina, Venezuela, and Saudi Arabia. Their expertise is widespread, including construction engineering, insurance, transportation, banking, and general business. Annual gross, $11 million to $15 million. They may be contacted, and they look at resumes. They make special efforts to recruit minorities and women: "We have a Practice Director devoted to Female Executive recruiting. Approximately 20 percent of our staff are women professionals." Retainer basis.

KEY PEOPLE	AREAS OF SPECIALIZATION
William A. Spartin, CEO	
Charles J. Chalk, president and COO	Insurance, general business
David R. McCarthy, executive vice president	Public broadcasting, transportation, general business

❧

Robert Murphy Associates
230 Park Avenue
New York, NY 10169
212-661-0460

SALARY RANGE—$50,000 and up

CHARACTERISTICS—In business more than 10 years, with working relationships in Europe. Their greatest expertise is in general management, marketing, and finance; least work in merchandising. They make special efforts to recruit women and minorities. Executives may get in touch with them by letter. They look at resumes. Gross revenue is reported at "several million dollars." They work on a retainer basis.

KEY PEOPLE
Robert Murphy, president
Thomas Cook, senior vice president
John Murray, vice president
Paul Hill, vice president
Rita Dreyfus, vice president

❧

Nicholson and Associates
230 Park Avenue
New York, NY 10169
212-686-7044

SALARY RANGE—$40,000 to $240,000

CHARACTERISTICS—Worldwide operation, with working relationship in the United Kingdom. They work in general management, finance, commercial and investment banking, MIS, data processing, retail merchandising and buying wholesale, and management consulting. Least work in manufacturing and operations. No special efforts to recruit women and minorities: "No special effort is required. We recruit without regard to race, sex, creed, etc. Our assignments are completed roughly equally with white male, female, and minority candidates." In business nine years. They look at resumes and may be contacted. Retainer basis.

KEY PERSON
Constantine Nicholson, president

❧

The Odessa Group
523 West Sixth Street, Suite H807
Los Angeles, CA 90014
213-629-9181

SALARY RANGE—$60,000 to $150,000

CHARACTERISTICS—Seven years old. They operate in the United States only. Greatest emphasis on engineering, marketing, and manufacturing, least emphasis on government. No special recruiting efforts on women and minorities. They report working with major aerospace and defense electronics companies in areas of electronics warfare, program management, and other sensitive disciplines. They work on a retainer basis. They look at resumes and may be contacted.

KEY PEOPLE	**AREAS OF SPECIALIZATION**
Odessa J. Felactu, president	Marketing/finance
Phillips Eastman, Jr., vice president	Manufacturing
Holly Anderson Bellows, vice president	Sales/marketing
John Reilly III, vice president	Human resources
Kimberley Crossley, associate	

∾

PA Executive Search Group
780 Third Avenue
New York, NY 10017
212-759-0532

SALARY RANGE—$50,000 to $500,000

CHARACTERISTICS—A leading worldwide firm, with branches and affiliates in Montreal, Toronto, Calgary, London, Birmingham, Manchester, Glasgow, Edinburgh, Dublin, Paris, Lyon, Madrid, Frankfurt, Hamburg, Dusseldorf, Stuttgart, Brussels, Copenhagen, Oslo, Stockholm, Helsinki, Rome, Tokyo, Hong Kong, Bangkok, Kuala Lumpur, Singapore, Sydney, Melbourne, and Auckland. Their greatest areas of expertise include general management, corporate governance, commercial and investment banking, information technology, university recruitment, and new engineering disciplines. They make special efforts to recruit minorities and women: "We believe the best way to assure that women and minorities receive appropriate consideration is to have them represented on our professional staff. Our professionals are selected for their competence and experience, but we happen to have strong female and minorities representation among them." In business more than 40 years. They do the least in advertising and public relations. They look at resumes and may be contacted. Annual gross, $23.8 million. They work on a retainer basis.

KEY PEOPLE	AREAS OF SPECIALIZATION
Robert G. Cox, president	General management and corporate directors
Michael Brenner, senior vice president	Information technology
Vance A. Howe, senior vice president	Financial services industries
Kenneth D. McCullough, senior vice president	Manufacturing
Bernard E. Brooks, vice president	Health and education institutions

Michael J. Illich, vice president
Linda S. Weiss, vice president
Diane Malanowski, assistant vice
   president and research director
Domenica Fero, assistant vice
   president

Hi-tech
Engineering and aviation

❦

Paul & Turner, Inc.
7616 LBJ Freeway
Dallas, TX 75251
214-386-9991

SALARY RANGE—not indicated

CHARACTERISTICS—They recruit for general management, marketing, and technical positions. Greatest expertise in telecommunications, computer, banking, and hi-tech. In business eight years. Executives seeking positions may get in touch. They read resumes. Branch in Morristown, New Jersey. They operate throughout the United States. Retainer basis.

KEY PEOPLE
Jerome T. Paul, chairman
Nat P. Turner, president
Gerard G. Hummel, supervisor

❦

Peat, Marwick, Mitchell & Co.
303 East Wacker Drive
Chicago, IL 60601
312-938-1000

SALARY RANGE—$50,000 to over $200,000

CHARACTERISTICS—They are a full-service recruiting firm, in business 24 years. Peat, Marwick, Mitchell operates on a broad scale, with branches and affiliates in Atlanta; Boston; Cleveland; Dallas; Houston; Kansas City; Los Angeles; Miami; Minneapolis; New York; Newport Beach, California; San Francisco; Short Hills, New Jersey; Stamford, Connecticut; and White Plains, New York. The firm has working relationships with recruiters in Argentina, Australia, Canada, Colombia, England, France, Germany, Hong Kong, Republic of Ireland, Italy, Japan, Mexico, Netherlands, Nigeria, Northern Ireland, Spain, Trinidad, and Venezuela. Their greatest areas of expertise are in management information services, financial services, health care, marketing, finance, and accounting. They do the least in technical engineering. They bill on a retainer basis. No special efforts to recruit women or minorities. They look at unsolicited resumes. Executives may get in touch with them.

KEY PEOPLE
Donald F. Dvorak, partner
Dwight E. Foster, principal
John H. Telford, principal
Lynn W. Dwigans, principal

❧

Pinsker and Shattuck, Inc.
P.O. Box 1235
Saratoga, CA 95071
408-867-5161

SALARY RANGE—$65,000 to $175,000

CHARACTERISTICS—They operate throughout the United States and have a branch in San Francisco. Greatest expertise in hi-tech, least in financial services. They look at resumes, prefer to be contacted only by mail. No special minority or female recruiting efforts. In business 19 years. Annual gross, $400,000 to $500,000. Retainer basis.

KEY PEOPLE
Richard J. Pinsker, founding partner
Mervin B. Shattuck, partner

❧

The PMS Group, Inc.
9200 South Dadeland Boulevard, Suite 516
Miami, FL 33156
305-667-6100

SALARY RANGE—$40,000 to $150,000

CHARACTERISTICS—A 14-year-old generalist recruiting firm. They work strictly in the United States. They make special efforts to recruit women and members of minority groups: We "have executed a large number of affirmative action searches in every category and in every discipline." Annual revenue is reported as $350,000 to $500,000. They charge on a retainer basis. They will look at resumes, and executives may get in touch with them.

KEY PERSON
Ned Tannenbaum, president

❧

Remer-Ribolow & Associates
507 Fifth Avenue, Suite 400
New York, NY 10017
212-808-0580

SALARY RANGE—over $40,000

CHARACTERISTICS—Specialists in publishing. They recruit (and place) in book and magazine editorial and support staff jobs, and space sales. In business 30 years. They cover the United States. They look at resumes and may be contacted. No special efforts to recruit members of minorities or women. Annual gross, $500,000. They work on a contingency basis.

KEY PEOPLE
Bob Remer, codirector
Adele Ribolow, codirector

❧

Russell Reynolds Associates, Inc.
245 Park Avenue
New York, NY 10167
212-953-4300

SALARY RANGE—over $70,000

CHARACTERISTICS—The second-ranking executive-search firm. World-wide in scope, highly professional. Founded in 1969. Offices in Boston; Chicago; Cleveland; Dallas; Houston; Los Angeles; Menlo Park, California; San Francisco; Stamford, Connecticut; and Washington, D.C. Also in London, Paris, Madrid, Hong Kong, Singapore, and Sydney. They recruit for the best candidates, without special efforts to seek out women or minority members, except in cases where clients request it. They do not wish to be contacted by executives. The stated policy of the firm is that they don't look at unsolicited resumes. Retainer basis.

KEY PEOPLE
Russell S. Reynolds, Jr., chairman
H. Leland Getz, vice chairman
Ferdinand Nadherny, president
Andrew D. Hart, Jr., managing director

❧

The RHE Group
333 East 46th Street
New York, NY 10017
212-682-7125

SALARY RANGE—over $75,000

CHARACTERISTICS—They operate in the eastern United States and in Western Europe. Branch in Philadelphia; working relationships with firm in Frankfurt, London, and Paris. Greatest areas of expertise are described as HR, engineering, general management, law, and international. No special efforts to recruit women and minorities: "We recruit equally among all groups." They look at resumes and may be contacted. Retainer basis.

KEY PEOPLE	AREAS OF SPECIALIZATION
K. J. Hackett, general partner	Generalist
F. C. Rockett, Ph.D., general partner	Psychological evaluation
G. L. Hoffer, Ph.D.	Management development

∾

Robison & McAuley
3100 NCNB Plaza
Charlotte, NC 28280
704-376-0059

SALARY RANGE—over $30,000

CHARACTERISTICS—They conduct a general search practice. In business seven years. No special efforts to recruit women and minorities: "We make no distinctions. We search for the most qualified individuals." Executives may contact them or send resumes. Gross revenues, $600,000 to $750,000. They work on a retainer basis.

KEY PEOPLE
John H. Robison, Jr., associate
A. L. McAuley, Jr., associate
John H. Robison IV (Rob), associate
Robert M. Frazer, associate

❧

Rogers & Sands, Inc.
Eight New England Executive Park
Burlington, MA 01803
617-229-2640

SALARY RANGE—$25,000 to $60,000

CHARACTERISTICS—Specialists in human resources, personnel and training, and development professionals. In business since 1959. They look at resumes and may be contacted. They seek out women and members of minorities as part of affirmative action plans. Area of operation is primarily New England. Contingency basis.

KEY PEOPLE
Reo N. Hamel, president
Dave Cronin, placement consultant

❧

Rourke, Bourbonnais & Associates
1808 Sherbrooke Street West
Montreal, Que. H3H 1E5 Canada
514-931-7675

SALARY RANGE—$45,000 to $150,000

CHARACTERISTICS—A large firm, working primarily in Canada. In business 15 years. Greatest focus on general management, sales/marketing, finance/control, and HR. Least work in computer/EDP and investment. Annual gross, $3 million. They look at resumes and may be approached. They make a special effort to recruit women executives: "Six of 22 members of our professional staff are women." Branches in Toronto and Calgary. Retainer basis.

KEY PEOPLE
Patrick W. Rourke, president
John J. Corso, partner
Anthony B. Mizgola, partner
Pierre Payette, partner
John F. Geci, partner
Roger Lachance, partner

✌

James J. Rust Executive Search
420 Lexington Avenue
New York, NY 10170
212-986-8011

SALARY RANGE—$50,000 to $300,000

CHARACTERISTICS—General management recruiting, with greatest expertise in transportation, least work in retail-design. They cover the United States and Europe, with an affiliate in Brussels. Rust is the successor to the long-established firm of Golightly Executive Search. Annual gross, $300,000. No special efforts to recruit women and minorities. They may be contacted, and they look at resumes. Retainer basis.

KEY PERSON
James J. Rust, principal

✌

Sales Executives, Inc.
755 West Big Beaver Road, Suite 2107
Troy, MI 48084
303-362-1900

SALARY RANGE—$30,000 to $200,000

CHARACTERISTICS—They are associated with Technical Executives and Financial Executives (at the same address). In business 12 years. The United States and the Far East. They look at resumes and may be contacted. No special efforts to recruit women or minorities. Contingency basis.

KEY PEOPLE
Dale E. Statson, president
William O'Neill, executive vice president

❧

Sampson, Neill & Wilkins, Inc.
543 Valley Road
Upper Montclair, NJ 07043
201-783-9600

SALARY RANGE—$40,000 to $350,000

CHARACTERISTICS—A leading recruiting firm, in business 18 years, operating worldwide, with branches and affiliates in London and Europe and the Far East. Their particular area of expertise is health industries, including pharmaceuticals, veterinary and animal health products, foods, biodevices, medical diagnostics, biomedical technologies, research institutes, advertising agencies, insurance corporate staffs, and hospitals. Also occupational and environmental health groups, all industries. Annual gross, $1.5 million to $2 million. They make special efforts to recruit women and minorities. They look at resumes, and executives may get in touch by letter only. Retainer basis.

KEY PEOPLE	AREAS OF SPECIALIZATION
Martin C. Sampson, M.D., F.A.C.P.	Medical administration, occupational health, environmental toxicology
Welldon C. Neill, executive vice president	Advertising and public relations
Robert J. Hodges, Ph.D., senior vice president	R&D, technical
Walter K. Wilkins, senior vice president	General management, marketing and production

∾

The Search Network
1669 South Voss Street, Suite 605
Houston, TX 77057
713-877-1214

SALARY RANGE—$35,000 to $100,000

CHARACTERISTICS—Ms. Lehrer specializes in recruiting only in the banking and finance areas for professionals. In business four years. Works nationwide. Special efforts to recruit women and minorities: "I try to find out which banks are hiring those people and then try to recruit to fill those positions." She looks at resumes and may be contacted but prefers only banking expertise. Retainer basis.

KEY PERSON
Myrna N. Lehrer, president

∾

Search West, Inc.
1875 Century Park East, Suite 1025
Los Angeles, CA 90067
213-203-9797

SALARY RANGE—$25,000 to $150,000

CHARACTERISTICS—They recruit in all technical, professional, administrative, marketing, management, and EDP areas. Annual gross, about $500,000. They operate throughout the United States, charging on a contingency basis. Yes on contacts and resumes. Branches and affiliates throughout California.

KEY PEOPLE
Lawrence G. Cowan, president
Robert A. Cowan, executive vice president

❧

Seitchik, Corwin and Seitchik, Inc.
1830 Jackson Street
San Francisco, CA 94109
415-928-5717

SALARY RANGE—$50,000 to $250,000

CHARACTERISTICS—They specialize in the apparel, textile, and sewn products industries, recruiting for all functions. In business 10 years. They have a New York branch and recruit worldwide. No special efforts to recruit women or minorities. Annual gross is reported as $1 million to $2 million. They look at resumes and may be contacted. Retainer basis.

KEY PEOPLE
Jack Seitchik, president
J. Blade Corwin, vice president
William Seitchik, vice president

❧

John Sibbald Associates, Inc.
5725 East River Road
Chicago, IL 60631
312-693-0575

SALARY RANGE—$70,000 to $150,000

CHARACTERISTICS—The firm, with one branch in Clayton, Missouri (near St. Louis), operates in the United States, the United Kingdom, and the Caribbean. In business 11 years. Their greatest areas of expertise are in consumer goods, financial services, durable goods, and not-for-profit organizations. They have a particular specialty in the area of clubs, having been endorsed by The Club Managers Association of America to screen candidates for management positions in country clubs, yacht clubs, city clubs, and other private clubs. They do the least work in computer systems and telecommunications. Annual gross revenues are about $2 million. John Sibbald makes a distinct effort to recruit women and members of minority groups: "We strive to have at least one of the final half-dozen candidates as a woman and/or a minority. We succeed in this goal 80 percent of the time." They charge on a retainer basis. They are open to unsolicited resumes.

KEY PEOPLE
John R. Sibbald, president
Carol S. Jeffers, vice president and administrative partner (specializing in clubs and resorts)
Betsy S. Tomlinson, vice president

ॐ

Skott/Edwards Consultants, Inc.
230 Park Avenue, Suite 902
New York, NY 10169
212-697-7640

SALARY RANGE—$60,000 to $200,000 (average, $100,000)

CHARACTERISTICS—Worldwide firm. Greatest areas of expertise are in financial services and technically driven businesses. They do the least in legal and merchandising. Branch in Rutherford, New Jersey. Annual gross over $4 million. They make special efforts to recruit women and minorities. They look at resumes and may be contacted. In business 12 years. Retainer basis.

KEY PEOPLE
Edward W. Golden, chairman
Skott B. Burkland, president

∾

Spencer Stuart & Associates
Park Avenue Plaza
55 East 52nd Street
New York, NY 10022
212-407-0200

SALARY RANGE—over $80,000 (over $120,000 in New York market)

CHARACTERISTICS—One of the largest executive-search firms, founded in 1956. They have offices in Atlanta; Chicago; Cleveland; Dallas; Houston; Los Angeles; San Francisco; and Stamford, Connecticut. Offices abroad are in Amsterdam, Brussels, Dusseldorf, Frankfurt, Geneva, London, Madrid, Manchester, Milan, Paris, Zurich, Tokyo, São Paulo, Hong Kong, Singapore, Melbourne, Sydney, Calgary, Montreal, and Toronto. Gross revenues, over $40 million. They recruit for senior-level management in all areas. They recruit the best candidates in all cases, usually making no special efforts to recruit women or members of minorities. One exception is that, today, there are often requests for female corporate directors. They may be contacted by executives at the appropriate level. They look at resumes (of those in the higher compensation levels); likely names go into the computer bank. Retainer basis.

KEY PEOPLE
CORPORATE OFFICERS
Arnold J. Tempel, chairman (Amsterdam)
Thomas J. Neff, president (New York)

U.S. OFFICERS
Robert W. Slater, U.S. managing director (Dallas)
Dayton Ogden, managing director (New York)
Robert L. Benson, managing director (Stamford)
Gerald J. Bump, managing director (Atlanta)
James J. Drury, managing director (Chicago)
George W. Henn, managing director (Cleveland)

Louis J. Rieger, managing director (Houston)
Daniel C. Wier, managing director (Los Angeles)
Joseph E. Griesedieck, managing director (San Francisco)

PRACTICE AREA LEADERS
Denis B. K. Lyons, managing director, banking (New York)
Carlton W. Thompson, managing director, communications (New York)
Richard T. Kalen, managing director, energy (Dallas)
O. D. Cruse, managing director, high technology (Dallas)
Edward C. Slowik, managing director, consumer financial services (New York)
Jack Lohnes, managing director, Board services (Stamford)

INTERNATIONAL REGIONAL OFFICERS
Richard W. Johnston, managing director, Canada (Toronto)
Paul Cheng, managing director, Southeast Asia (Hong Kong)
Kerry McInnes, managing director, Australia (Sydney)
Christopher D. Power, managing director, United Kingdom (London)

❧

William Stack Associates, Inc.
230 Park Avenue
New York, NY 10169
212-490-0490

SALARY RANGE—over $75,000

CHARACTERISTICS—They work in the United States and Canada, with branches and affiliates in London, Hong Kong, Wiesbaden, and Zurich. They make special efforts to recruit women and members of minorities. They may be contacted, and they read resumes. In business 18 years. They work on a retainer basis.

KEY PEOPLE
J. William Stack, Jr., president
Christopher D. Stack, vice president
Edward J. Dwyer, vice president
George H. Orgelman, vice president

ॐ

Paul Stafford Associates, Ltd.
45 Rockefeller Plaza
New York, NY 10111
212-765-7700

SALARY RANGE—$50,000 to $200,000

CHARACTERISTICS—A large generalist firm "with some emphasis on financial operations, human resource, marketing, not-for-profit, etc." They make special efforts to recruit women and minorities: "On a number of occasions we have placed women in senior management positions, Board of Directors, and the like. We have also recruited some blacks for senior positions, the most notable of which was a president of a major insurance company." Branches in Chicago; San Francisco; and Washington, D.C. Working relationship with firm based in London with branches in Europe. They look at resumes. Executives may get in touch "only after having submitted resignation." Revenues, over $3 million. They charge on a retainer basis. In business 27 years.

KEY PEOPLE	AREAS OF SPECIALIZATION
Norman F. Moody, chairman	Financial community
Robert M. Flanagan, president	Industrial and operations
A. S. Blodget, Jr., vice chairman	Finance, insurance
Franklin Key Brown, vice chairman	Investment banking

ॐ

The Stevenson Group
720 Palisade Avenue
Englewood Cliffs, NJ 07632
201-568-1900

SALARY RANGE—$50,000 to $250,000

CHARACTERISTICS—In business nine years, they work throughout the United States. Branches in Hartford and Southbury, Connecticut. Greatest strengths in general management, human resources, administrative departments, sales, and marketing. Industries: insurance, medical and pharmaceutical, financial services, health, beauty aids, and cosmetics. No special efforts to recruit women or minorities. They look at resumes and may be contacted. Annual gross reported at $1.8 million. Retainer basis.

KEY PEOPLE
Stephen M. Steinman, chairman and CEO
James Johnston, president and COO
William Rutledge, vice president and senior consultant
Theodore Lewis, vice president and senior consultant

❧

S. K. Stewart & Associates
The Executive Building, P.O. Box 40110
Cincinnati, OH 45240
513-771-2250

SALARY RANGE—$40,000 to $120,000

CHARACTERISTICS—In business 18 years, covering North America. Recruit in areas of hi-tech, health care, food, feed and pet food, insurance, and manufacturing. They do the least in retailing. Revenues, $300,000 to $500,000. No special efforts to recruit women or minorities. They look at resumes and may be contacted. Retainer basis.

KEY PEOPLE
Stephen K. Stewart, president
L. Christine Visnich, associate

❦

Straat Group, Inc.
999 Summer Street
Stamford, CT 06902
203-967-3334

SALARY RANGE—$70,000 to $200,000

CHARACTERISTICS—A small, professional search firm operating nationwide. In business 13 years. They have the greatest expertise in industrial companies in higher technologies, although they work across the board—for example, in publishing. They do the least work in consumer products. While Straat makes no special effort on women and minorities, they recruit on a "sex-blind" and color-blind basis. They represent foreign clients for work in the United States. Annual gross revenues are about $250,000. They charge on a retainer basis. They may be contacted, and they look at resumes.

KEY PERSON
Kent L. Straat, president

❦

Stricker & Zagor
717 Fifth Avenue
New York, NY 10022
212-308-7272

SALARY RANGE—$60,000 to $500,000

CHARACTERISTICS—They recruit worldwide for a wide range of functional areas. Working relationships with firms in Chicago, Los Angeles, London, Stockholm, and Sydney. Greatest concentration on general management, marketing, sales—"for image-driven consumer packaged goods companies." Least in heavy industries and technology. In business 12 years. No special efforts on women and minorities: "We make the same effort to recruit *all* candidates and make *no* distinctions pro or con." They look at resumes and may be contacted. Annual gross, over $1 million. Retainer basis.

KEY PEOPLE
Sidney G. Stricker, Jr., senior partner
Howard S. Zagor, partner
Sally M. Bailey, associate

∾

John J. Sudlow & Company
625 North Michigan Avenue, Suite 500
Chicago, IL 60611
312-944-5127

SALARY RANGE—$35,000 to $150,000

CHARACTERISTICS—Their greatest expertise is in general management, marketing and sales, and distribution, least in data processing. In business 11 years, they operate in the United States. They have a branch in Seattle. They make special efforts to recruit members of minority groups and women. ("Two of our officers are women, they are directly involved in search activity and are in contact with women's professional organizations in order to bring qualified women candidates to the foreground for all of our searches.") They look at resumes. Executives seeking jobs should get in touch with them by mail only. Annual gross, $800,000. Retainer basis.

KEY PEOPLE	AREAS OF SPECIALIZATION
John J. Sudlow, president	General management
Michael Dalzell, research director	General management
Juelanne B. Dalzell, vice president	Marketing
George R. Herman, vice president	Transportation and distribution

∾

The Systech Organization, Inc.
2825 Cub Hill Road
Baltimore, MD 21234
301-665-6033

SALARY RANGE—$25,000 to $150,000

CHARACTERISTICS—This is a management consulting firm with a search division. The consulting practice is primarily in the management, marketing, and HRD areas. In recruiting, they do the most in financial services, least in government. In business 12 years. They make special efforts on women and minorities: "involvement in community activities and approximately 20 associations." They look at resumes and may be contacted. The firm has branches/affiliates in New York, as well as other offices in Baltimore. They operate throughout the United States and have worked in Europe. Annual gross, $300,000 to $500,000. Retainer basis.

KEY PEOPLE	AREAS OF SPECIALIZATION
Walter J. Sistek, C.M.C., president	HRD, financial, real estate
F. Michael Herman, C.P.A., principal	Financial
Robert Pfeifer, managing director	
C. Beverly Sistek, corporate secretary	Management
Donald L. Hartman, managing director	Construction

❧

TASA, Inc.
875 Third Avenue
New York, NY 10022
212-486-1490

SALARY RANGE—$60,000 and up

CHARACTERISTICS—A 14-year-old large worldwide firm that recruits across the board. TASA has branches and affiliates in Miami, Mexico City, Bogotá, Caracas, São Paulo, Buenos Aires, Brussels, Paris, London, Zurich, Frankfurt, Milan, Madrid, Barcelona, Johannesburg, and Hong Kong. No special efforts to recruit women or minorities. Their gross revenues are over $10 million (U.S.). They charge on a retainer basis. Executives seeking jobs may get in touch with them. They look at resumes.

KEY PEOPLE
Klaus Jacobs, president
R. Fred Rijke, managing partner (New York)

❧

Taylor, Johnston, Inc.
240 Crandon Boulevard, Suite 202
Key Biscayne, FL 33149
305-361-5400

SALARY RANGE—$100,000 to $500,000

CHARACTERISTICS—A newly established firm, operating worldwide on relatively high-level searches. Greatest expertise in international, health products, advertising, and communications. They have a branch office in New York City. They look at resumes and may be contacted. No special efforts to recruit women or minorities: "We normally include women executives and members of minority groups in any search that we do but we do not make any special effort in their direction." They are aiming at $1 million annual volume. (A. Robert Taylor founded TASA, one of the largest recruiting firms, leaving in 1984 when he reached age 65.) Retainer basis.

KEY PEOPLE
A. Robert Taylor, chairman
Harold C. Johnston, president
Rosemary Casey-Freeman, secretary/treasurer

❧

Thomas-Pond Enterprises
520 Speedwell Avenue
Morris Plains, NJ 07950
201-540-0160

SALARY RANGE—$50,000 to $200,000

CHARACTERISTICS—They recruit for practically all functional areas, working throughout the United States. Special efforts are made to recruit women and minorities "as typically required by clients." In business 11 years. Executives may get in touch with them, although they do not look at unsolicited resumes. Branches/affiliates in Atlanta; Danville, California; and Oak Park, Michigan. Retainer basis.

KEY PEOPLE
Cole G. Thomas, president
Audrey J. Penney, vice president
Robert Conte, vice president

❧

Thorne Stevenson & Kellogg
2300 Yonge Street
Toronto, Ont. M4P 1G2, Canada
416-483-4313

SALARY RANGE—over $50,000

CHARACTERISTICS—This is the search division of a 50-year-old management consulting firm. They recruit for all functional areas—general management, finance, marketing, human resources, and manufacturing; also public-sector management. They usually do the least in the scientific area. They have branches in Vancouver, Edmonton, Calgary, Regina, Saskatoon, Winnipeg, Kitchener, Ottawa, Montreal, and Halifax. Working relationships worldwide. An equal-opportunity recruiter: They "strongly support growth of women in management. Client receptivity increasing." They look at resumes, and they wish to be contacted in writing, preferably. They operate throughout Canada. Annual gross for the search division (in business 25 years) is $1.5 million (for the entire firm, $2.5 million). Retainer basis.

KEY PEOPLE
James A. Parr, partner-in-charge
Robert E. McMonagle, principal
Robert E. Nemish, senior consultant

❧

Trotter, Mitchell, Larsen & Zilliacus
523 West Sixth Street, Suite 737
Los Angeles, CA 90014
213-489-7120

SALARY RANGE—$50,000 and up

CHARACTERISTICS—A worldwide firm recruiting in the upper-level management areas. Branch in Newport Beach, California; working relationship in Japan. In business five years. They look at resumes but do not wish to be contacted by executives seeking new positions. No special efforts to seek women and minorities. Annual gross, approximately $2 million. Retainer basis.

KEY PEOPLE	AREAS OF SPECIALIZATION
Hugh B. Trotter, partner	General
Thomas M. Mitchell, partner	Technology
Richard F. Larsen, partner	Financial services
Patrick W. Zilliacus, partner	General
Robert S. Divine, partner	General
Oscar W. Montano, associate	Medical

❧

Thomas L. Trout & Associates, Inc.
30423 Canwood Street, No. 123
Agoura Hills, CA 91301-2089
818-706-1980

SALARY RANGE—$40,000 to $150,000

CHARACTERISTICS—Heaviest emphasis is on generalist organization, hi-tech aerospace, and commercial companies; engineering, manufacturing, and support. Least work in the administrative area. They may be contacted, and they look at resumes. No special efforts to recruit women and minorities. In business 14 years. Retainer basis.

KEY PEOPLE
Names are confidential

༄

Tully and Hobart, Inc.
333 North Michigan Avenue
Chicago, IL 60601
312-332-4545

SALARY RANGE—$50,000 to $200,000

CHARACTERISTICS—Generalist, in business nine years. They make special efforts to recruit women and minorities. They look at resumes and may be contacted. Retainer basis.

KEY PERSON
James Tully, president

༄

VanMaldegiam Associates, Inc.
150 North Wacker Drive, Suite 2160
Chicago, IL 60606
312-648-0807

SALARY RANGE—$40,000 to $150,000

CHARACTERISTICS—In business six years, covering the United States. Recruiting for middle- and top-management positions. Least work in international, governmental, and not-for-profit areas. No special efforts to recruit women and minorities: "Recruit executives identified by direct sourcing for talent who . . . are the best qualified without regard to the race, sex, etc." May be approached and sent resumes. They work on a retainer basis.

KEY PERSON
N. E. VanMaldegiam, president

❧

Vine Associates, Inc.
4719 Morse Avenue, Suite B
Sherman Oaks, CA 91423
818-906-3368

SALARY RANGE—$40,000 to $250,000

CHARACTERISTICS—They work in the United States, Europe, and the Far East. They specialize in emerging growth industries—e.g., health maintenance, hospital-related, biotech, and international medical services. In business 13 years. Branch in New York, affiliate in London. They make special efforts to recruit women and minorities. They look at resumes but are not enthusiastic about being contacted. The firm's annual gross is in the "low seven figures." Retainer basis.

KEY PEOPLE	**AREAS OF SPECIALIZATION**
Dr. Neil M. Levine, president	Health maintenance, corporate studies, U.S.A.
Robert Barton, vice president	Health maintenance, corporate studies, Europe
Dr. Sharon Burns, vice president	EEO, U.S.A.
Lord Wesley-Thomas, managing director, London	European Common Market

❧

Albert J. Walsh & Associates, Inc.
The Commons West, 638 Newtown-Yardley Road
Newtown, PA 18940
215-968-0707

SALARY RANGE—"new grad to unlimited"

CHARACTERISTICS—Their areas of concentration include engineering, financial, manufacturing, general management, marketing, and technical. Least work in R&D. They recruit for all management functions. In business 13 years. Branch in Boston. Special efforts to recruit women and minorities. They look at resumes and are open to contacts. They work mainly in the United States but have recruited executives from the United Kingdom and Italy. Retainer basis.

KEY PEOPLE
Albert J. Walsh, president
Nicholas Burkholder, vice president
Andrea Hop, corporate secretary
James J. O'Kane, senior consultant
Samuel Lieberstein, senior consultant

∾

Werner Management Consultants, Inc.
111 West 40th Street
New York, NY 10018
212-730-1280

SALARY RANGE—$75,000 to $150,000

CHARACTERISTICS—A recruiting branch of a general management consulting firm. They work in all functional areas of management. They are particularly experienced in soft goods: primary textiles and sewn products. While there are no special minority efforts, "We take particular pains to avoid discrimination, either positively or negatively, of women or minority groups." Gross is approximately $1 million. They operate worldwide, with particular emphasis on the United States. The consulting company has been in business 45 years; the recruiting division, 20 years. Yes on contracts and resumes. They charge on a retainer basis.

KEY PEOPLE
Martin H. Rubenstein, vice president
Walter A. Croen, vice president
Douglas G. LaPasta, director

❧

Whatman, Payne, Inc.
1617 Selkirk Avenue
Montreal, Que. H3H 1C7, Canada
514-932-7460

SALARY RANGE—$45,000 to $175,000

CHARACTERISTICS—They have a branch in Toronto and a working
relationship with a firm in London, England. They have the greatest
expertise in hi-tech, specifically telecommunications and data processing, the least in health services. In business eight years, working in
Canada and the United States. "Quebec-based organizations often
express a preference in having a francophone (French Canadian) in an
executive role and we place the emphasis in our search efforts
accordingly." Gross revenues, $250,000. They look at resumes, and
they talk to executives who contact them. Retainer basis.

KEY PEOPLE
Trevor G. Payne, president
Gordon G. Whatman, vice president
Lise Averill, researcher

❧

Whittlesey & Associates
300 South High Street
West Chester, PA 19382
215-436-6500

SALARY RANGE—$40,000 to $150,000

CHARACTERISTICS—Whittlesey has been in business for seven years. They cover North America. They focus most heavily on finding sales and marketing executives for marketing information firms, consumer packaged goods marketing services (market research, promotion, advertising), accounting/controllership, and manufacturing. They work least in data processing and research development. No special efforts to recruit women and minorities. They look at unsolicited resumes, and executives seeking positions may get in touch with them. Retainer basis.

KEY PEOPLE
James G. Hogg, Jr., president
Colin A. Hanna, principal
Glenna Geiger, administrative manager
Elizabeth Landreth, research manager

∾

Williams, Roth & Krueger, Inc.
101 North Wacker Drive, Suite 675
Chicago, IL 60606
312-977-0800

SALARY RANGE—$65,000 to $300,000

CHARACTERISTICS—They recruit senior-level executives ($100,000 to $300,000) in all major industries and all major functions. They work least in automotive and basic industries. In business five years. Yes on resumes and contacts. Annual gross revenues, over $1.5 million. They operate throughout the United States. They work on a retainer basis.

KEY PEOPLE
Roger K. Williams, chairman/partner
Robert J. Roth, vice chairman/partner
Clarence F. Krueger, president/partner
Andrew R. Zaleta, senior vice president/partner

❧

Winchester Consultants, Inc.
49 Locust Avenue, P.O. Box 1334
New Canaan, CT 06840
203-972-0011

SALARY RANGE—$50,000 to $200,000

CHARACTERISTICS—A general management recruiting firm with greatest expertise in information processing, telecommunications, and related hi-tech areas. Least concentration on "pure and classical and soon to be obsolete manufacturing areas with no emphasis on technology." In business over five years. They "very definitely" make a special effort to recruit women and minorities. They look at unsolicited resumes ("Always!") and may be contacted. Primarily in the United States. Retainer basis.

KEY PEOPLE
Anthony F. Piotrowski, Sr., president
Beverly J. Piotrowski, corporate secretary
Anthony F. Piotrowski, Jr., vice president

❧

Winguth, Schweichler, Velcamp Associates, Inc.
24 California Street, Suite 750
San Francisco, CA 94111
415-495-8255

SALARY RANGE—$50,000 to $400,000

CHARACTERISTICS—They work "with the rapidly growing or changing organization; especially with emerging companies; almost half the client base is high technology/high science. . . ." They do the least in "insurance and similar slowly changing or declining industries; advertising; home consumer products (computer-related excepted); 'smokestack' industries; textiles." They look at resumes and may be contacted. They operate in North America, Europe, and the Pacific Basin. Branches/affiliates in Santa Clara, California; Brussels; and Tokyo. They make special efforts to recruit women and minorities: "Women and minority executives are presented as part of the slate of candidates. Special recruiting efforts are made when requested . . . by contacting the appropriate 'communities' and 'networks.'" In business nine years. Gross revenues, $1 million to $2 million. Retainer basis.

KEY PEOPLE
Erwin W. (Ed) Winguth, president
Lee J. Schweichler, executive vice president
John T. Velcamp, vice president
William J. Docker, treasurer

❧

Witt Associates, Inc.
724 Enterprise Drive
Oak Brook, IL 60521
312-325-5070

SALARY RANGE—over $45,000

CHARACTERISTICS—They work in the health care field exclusively, recruiting for all executive/management positions. In business 17 years. Annual gross revenues, $3.5 million. They make special efforts to recruit women and minorities. They look at resumes and may be contacted. Branch in Dallas. They work primarily in the United States, although they have handled international assignments. Retainer basis.

KEY PEOPLE
John A. Witt, president
John S. Lloyd, executive vice president

❧

Yelverton & Company
353 Sacramento Street
San Francisco, CA 94111
415-981-6060

SALARY RANGE—$60,000 to $200,000

CHARACTERISTICS—Heaviest concentration in emerging hi-tech enterprises, least in transportation. Working relationships in London and
Sydney. In business 20 years. Annual gross revenues, about $500,000.
No special efforts to recruit women and minorities. They look at
resumes and may be contacted. Retainer basis.

KEY PEOPLE
Jack R. Yelverton, president
Linda J. Hall
Katherine A. Styles

❧

Arthur Young Executive Resource Consultants
One Sansome Street
San Francisco, CA 94104
415-951-3300

SALARY RANGE—$50,000 to $350,000

CHARACTERISTICS—A large general line firm, in business 21 years,
operating in the United States, but also worldwide through their joint
operating relationship with TASA. Branch offices in New York;
Boston; Chicago; Minneapolis; Los Angeles; Dallas; and Washington,
D.C. Working relationships with firms in Europe, South Africa, Latin

America, Australia, and China. Yes on women and minorities: "Our methodology and approach will uncover the top candidates on a search assignment, including women and minorities." They look at resumes and may be contacted. Retainer basis.

KEY PERSON
Dan K. Metz, national managing partner

❧

Egon Zehnder International, Inc.
One First National Plaza, Suite 3004
Chicago, IL 60603
312-782-4500

SALARY RANGE—over $100,000

CHARACTERISTICS—A very large international firm, with branches and affiliates in Atlanta, Brussels, Buenos Aires, Copenhagen, Dusseldorf, Frankfurt, Geneva, The Hague, London, Madrid, Melbourne, Mexico City, Paris, São Paulo, Singapore, Sydney, Tokyo, and Zurich. They recruit across the board. Least emphasis on the public sector. They look at resumes, and executives may contact them. In business 22 years. Annual gross revenues, $24 million. "Whenever possible, particular attention paid to identification of minority groups and women." Retainer basis.

KEY PEOPLE
Kai Lindholst, managing partner, North America
Victor H. Loewenstein, managing partner, New York (Latin America)
Samuel H. Pettway, managing partner, Atlanta

❧

APPENDIX III: SOURCES OF INFORMATION ON EXECUTIVE SEARCH

Association of Executive Search Consultants
151 Railroad Avenue
Greenwich, CT 06830
203-661-6606

The AESC promulgates a code of ethics for the search industry. The association publishes a list of its member firms.

National Association of Corporate & Professional Recruiters
197 Cedarwood Road
Stamford, CT 06903
203-329-2349

The NACPR is an association of recruiters from corporations as well as executive search firms.

Kenneth J. Cole is an outstanding source of information and analysis for executive recruiters and those to whom the recruiting industry is important. Cole, who has experience as a search consultant, publishes a newsletter, *The Recruiting & Search Report,* which focuses on information and recommendations rather than on industry gossip. In addition, Cole publishes special reports on topics of interest to the search community.

Cole has published an updated listing of independent researchers. Called *Independent Researchers—Services, Special Report #6, 2nd Edition*, it is available for $51.50. Cole has a variety of other interesting material: a full list is available on request. His organization can provide lists of recruiters in most functional and industry specialties. (As an example of price range, three categories—a functional list and two industries—might cost $25.) Cole also publishes a detailed listing of 58 independent researchers. His address and phone number are:

Kenneth J. Cole
The Recruiting & Search Report
P.O. Box 9433
Panama City Beach, FL 32407
904-235-3733

Kennedy & Kennedy publishes *Executive Recruiter News* as well as a directory of search consultants. The firm also carries on a mail-order business offering information on consulting and recruiting.

Kennedy & Kennedy, Inc.
Templeton Road
Fitzwilliam, NH 03447
603-585-6544

The Executive Grapevine, published by Robert Baird, has been a successful directory of recruiters in the United Kingdom. Mr. Baird is now publishing *The Executive Grapevine* (in two volumes, one for retainer and one for contingency) to cover United States recruiters. Baird will also publish a journal of executive recruiters in the United States on a regular basis.

Robert R. Baird
Executive Grapevine, Inc.
575 Madison Avenue, Suite 1006
New York, NY 10022
212-605-0414

National Association of Executive Recruiters
P.O. Box 3346
Alexandria, VA 22302
703-998-3008
Contact: George Ridenour

Index

Abbott Smith Associates, 155
Accounting Resources International, 155–56
Aetna, 105
Alexander Edward Associates, Inc., 156
Allerton, Heinze & Associates, Inc., 156–57
Allied Stores, 105
Alumni associations, 59
Amansco, Inc., 157
American Executive Management, 157–58
American Executive Search Services, Inc., 158–59
American Men of Science, 21
American Standard, 105
Ames Associates, Inc., 159
Amory Associates, Inc., 159–60
Andre Group, 160
Annas/Clancy Associates, 151
Apple Computer, 8
Art & Science of Negotiation, The (Raiffa), 98
Association of Executive Search Consultants, 10, 70, 263
 code of ethics of, 13, 70, 77
AT&T, 114

Baird, Robert, 79
Baker International Corporation, 109
Bargaining process, *see* Negotiating

Bartholdi Partners, 161
Barton Business Research, 147
Bason Associates, Inc., 161–62
Battalia & Associates, Inc., 162
Beedle, Rick, Associates, Inc., 163
Bentley & Evans, International, 163–64
Billington, Fox & Ellis, Inc., 164
Blackshaw & Olmstead, Inc., 164–65
Blau Kaptain & Associates, 165
Board memberships, 60
Bonuses, 105–13
Booz, Allen & Hamilton, 106
Borden's, 105
Bowden & Company, Inc., 165–166
Bowersox & Associates, Inc., 166
Boyden Associates, Inc., 167
Boyer, Heath C., 69
Boyer, Heath C., Company, 167–168
Brand Company, Inc., 168
Bridgeport (Conn.) *Sunday Post*, 8
Brissenden, McFarland & Wagoner, Inc., 169
Browne, Kevin, Associates Research Services, 144
Bryant Associates, Inc., 169–70
Buell Associates, 170
Buffum, Tom, 86
Bushee, Robert J., 170–71

ABOUT THE AUTHOR

JOHN TARRANT has written numerous books, mostly about business, including *Perks and Parachutes: Negotiating Your Executive Employment Contract; Drucker: The Man Who Invented the Corporate Society; How to Negotiate a Raise; The End of Exurbia*—and a dozen others. With his wife Dorothy he writes about American art and artists, in books (*A Community of Artists*) and articles for magazines including *Smithsonian, New York,* and *Savvy,* as well as *Cosmopolitan, Family Circle,* and *Working Woman.* Tarrant is also a consultant, serving clients like General Electric, PepsiCo, Texaco, Chase Manhattan, and others. Before becoming a freelancer, John Tarrant worked as Vice President for Training and Development, Benton & Bowles, and Director of Management Programs, Research Institute of America. He lives in Westport, Connecticut, with his wife.